INNOCENCE LOST

(more . . .)

Books by Carlton Stowers

Careless Whispers
Innocence Lost

Published by POCKET BOOKS

INNOCENCE LOST

CARLTON STOWERS

POCKET STAR BOOKS

New York   London   Toronto   Sydney   Tokyo   Singapore

A Pocket Star Book published by
POCKET BOOKS, a division of Simon & Schuster Inc.
1230 Avenue of the Americas, New York, NY 10020

ISBN: 0-671-66818-8

First Pocket Books paperback printing September 1991

10 9 8 7 6 5 4 3 2 1

POCKET STAR BOOKS and colophon are trademarks of
Simon & Schuster Inc.

Cover photo by Pat Stowers
Cover photo retouching by Michael Shen

Printed in the U.S.A.

To the memory of George W. Raffield, Jr.
Midlothian Police Department
Badge Number 112 (retired)

Acknowledgments

There is both a comfort and a danger in writing about one's own neighborhood, talking to people who frequent the same eating spots and grocery, traveling territory so familiar one need not stop and ask for directions.

Which is to say I felt no small degree of reluctance when the idea of writing this book was first suggested.

My initial awareness of the tragedy in Midlothian, Texas, came not from radio reports or newspaper headlines, but from a disturbing telephone call from the most unlikely of sources. A young woman named Karen Hufstetler, who professes to have psychic abilities, had taken to calling me on occasions when she experienced "feelings" about possible criminal activity. It was on Saturday morning, October 24, 1987, that she telephoned to tell me that she had wakened from a dream in which a friend of hers named Jeff Bryant, a deputy in the Ellis County Sheriff's Department, was walking through a field while involved in some kind of search. "I think he's looking for a red pickup," she volunteered.

Certain that Deputy Bryant had not yet located the truck, Karen had placed a call to the Sheriff's Department, identified herself, and told the dispatcher she was under the impression that Bryant was looking in an area somewhere between Midlothian and the Cedar Hill neighborhood where I lived.

"Tell him that he's looking in the wrong area," she had said. "He needs to be farther south."

The stunned dispatcher, who hadn't even acknowledged that a search was under way, asked Karen if she had any other information.

"When they find the pickup," she said, "the keys will be missing."

The conversation took place six hours before the truck, its keys nowhere to be found, was located—several miles south of where Deputy Bryant had begun his search.

It was not until the evening news that I actually learned that an undercover police officer had been found dead less than a twenty-minute drive from my home.

In the days to come I read and watched news accounts of the event closely but fought against my journalist's instinct to look into the case. Even when an editor from a New York publishing house called to express his interest in the story, I hestitated. The deadline for another project on which I was working loomed uncomfortably near, and frankly, I had grave misgivings about entering into the writing of a book which, in a manner of speaking, would lay bare the life-style of friends and neighbors.

For years I had been making the short drive down Highway 67 to Midlothian to attend my sons' Little League games, to cheer on the Cedar Hill Longhorns in their grudge football games with Midlothian's Panthers, and to regularly order chicken-fried steak and cream gravy at Dee Tee's Restaurant.

I was not at all sure I wanted to delve beyond the picturesque image—to search the community's dark side, seeking some answer to how and why this nightmare had been played out in such a pastoral setting.

Adding to my reluctance was the fact that the story, already well chronicled by members of the Dallas media, lacked some of the standard elements required of a nonfiction crime story. A case solved quickly—as this one was— is a boon to law enforcement but provides great problems for the journalist seeking to develop a story into book length.

What remained to be told, then, was not so much what had happened, but why. Finding a satisfactory answer, if, in fact, one existed, would be no easy task.

Help in the ultimate decision to enter into the project came from three women to whom I am indebted: my wife Pat, who persuasively insisted the story needed to be told; and my agent Janet Wilkens Manus, whose enthusiasm is infectious; and Jane Chelius, who helped point the way. In retrospect, I am grateful for their gentle nudgings, for in the process of researching and writing the book I gained new—though sometimes troubling—insight into the part of the world I call home.

Too, my task was made easier by the generous help of many, some who asked only that they remain anonymous. My gratitude to them is in no way less than to these: Roy Vaughn, Billy Fowler, Fran Ross, Steve Egan, Don Blanton, Jesus Chao, and Sonny Pfeifer of the Midlothian Police Department; Phil Hambrick and Jack Wallace of the Cedar Hill Police Department; Texas Ranger George Turner; Stan Ferguson of the Fort Worth Police Department; Tom Wafer of the Dallas Police Department; John Gage and Robert Browning of the Ellis County Sheriff's Department; Norman Kinne of the Dallas County District Attorney's Office; and Detective J.W. Greene of the Coconino County (Arizona) Sheriff's Department.

Kevin Chester, formerly with the Ellis County District Attorney's Office, patiently addressed my questions as did District Judge Gene Knize and Justices of the Peace Glen Ayers and Maurice Lowrey. The input of attorneys Brad Lollar, Don Ellyson, Jim Jenkins, Joe Grubbs, and Lee Johnson was also beneficial.

Special thanks to Midlothian City Manager Chuck Pinto, Mayor Maurice Osborne, and Midlothian High School principal Wilburn Roesler. And to Fred Turner, Jr., Lane Turner, Lance Turner, Dana Turner, Patsy Day, Scott Lindsey, Rick Simmons, Robert Campbell, Jerry Reeves, Kirk Reeves, Steve Womack, and Gabe Smith. And literally dozens of Midlothian residents, young and old, who shared recollections and offered insight.

Fellow journalists Bob Walton, Bobbi Miller, David Bloom, Tom Dodge, and Robert Tomsho not only shared observations but helped pass the time during lengthy trial recesses and lunch breaks. Thanks, too, to Jim Henderson, Dr. Richard Fullington, and Troy Dungan for special favors.

A gracious nod is also due the photographers whose names are carried alongside the photographs used.

Had it not been for the belief in this project on the part of the relatives and loved ones of George Raffield, the undertaking would have been impossible. A simple thank-you hardly suffices to Don and Shirley Moore, Sherrie and Mark Prine, and Sheryl and David Zanolini. If this book carries the message I hope it does, it is because they were willing to share their memories of both good times and bad.

To Dr. Linda Kelley of the Green Oaks Resource Center; Dr. Gary Malone; Carol Steele, executive director of the Crisis Center of Collin County; and DeSoto Police Department Sergeant J. D. Horvath I am indebted for the patient explanations of the growing problem of teenage involvement in satanic activities. And it was Austin Police Department Sergeant Dusty Hesskew who made the forensic magic of blood splatter re-creation understandable. Thanks also to Los Angeles Police Department Detective Everett Berry.

All occurrences and conversations in the book are based on court and police records, personal observations, and the remembrances of the parties involved. In some instances dialogue has been re-created but is as close to exact as the memories of my sources permit.

And, in the interest of fairness, the names of certain minor characters—people in no way directly involved in the crime—have been changed.

To all, I have done my utmost to keep a promise: that I would tell the story as truthfully and honestly as possible.

Prologue

The pretty young woman, dressed in mourning black and visibly weary from the stress and sleeplessness that preceded her arrival at the funeral, could not get the thought out of her mind. It was there, buzzing in her brain like some silly jingle one hears on the radio and can't forget.

What was she going to do with all those candied apples?

That the concern should grip her as she walked toward the entrance to the church, past solemn faces and honor guards standing at rigid attention, she knew, was foolish. Like so many other things that had occurred in the shadowy numbness of the past few days, it made no sense.

All she knew for certain in her fragile state was that her brother—half brother, actually, though she had never thought of him as such—was dead at age twenty-one. He had been a policeman just beginning a career he had aspired to since childhood. He was someone she had loved a great deal.

And he had been crazy about candied apples.

The woman thought back to days when she and her brother had dressed as goblins and visited the houses in their neighborhood, collecting Halloween cookies and candy. It was a neighbor, she remembered as the tears began to moisten the corners of her eyes, who had introduced her brother to the delight of candied apples.

She had been making some on that damp October evening just four days earlier, the twenty-third, planning to take them with her on Saturday night when she and her husband were to have dinner with her brother and his fiancée.

But while she was in her kitchen, dipping apples into a hot, sticky caramel mixture, a tragedy that would forever alter her life was taking its ugly shape.

It was not until the next day that they found him, lying face down beside his pickup, in which she had so often ridden.

For most of that Saturday she had waited at the home of her parents for news as law enforcement officers searched for her brother. She had been seated at the kitchen table with her mother, listening to a police scanner, when the chilling words finally came late in the afternoon. The monotone voice of a police officer confirmed the family's worst fear: "Vehicle and victim located . . . discontinue search . . . notify family."

The girl's mother began to sob as she heard the word *victim,* slumping forward onto the tabletop, burying her face in her hands. Her shoulders heaved in spasms as she cried uncontrollably. Her husband tried briefly to comfort her, then walked silently into the backyard.

In the living room, the young woman's five-year-old son was lying on the floor in front of the television when the program he was watching was interrupted by a news bulletin. Jumping to his feet he ran to the kitchen, a terrified look on his face. What he had seen was a picture of his uncle's truck, a prone body next to it. "The man said he's dead," the little boy said. He burst into tears even before his mother could rush to cradle him in her arms.

Now, on this bright and warm Tuesday afternoon as she accompanied the rest of her family and her brother's fiancée to the places reserved for them in the front row of the First Baptist Church in Waxahachie, it seemed to the woman that it had all happened a lifetime ago.

Life seemed to pass in agonizing slow motion, fueled by a

range of emotions that jumped out at her at the most unexpected times. Like others in the family, she had cried. And there were the moments when she would sit alone, oblivious to the passage of time and numb to those around her, feeling nothing, hearing nothing, a brief escape from her overwhelming grief. But the respite from the pain never lasted long. Reality would again grip her, and a sudden boiling anger would make her want to scream.

And then, just as quickly, she would find herself thinking of some good time, reaching out to it as to a comforting touchstone.

That, she had decided, was why she thought about the candied apples even as she walked down the carpeted aisle toward the silver casket, her eyes fixed on the red and white carnations resting on top of it.

The church had been selected for the service because Waxahachie was the largest in the triangle of small Ellis County communities most directly affected by the tragedy. Midlothian, where the young officer had worked, was eleven miles to the west; Red Oak, where he had lived with his parents until he moved into his own apartment just twenty-three days before his death, was only ten miles to the north.

His mother had decided to have him buried in the Waxahachie City Cemetery next to his grandmother, who had died a year earlier. "I don't want him to be alone," she had told her husband.

From the elevated pulpit the minister looked out on the largest crowd ever assembled for a funeral in Waxahachie. Every seat was filled, and many mourners stood, lining the walls of the church. The parking lot outside held several hundred more; they stood quietly, listening over a loud-speaker as the pastor spoke of the young officer's courage and dedication to duty.

The officer's grandfather, who had traveled from Georgia for the funeral, tried to count the men in uniform who had come from throughout the state of Texas to pay their respects before finally giving up. Had he been able to complete his task he would have found there were 576, all with a ribbon of black draped across their badges.

3

And there were the journalists—dozens of newspaper reporters and photographers and television cameramen, some from as far away as New York—who had followed the tragic story since the first alert that a police officer had been slain. For most of them it was an unpleasant assignment, one that required them once again to intrude on the private grief of people they did not know. Still, for even the most hardened reporters it was impossible not to be moved by the service they had been dispatched to chronicle. Their reports would estimate that almost a thousand people had attended.

A police chaplain delivered the eulogy, describing the officer as a young man whose mission should live on in the memory of all in attendance: "He gave his life in an attempt to make a difference; to make the world a safer, better place for us all."

The service ended with the playing of "Amazing Grace" as the honor guard silently saluted the casket.

Officers standing at attention then formed a double column from the church to the hearse that would carry the fallen officer to the cemetery.

Led by twenty motorcycle policemen and followed by one hundred police cruisers, the funeral cortege slowly made its way downtown past the historic old Waxahachie courthouse through streets lined with people. At the corner Texaco station, a group of elderly men stood, their hats over their hearts. The flag in front of the fire station had been lowered to half-mast. Even the residential streets of proud old gingerbread-trimmed homes were crowded. Mothers stood holding the hands of small children, still too young to comprehend the magnitude of the event. Someday they would remember the day, however, and ask questions.

The crowd at the cemetery was even larger than the one at the church. Grim-faced high school students from Midlothian, many experiencing for the first time the death of someone they had known, stood in small groups, some talking quietly, others standing alone, looking uncomfortable in Sunday suits and dresses. Officers from the nearby Mansfield Police Department had agreed to man the Midlothian station so that all thirteen of the dead man's fellow officers could attend the services.

And many strangers came to pay their respects. An elderly woman stepped quietly to the side of the officer's mother, touched her hand, and said, "Your son was a hero. I just wanted to come and say thank you for what he did." Another woman, a mother from Midlothian, slipped an envelope into the grieving mother's hand. In it was a handwritten note, explaining that she had children whose lives had been steered in the right direction by the impact of the tragic event.

The woman's brief message meant even more to the dead officer's mother than the letter of condolence the parents would later receive from President Reagan.

With a gentle breeze humming through the nearby cedar trees and flapping the green canvas canopy that had been erected over the freshly dug grave, the pastor briefly spoke again of this "fallen soldier."

A member of the honor guard presented folded American flags to the mother and fiancée, and from a hill behind those who had crowded near the casket to pass and pay last respects came the clear, chilling bars of taps, played by an officer from the Dallas Police Department.

Then the honor guard took its orders and began the firing of the traditional twenty-one-gun salute.

As the shots echoed into the blue cloudless sky, the smell of gunpowder floated over the gathering.

And the young woman thought no more of candied apples.

Instead, she found herself wondering if her brother had heard the shots that were fired into the back of his head.

Part
ONE

"The undercover cop was found face down in a field . . ."

—*from "Tweeter and the Monkey Man"
by the Traveling Wilburys*

1

The phone woke Police Chief Roy Vaughn from a pleasant dream about towering pine trees and hidden lakes brimming with bass. In his half-awake state he first thought the ringing was the alarm clock, signaling time to get up and finish packing the van for the getaway weekend into the east Texas and Louisiana woodlands that he and his wife had been planning.

But by the third ring he had the receiver in hand. During a lifetime of law enforcement work, first as a Dallas patrolman and now as chief of the small force of the community of Midlothian, Texas, middle-of-the-night phone calls had become a way of life. Seldom did they bring good news.

This one was to be no exception. The voice on the other end was that of Lieutenant Billy Fowler. Sitting on the edge of the bed, the chief finally replied. "I'll meet you at the station in ten minutes."

Margie Vaughn sat up and turned on a bedside lamp and watched as her husband hurriedly pulled on a pair of jeans. "What's the matter?" she asked.

"We've got an officer missing," he said, now fully awake. "Billy and I are going to go look for him."

Studying the look of concern on her husband's face, she asked if he wanted her to fix him a cup of coffee. No, he said, he didn't have time; then he urged her to go back to sleep.

"Who is it?" Margie asked.

"George Raffield," her husband replied, squinting into an unlit closet in search of his windbreaker.

Margie enjoyed a friendly relationship with most of the men under her husband's command, but she knew very little about the missing officer. Though he had been a member of the force for three months, she had seen him only a couple of times in passing. Hired to work as an undercover officer in the local high school, Raffield had not been part of any social activities involving the department. In fact, her husband had sworn him in at Lieutenant Fowler's home in secrecy rather than at the police station or City Hall as was the general practice. Margie had to think for a second to connect a face to the name. Her husband had told her only that the young officer was posing as a senior to investigate drug trafficking among high school students in the community. Aware that the operation was of the utmost secrecy, she had not pressed for details. Part of being a police officer's wife, she had learned, was not to ask too many questions.

"Is it serious?" she said.

"Billy sounded worried. George hasn't reported in since around seven. His fiancée just called to say he hadn't come home."

Margie glanced at the clock radio. It was a few minutes before 3:00 A.M.

"Go back to bed," Roy told his wife as he kissed her good-bye. "I'll call you." Though neither mentioned it, both knew that the weekend trip was off.

As Vaughn made his way through the darkened house, Sarge, the family cocker spaniel, roused from sleep, followed him to the front door, puzzled by his master's sudden departure and the fact he didn't get the customary pat on the head.

The chief stepped out into the drizzle and fog of that night of October 24, 1987, and pulled the collar of his windbreaker closer around his neck. A knot was already forming in his stomach.

From Vaughn's house in a quiet residential neighborhood it was only a five-minute drive to the police station. Unlike the days when he had worked in Dallas, where a trip to the station could take forty-five minutes to an hour depending on the traffic, any place the chief or his men needed to be was only a few minutes away in rural Midlothian, population 7,500.

The only thing that ever slowed the officers' response time was the passing of a Santa Fe freight train blocking Ninth Street, the city's main thoroughfare, twice daily. That, or the red lights that greeted travelers approaching the downtown area from Highways 67 and 287.

His windshield wipers sweeping away the drizzle, Vaughn drove past the First National Bank and glanced at the time and temperature sign flashing from the empty parking lot. It was sixty-one degrees—warm for that time of the year—and five minutes past three. Making the turn that led to the abbreviated downtown area, he saw the lighted billboard that proclaimed the city as the "Cement Capital of Texas." It also bore a message reminding residents of an anti-drug rally that was scheduled for the high school the following week. Vaughn and Lieutenant Fowler, who would be coming from his home on the opposite side of town, should be arriving at the station at the same time.

As he drove, Vaughn tried to convince himself that there was really no cause for alarm. Since Lieutenant Fowler and his wife were planning to accompany the Vaughns on their weekend trip, Raffield had been told not to work Saturday or Sunday. Fowler, who was the undercover officer's contact, had instructed him to stay out of Midlothian over the weekend and not to return until Monday morning for classes. Maybe, the chief thought, Raffield had already left town.

But why, then, hadn't he returned to the apartment he shared with the young woman he planned to marry in April?

Perhaps he had gotten involved with some of the teenagers he had become acquainted with—the "dopers," as

11

students at the school called them—and was still out protecting his cover. Or maybe he had had an accident in the wet weather and was stuck in a ditch down one of the tangle of back roads that surrounded the town.

Each imagined scenario, however, was unrealistic, leaving troubling questions. One of the key elements of Raffield's undercover training was the importance of keeping his contact—Fowler—aware of his whereabouts and activities by reporting at regular intervals. Raffield had been late with his check-in call a couple of times but only by an hour or so at most.

The fact that it had been almost eight hours since the lieutenant had heard from the officer justified Vaughn's concern. That feeling was quickly reinforced when the chief, pulling into the parking space in front of the station, saw the expression on Fowler's face.

"What do you think?" the chief asked as the two stood under the yellow glow of the light which burned above the station entrance.

"I don't know," said Fowler, drawing on a cigarette. It was the third he had smoked since being awakened by the call from George Raffield's fiancée. "But I don't feel good about it."

Like the man he now worked for, Fowler had spent almost twenty years with the Dallas Police Department before retiring. When they had met many years earlier, neither had suspected that one day they would be the two top men in a small-town police department. Over the years their relationship had evolved into something that went far beyond their common profession. They had become close friends.

If Billy Fowler was worried, Chief Vaughn knew there was good reason for concern.

Just hours earlier the two men and their wives had sat in a seafood restaurant in nearby Waxahachie, eating catfish and enthusiastically discussing the coming trip. Fowler mentioned that the undercover officer had called to check in just before he and his wife left for the restaurant.

Now the chief wanted to know exactly what young Raffield had said to Billy.

"There wasn't any kind of a buy set up for tonight," Fowler said. "He called just before seven. I think he was at the Pizza Inn. I asked what his plans were for the evening, and he said he was on his way to pick up Sparky Knighten and go messing around. They didn't have any specific plans."

Their conversation, Fowler said, had been brief. He had reminded Raffield not to go to the football game in Red Oak, where Midlothian High would be playing that evening. Raffield had come to the Midlothian Police Department from that nearby community, where he had worked as a reserve officer and civilian dispatcher. It was there that he had lived with his parents until the recent move into his own apartment. Fowler knew that Raffield had regularly worked as a security guard at Red Oak football games the season before and didn't want him to risk being recognized.

"Where do we start?" the chief asked as the two men climbed into Vaughn's Ford.

Fowler knew some of the spots that George had visited since his enrollment in school, hangouts of the kids he had become friendly with during the course of his operation. "We'll try them first," the lieutenant said. "After that . . ." He shrugged.

"What?" Vaughn asked.

Fowler flipped the butt of his cigarette out the window. "We start looking for a needle in a haystack."

Under normal circumstances, Fowler would have liked being out at that time of night. The most enjoyable hours he had spent with the Dallas Police Department had been working "deep nights," midnight until dawn. There had always been a special excitement about the facade of quiet and calm that masked the criminals' busiest hours. Violent rages, breaking and entering, drug transactions, pimps and hookers—beneath the mirage of tranquil dark, Lieutenant Fowler well knew, there was a great deal happening. And back in those days, before his wife's worry and loneliness had led him to change shifts, he had been more successful than most at finding the action that waited in the alleyways and back streets of Dallas.

On this particular night, however, he felt none of the old excitement as they pulled away from the station and drove through the block-long business district of the community he now called home.

Dee Tee's Restaurant was dark; it would be a couple of hours before it would open for the early morning arrival of coffee drinkers gathering to discuss the previous night's game. Aside from the neon Western Auto sign shining dimly through the heavy fog and the lights of the corner washateria, the town was quietly sleeping. There was not a single car or pickup in any of the downtown parking spaces.

The two said little as they made their rounds. Not yet ready to discuss the possibility of foul play, they were searching only for George Raffield's red GM pickup. Once they located it, they felt sure their questions would be answered.

Out Farm-to-Market Road 663 they drove past the deserted parking lot of the high school, then down a nearby road that led to City Lake, which had once served as the community's water supply. Now abandoned, the small lake was frequented only by occasional fishermen and teenagers who favored its isolation to smoke pot or to find the privacy young love demanded.

Vaughn navigated the maze of rutted road that circled the lake, constantly fearing that he would get stuck. While there was evidence that a few other drivers had come before them, they did not encounter a single vehicle before returning to the firm blacktop that led back to the main road.

On the drive back toward the Farm-to-Market Road they passed the old two-story house where Vaughn had lived when he first moved his family out of Dallas in the summer of 1968. To him that was a lifetime ago. He had married a woman with four children from a previous marriage; later, when they had a child of their own, the search for a home large enough to accommodate their family had led them from the cramped house they owned in Dallas to the rural quiet of Midlothian.

As they passed the house, Vaughn made no mention of it.

Any good memories had been destroyed by a bitter divorce he had not spoken about in years. Long before he met Margie, he had given up the comfortable old place and sold the few cattle he had bought for the boys as Future Farmers of America projects. To escape the pain of the divorce, he had put the house up for sale and moved briefly to nearby Lancaster.

Again they drove past the new high school, built on the land where Vaughn's small herd of cattle had grazed years before, and turned south.

Vaughn sped up, heading in the direction of a housing development located a few miles farther out of town. Sitting just off the Farm-to-Market Road, barren of even the scrub cedars generally found in the area, the tidy collection of new brick homes hardly justified its name. It was known as Camelot, and among those who called it home was the family of a Dallas police officer named Tom Knighten.

Vaughn and Fowler had known him when he served as an instructor at the Dallas Police Department's shooting range. A man with a trim athletic build and a boyish face that seemed always to be smiling, Corporal Knighten had been one of the first to appear at the Midlothian station and extend his congratulations after Vaughn was named chief.

Like many Dallas police officers, Knighten had opted to live somewhere other than the city where he worked. For a while, the bedroom community of Duncanville, just a few miles up Highway 67 toward Dallas, had been the Knightens' home. His wife taught in a Christian academy there where his children also attended school. It had been a quiet, safe place to live until the drug problem began to creep out of south Dallas and into the suburbs. For that reason the Knightens had decided to move farther away, to Midlothian and its Camelot.

The move, however, had not provided the isolated protection the Knightens had hoped for. It was their sixteen-year-old son Greg—nicknamed Sparky—whom George Raffield was en route to pick up when he had last contacted Lieutenant Fowler.

Tom Knighten did not know that the undercover officer had already made several drug cases against his son. Greg Knighten, in fact, had quickly emerged as one of the most active drug dealers in Midlothian High School. Fowler and Vaughn both privately dreaded the day when Raffield would complete his undercover work and arrest the youngster.

Vaughn wound through the maze of darkened houses, slowing as he approached the Knighten home. There was no sign of a red pickup. They discussed waking the family and asking the youngster if he knew where George might be, but they finally decided not to chance compromising their officer's cover. There were other places Fowler wanted to look before taking such measures.

Heading back to town, Vaughn drove to the P&S Grocery, a small all-night convenience store he knew to be a popular hangout of high school students. To his disappointment the parking lot was empty. Through the window he could see a large woman, her back to him, leaning forward with her elbows on the counter, watching a black-and-white movie on a small television near the cash register. The electronic games that lined one wall were quiet, and no one was seated in either of the small booths.

"Damn," Vaughn said, pounding his fist against the steering wheel.

"Let's check Oxford Square," Fowler suggested. Though neither mentioned it, they were getting nervous, two middle-aged men who suddenly had to try to think like teenagers and who weren't having much success. The only ideas they had were the places Raffield had mentioned to Fowler in his regular check-ins.

The Oxford Square Apartments, located just across the highway from the P&S Grocery, were a federally funded low-income housing project populated primarily by the elderly. One exception was twenty-three-year-old Cynthia Fedrick, who lived in apartment 31.

Just a few days earlier, Raffield had gone there with Greg Knighten. George had told Fowler that a number of kids went there frequently to smoke marijuana. He had also told the lieutenant about an expensive stereo system the woman had just received—a stereo system that had recently been reported stolen.

Fowler drove to the back of the apartment where Cynthia Fedrick lived. There were several pickups parked in the complex, but George's was not one of them.

"Let's go back to the station and get on the telephone," the chief suggested. "We need to call Dallas and have them look around in the area where George was buying drugs with the other kids."

Fowler had told Raffield's fiancée to stay home in case George returned or called, in which event she was to phone the police station immediately. He had been silently hoping since leaving his house that he would hear the dispatcher's voice crackling on the radio to say she had called.

"We're going to have to call Knighten," Fowler said, speaking more to himself than to the man sitting beside him.

Before returning to the station, Fowler wanted to check one more place. He directed Vaughn to a side street not far from the downtown area and told him to slow down when he approached a rutted dirt road. In the early morning darkness, it appeared to lead nowhere, but one hundred yards back from the street stood an old abandoned house. Once an impressive structure surrounded by stately oak trees, the paintless, crumbling two-story house had become an eyesore that many of the community leaders had complained about for years. Most of the outside walls had been torn away, leaving only skeletal beams to show where rooms had once been. The roof, which had once shielded a porch running the full breadth of the house, had fallen away.

Several times the police had received late night complaints from nearby residents who told of strange noises and weird chants coming from the old house. One elderly woman, who had called to complain several times, was convinced the sounds were from devil worshipers. A daylight trip onto the property had convinced her she was right, and she phoned the police again.

What patrolmen found upon inspecting the old house was, in fact, disturbing. Pentagrams, swastikas, and vulgarities were drawn on the walls in chalk. Near an old fireplace that had obviously been recently used was the message, "By the rites of the Black Mass evil will speak in this house." On the floor upstairs someone had drawn the outline of a prone body, much like the diagrams used at murder scenes. The remnants of burned candles encircled the outline.

Concerned by what his officers had found, Chief Vaughn had summoned an expert in satanic cults from the Fort Worth Police Department to come to Midlothian and look at the writings and drawings. The last thing he needed was a community terrified by rumors of a satanic cult.

The Fort Worth officer, after a trip out to the house, had said the messages and symbols were most likely those of juvenile pranksters with no serious involvement in devil worship.

Though relieved, Vaughn had ordered that the area be patrolled more frequently. He also began an effort to find out who the property belonged to. He wanted to advise the owner that the old house presented a danger and should be torn down or at least fenced off. City records revealed that the property was owned by a corporation with headquarters in Hong Kong.

George had told Fowler that the house was a favored meeting place for some of the high school kids. On a couple of occasions he had gone there with several students after school to listen to heavy metal music and smoke pot. There had been no satanic activity, George reported, but he did recall someone mentioning a student who bragged that he'd done some devil worshiping before moving to Midlothian.

Vaughn drove down the dirt road, which was sheltered by a canopy of trees, toward the old structure. In the beam of his headlights the house looked evil. An old yellow tomcat stood on the porch and briefly stared at the intruders before scurrying off to the protection of darkness.

George Raffield's truck wasn't there, and Vaughn began backing down the road. "We're going to get rid of this fucking place if I have to tear it down myself," he said.

Back in his office at the police station, Fowler placed a call to Sergeant Eddie Silva at Dallas's southwest substation. Silva had worked as an undercover narcotics investigator for Fowler several years earlier, posing as a student at Southern Methodist University.

A dispatcher said that Silva had just checked out to go to a nearby restaurant for breakfast. Fowler explained that it was an emergency and asked that Silva be contacted by beeper and asked to call him as quickly as possible.

He then dialed Tom Knighten's number.

"Tom, I'm sorry to wake you," Fowler said, carefully measuring his words to disguise his concern. "We're working a missing persons report on a kid named George Moore."

"Yeah, I know him."

"Well, he hasn't made it home, and we're told he was with your boy last night. Has Greg come in?"

Knighten said he had wakened during the night to use the bathroom and was under the impression then that his son was in his room but would check to make sure. Only a few seconds passed before he returned to the phone. "He's in bed, asleep," Knighten reported.

"I hate to ask you to do this," Fowler said, "but would you mind waking him up and asking him if he knows where George might be?"

Again Tom Knighten left the phone. This time it was several minutes before he returned. "Yeah, Billy, Greg says he saw George around seven o'clock last night. He says George came by and gave him a ride out to his girlfriend's house. Dropped him off there and left. Greg says he was out there, at the Cadenheads' place, until her daddy brought him home around midnight."

"I appreciate it, Tom. Sorry to bother you."

"No problem. I hope you find the boy."

Fowler hadn't even had time to relate the conversation to Vaughn before Sergeant Silva called from a restaurant pay phone. "You're working pretty late hours for a man your age," he joked.

Fowler didn't laugh. He immediately explained the problem and asked if Silva would have some patrolmen look for the red pickup in the Dallas neighborhood where Raffield had been making his drug buys.

"We'll get a detail on the way," said Silva. As one who had worked undercover, he knew full well the concern Fowler was feeling. "If he's in our neighborhood, we'll find him. I'll be in touch."

The dispatcher knocked on the door of the office and entered with two cups of coffee, setting them on the desk in front of the lieutenant. Fowler was already dialing the phone again.

When Martha Asbury answered on the first ring, his question was answered. She had still not heard from her fiancé. When Fowler said he had no news, she burst into tears.

"Martha," he said, trying to calm her, "we're out looking. We've got other people looking. We're going to find him."

Between sobs she told him things he already knew. It was unlike George not to get in touch if he was going to be out late. He was too reliable, too conscientious for that. He would have found some way to contact someone—her or Billy or somebody in the family who would spread the word not to worry.

"I've got to ask you something," Fowler said. "Did you and George have an argument of any kind? Is there some reason he might not have come home tonight?"

There was a long pause before she replied. "No, everything was fine." George, she said, was looking forward to having the weekend off. His sister and her husband were planning to come over for dinner on Saturday.

"We're just trying to think of any explanation," Fowler said apologetically.

"I know," Martha replied. Then, after another pause: "Lieutenant Fowler, something's happened to him. I'm scared."

Billy Fowler did not tell her so, but he was, too.

Sitting in the office, even just to make the necessary phone calls, had become an exercise in frustration. Tom Knighten's mention that George had driven Greg out to his girlfriend's house provided a new area to search, something to do besides sitting and waiting.

After calling Raffield's parents in Red Oak to make sure he had not gone there, Fowler followed Vaughn to the car. The country roads leading out to the Cadenhead place, both knew, could be dangerous in weather like this. And there were winding, little-traveled back roads that would have taken Raffield to the main highway, then to his apartment, without coming back through Midlothian. Perhaps George had, in fact, taken young Knighten to his girlfriend's house, decided to go on home for the night, and then skidded off the road. Maybe they would find him stuck in a ditch, sleeping in the cab while awaiting help from some passerby.

For the next hour they drove along the country roads, finding nothing. Though it would not be light for another two hours, Roy Vaughn was already planning to organize a full-fledged search party.

It was also time, he decided, to telephone City Manager Chuck Pinto, his boss and the man who had initially given the okay to put an undercover officer into the high school.

Though neither mentioned it, both Vaughn and Fowler had given up their attempts to ignore the worst-case scenario that had been running through their minds.

Their experience and the gut feeling that all good police officers seem to develop told them that something tragic had happened to George Raffield. The feeling grew when Sergeant Eddie Silva telephoned from Dallas to say that his officers had been unsuccessful in locating Raffield's truck.

As he stood at the front door of the small police station, silently staring out into the damp darkness, Fowler felt a sudden cold shiver run through his body.

2

Time was when Midlothian was isolated despite the fact it was only a thirty-minute drive south from Dallas, anonymous for the simple reason there really was nothing about the little Ellis County community to set it apart from the hundreds of other small tradition-steeped Texas towns just like it.

In the town's one-hundred-year history there has been no significant boom or bust, no blue ribbon list of favorite sons who have gone off into the world to gain fame or fortune as war heroes, politicians, or wheeling-dealing entrepreneurs. In this town, dairy farming shares commercial importance with a cement factory, and a steel-recycling plant hides no horrible secrets. And although many of its townspeople still cling jealously to old frontier ideals, there is no colorful history of passionate violence or criminal mayhem to be passed down.

In another time Clyde Barrow and Bonnie Parker did roam and hide nearby, robbing a few area banks, but mostly they used the woods around Midlothian as peaceful meeting places where they could have an occasional midnight picnic with their Dallas kin while on the run from the big city sheriffs and police. Even notorious gangsters back then sought out Midlothian because of its tranquillity.

The town was established on the high rolling north Texas plains in 1877 by officials of the Gulf, Colorado, and Santa Fe Railroad companies who laid out two hundred acres and decreed that a community would be born from the sweat and dedication of those farsighted enough to purchase parcels of the rich farmland. Four years later the town had a church, a post office, and a name: Baker, after a fire-and-brimstone preacher named Charles Baker who had been among the first to take up the railroad on its land offer.

It wasn't until 1883 that a Scottish engineer, upon making his first pass through the community growing up along the banks of Waxahachie Creek, remarked on how closely it resembled Midlothian, Scotland, the village where he had spent his youth. Residents were flattered by the comparison and charmed by the lyrical quality of the name, and in short order the city fathers had, by a quick and unanimous vote, decided that Baker would officially become Midlothian.

It would be fifty years before the population grew to 1,000. And, as late as 1950, the census counters collected only 1,175 names.

Until the late sixties, when weary Dallas residents began looking upon the suburbs as an escape to a more peaceful way of life, Midlothian was primarily populated by those who had been born and raised there. From great-grandfather to grandfather, father to son, brothers to sisters, cousins to second cousins, the residents were united in what could generally be described as one big happy family.

Many of those earning weekly paychecks at Chaparral Steel or the BoxCrow Cement plant had begun their education at the local elementary school, completed it with high school graduation ceremonies, then remained in Midlothian to marry, have children of their own, and maintain the traditional cycle.

At the coffee shops and pharmacy, the post office and the local grocery, the greatest social sin was a failure to greet everyone, strangers included, with a warm hello and a smile.

It was, and remains, a place where a God-fearing faith is firmly held to. Charles Baker's one-room church has spawned a dozen others, many of them almost as old as the community itself. Their parking lots and pews are filled not only for Sunday morning services but for Wednesday night prayer meetings as well.

The newcomers were greeted by what they perceived to be a much welcomed understanding of their own desire for privacy. Those fleeing from Dallas, with its racial problems, its economic caste system, its cannibalizing workplaces, did not mind that some longtime residents might begrudge their arrival. It made little difference to those looking for a place to raise their families in peace that they had no blood ties, no grandfather who had once farmed the rolling black lands, no heritage that linked them to the town's unremarkable history. To the modern-day pioneers, searching for open spaces, unpolluted skies, and a gentler life-style, Midlothian represented a new beginning.

They were not deterred in the least by the unwritten law of small towns everywhere: He who is not born and raised there is, regardless of the years he might call it home, forever an outsider, to be held at arm's length from the heart and soul of the community.

It was a state of affairs most new arrivals quickly learned either to accept or to ignore, a fair trade for escape to a more pastoral way of life.

And as more and more people found their way to Midlothian, the reserved welcome evolved into a resigned acceptance. It was, after all, the new people who were moving into the expensive housing developments, ultimately prompting the building of a new high school and elementary school, causing the boundaries of the town to expand, raising the tax base, and bringing prosperity in the construction of new places to eat, a modern grocery, even a small shopping center.

It was easy to tell the natives from the newcomers. Those who had been born and raised there lived on the small farms and dairies on the outskirts of town or in the neat rows of frame houses on narrow blacktopped streets shaded by ancient oaks and pecan trees. With the exception of those adventurous couples who bought old homes for restoration, the late arrivals flocked to the treeless new subdivisions where it is difficult to differentiate one brick house from another.

In a sense, then, Midlothian became two communities— one old, one new. The newcomers brought with them creative new ideas and talk of progress. It was the new citizens of Midlothian, growing in number almost daily, who woke the town from its sleep and gently coaxed it into the twentieth century.

Such were the things considered by thirty-six-year-old Chuck Pinto, who was serving as city manager of the south Texas community of Live Oak in the spring of 1986 when he was approached about assuming the duties of directing Midlothian toward even more rapid progress. If full-blown prosperity was to come, it would be best achieved by proper planning. And in the minds of the city council members, Pinto, with his vision, know-how, and keen understanding of the inner workings of a rural community, was the man for the job.

Before visiting, Pinto did his homework. He learned that in the previous fifteen years the population had nearly doubled, from less than 4,000 to over 7,000. The median income had climbed from $23,000 to $34,000 in a five-year period. And while the city had recently developed the reputation of a bedroom community, with only 10 percent of its residents working at the cement and steel plants, the opportunity for economic growth was there. A federal grant had been awarded Midlothian and nearby Waxahachie for the construction of a commercial airport; the city had begun to turn a profit with a new electrical franchise, selling power to neighboring communities; and word out of Washington was that there was a good chance that Ellis County's bid to land the U.S. Department of Energy's $4.5 billion superconducting super collider—a high-tech research facility— would ultimately turn the area into an economic gold mine.

Midlothian, the perceptive Pinto determined, was on the verge of an economic boom, and the idea of directing the community's rise was attractive enough to prompt him to travel north from the picturesque Texas hill country to take a look.

What he found on a rainy Saturday afternoon as he and his wife made their unannounced arrival was disappointing. Following a five-hour drive from their home in Live Oak, the Pintos finally turned off Highway 67—and entered a time warp. The research Pinto had done had not prepared him for the rows of dilapidated houses that greeted him as he slowly drove through the town toward the business district. Midlothian had been built without design. The streets had no curbs or drainage. In one residential area, several houses had flooded. There was no hotel, shopping facilities were limited, and what new construction had been done was often in the shadow of ancient empty buildings, ugly ghosts from bygone days. He immediately realized that little thought had been given to growth and development over the long term.

After driving around town for a couple of hours, he had seen more than enough and turned toward home, his mind made up. The challenge the city fathers had offered was more than even he was willing to take on.

What he did not anticipate was the almost desperate persistence of those seeking his help. He was ultimately persuaded to return for an interview. His weekend visit, he was told, had not afforded him the opportunity to acquaint himself with the town's greatest commodity—its residents. Meet the people, he was told. Then make a decision.

A conservative man who gives high marks to community values, Pinto had, during his six-year tenure in Live Oak, managed to transform the town into something of a municipal hybrid. Under his direction, the small town just north of San Antonio had become a modern community while retaining the rural atmosphere so important to its heritage. He had patiently battled the small town politics and the distrust of set-in-their-ways community leaders, gradually gaining the confidence of those who had appointed him guardian of their future. In time he was no longer looked upon as an ambitious outsider eager to undermine tradition in favor of drastic change. Chuck Pinto became a hero, the savior of a dying town.

It was that accomplishment which attracted the attention of Midlothian. That, and Pinto's background.

An air force veteran, he had a bachelor's degree in criminal justice and a master's in public administration. He had briefly served as a traffic accident investigator for the Houston Police Department, but like millions of other Americans beginning a family, Chuck Pinto wanted out of the metropolitan rat race and began looking for a quieter community where his wife and children would be safer and happier. He applied for the police chief's job in Live Oak, Texas, won the position, and immediately set about the task of adapting modern big-city law enforcement techniques to a small-town department. He computerized and he organized. He persuaded the city council to increase the budget so that he might hire more qualified officers and provide them with better equipment. He introduced crime prevention programs that involved the community in its own safety. In time, it was determined that this aggressive, hardworking young outsider could serve the community even better if he was moved from the police department into the office of the city manager.

Having gained the community's confidence as police chief, Pinto was able to continue with his master plan to make Live Oak an even better place to live.

Midlothian wanted the same kind of direction, and it was the townspeople who persuaded him to meet the challenge. On his return for an interview, Pinto toured the schools and visited the businesses. He sat in coffee shops listening to friendly conversation and country and western music playing on the juke boxes. He saw smiling faces and felt an energy that was almost tangible. Most of all, he liked the stability of those he met, their honesty and values.

In July of 1986 Pinto moved his family into a new brick

home near Midlothian High School, leaving one success behind and making plans for a new one.

Even before the move, he knew what he wanted to accomplish. His plan was to modernize Midlothian and at the same time make sure the small-town atmosphere he found so charming was not disturbed. It would, he told his wife, be no easy task.

He attacked the job with a vengeance, poring over the city budget to bring immediate attention to the most pressing needs. He urged the annexation of more land into the city limits, convinced the city council of the need for computerization, pumped new enthusiasm into the Chamber of Commerce, and personally watched over the improvement of virtually every public service offered the community.

He went to his City Hall office only to conduct meetings and check on telephone messages. To the immediate delight of those who hired him, Pinto considered the community his workplace. He made a point of getting to know the local businessmen on a first-name basis. He visited their stores, attended their weekly service organization meetings, went to Little League games, and joined a church.

He also made it a point to find out how the local police department functioned. Though he enjoyed the challenges of his administrative position, Pinto was, in a sense, still a cop at heart. Occasionally he would drop by the station in the evenings and ride with the patrolmen. He regularly stopped in to have coffee with the chief and to discuss the problems he and his men were facing.

What Pinto found was easygoing, outdated law enforcement. Filing systems were virtually nonexistent, the relationship between the Midlothian department and other agencies in the area was strained at best, and there was little indication that the chief was interested in the innovations he suggested.

Pinto was privately pleased when he learned that the chief was planning to retire at the end of the year. It would afford him the opportunity to seek a man who would instill new direction and enthusiasm into local law enforcement.

It was a few days before Christmas, only two weeks before the application deadline for those seeking the post of police chief, when burly Roy Vaughn ran into Pinto in City Hall.

Pinto had met Vaughn and knew that he had been a police officer in Dallas before retiring to operate a glass and mirror business in Midlothian. He had watched with interest as Vaughn campaigned vigorously for justice of the peace on the Democratic ticket, only to lose by twelve votes.

What he didn't know was that several townspeople had been encouraging Vaughn to apply for the chief's job. Though he had had several opportunities to return to active duty with the Dallas Police Department since his retirement in 1980, Vaughn had expressed little interest in getting back into law enforcement. But, when the Midlothian job opened, he found himself thinking about it and finally discussed it with his wife, who encouraged him to apply.

Before doing so, however, he wanted to know what Pinto's thoughts were about a man in his fifties seeking the position. It stood to reason that the youthful city manager might be looking for a younger man who would likely be more receptive to new ideas.

"All I'm looking for," Pinto said, "is someone who is qualified, someone who can come in and upgrade the department. Age won't be a factor." In the short time he had known Vaughn, Pinto had learned that he was well respected; he had a friendly but no-nonsense manner and was clearly interested in the community; he had put five children through the local school system; though Vaughn himself was not a native Midlothian, his wife had been born and raised there; and he had twenty-two years of experience with the Dallas Police Department. "I'd like to see you apply," Pinto told him.

By mid-January the list of candidates had been whittled to six, and Vaughn was one of those asked to appear before an executive session meeting of the city council for a formal interview. A week later he received a call from Pinto, instructing him to take a physical and renew his Texas Law Education Standards license.

On February 1, 1987, in a brief ceremony at City Hall, Roy Vaughn was sworn in as the city's new police chief. On that same day he walked into the Midlothian Police Department headquarters for the first time.

In his first meeting with those under his command, Vaughn outlined his uncompromising philosophy of police work. Fairness and honesty would be the cornerstones of his department. If there were those who felt it right to overlook a speeding violation by some pillar of the community, they should look elsewhere for employment. If there were those who saw nothing wrong with occasionally helping themselves to confiscated property, they would no longer be needed.

Roy Vaughn, it was clear, knew police work and the men who performed it—the good and the bad—and he was not going to tolerate the latter, no matter how minor the rule-bending might be.

Neither was he going to be simply an administrator. In a department with limited manpower, he saw himself as an active member of the force. Vaughn reported for work each morning in full uniform rather than in a suit and tie. Members of his staff were surprised to see him directing traffic near the high school in the early mornings, then sitting in for the dispatcher in the evenings.

Vaughn restructured his staff, dismissing those he felt would not fit into his plans and hiring new officers who shared his philosophy and enthusiasm. He made fence-mending trips to neighboring police departments, and his message to them was clear and to the point: Midlothian would no longer refuse to cooperate with visiting agencies investigating criminal activity. Much of the crime in suburban and rural communities overlapped from one city to another, he knew, often spilling out of nearby Dallas and Fort Worth. He vowed to cooperate with them and made it clear that he would welcome their help if an investigation took his men beyond Midlothian. To neighboring police departments, Roy Vaughn was a breath of fresh air.

In time, the statistics that he regularly presented to Pinto mirrored a dramatic reduction in local criminal activity. Arrests for theft and burglary were up, and the three jail cells in the rear of the police station were filled virtually every weekend following arrests for drunk driving, breaking and entering, and domestic violence. Cases being sent to the Ellis County District Attorney's office in greater numbers than ever were well made, and indictments were routinely handed down.

The newly appointed chief was doing his job well. Privately, Chuck Pinto viewed the aggressive attitude of the police department as his first major accomplishment.

Vaughn, however, was just getting started. Things he heard in the coffee shops and saw as a Midlothian businessman had convinced him that beneath the quiet surface of the town was a dark, threatening evil that had gone virtually unchecked. He had only to read reports in the Dallas papers to know that Ellis County, thanks to its rural isolation and sparse population, was a hotbed of methamphetamine lab activity. More than one Dallas police officer had suggested to him that Midlothian had become a favored drop-off spot for big-city drug dealers. Too, there had been a steady stream of anonymous calls and unsigned letters warning him to be aware of drug-related activities involving certain Midlothian residents.

Almost every arrest his men made, Vaughn soon became aware, was somehow connected to drug activity. He knew the townspeople would not willingly accept the fact that their community was infected by the same cancer that was gnawing away at nearby metropolitan areas.

Persuading the citizens to confront the problem would be no easy task. But the chief was pleasantly surprised to find that he had a strong ally outside his department.

Chuck Pinto shared Vaughn's concern. In Live Oak he had seen the trafficking of drugs spread into his community from nearby San Antonio. There was no reason to believe Midlothian, just a short drive from a Dallas neighborhood that was heavily populated by Jamaican crack dealers, had remained drug-free.

Pinto knew his concerns were justified one evening when he stopped at P&S Grocery and witnessed an open exchange of drugs and money in the parking lot.

Thus he was more than receptive when Vaughn came to him and suggested the first-ever undercover drug operation in Midlothian history. At the same time, the city manager knew that setting up such an operation, particularly in a community with limited money and manpower, would be difficult. Some smaller towns, Pinto knew, had conducted undercover programs with state and federal money, but the bureaucratic process of securing a grant often took months, and there was no assurance that funds would ever be made available.

Vaughn, convinced that waiting would only allow the problem to worsen, had anticipated Pinto's argument. "You give me the go-ahead," he said, "and I'll put it together."

In the next few days the police chief and city manager paid private visits to local businessmen, soliciting funds for what they described as an operation whose purpose was to deal with the drug problem they were convinced existed in the community. By the end of the week the Chamber of Commerce had pledged $1,000, and a local bank and two business leaders added another $1,000.

With $2,000 in "buy money," to be used by an undercover officer to purchase drugs from local dealers, Vaughn set out to find an undercover agent.

He didn't have to look far.

Jack Wallace had been honorably discharged from the Marine Corps in the spring of 1980, returning home with a Japanese wife and a strong desire to follow his father's footsteps into law enforcement. For a quarter-century the elder Wallace had served with the Dallas Police Department, for eighteen years as a patrolman, then as one of the first officers recruited into the newly formed helicopter section.

Fascinated by stories his father had told him, Wallace knew even before he enlisted in the service that his life's profession would eventually be in law enforcement. Rather than becoming a policeman, however, his ambition was to join the Texas Department of Public Safety, secretly hoping to become a Texas Ranger. Only when he failed to meet the eyesight requirement did he revise his plans and begin looking for a job with a small- to medium-sized police department where experience and advancement would come more quickly than on a metropolitan force. At twenty-four, he felt he was getting a late start on his career and wanted to make up for time lost as quickly as possible.

It was in June of 1980 that the angular, boyish-looking Wallace was hired by Chief Steve Campbell in Cedar Hill, just eight miles up Highway 67 from Midlothian.

Wallace was in his fourth year as a patrolman when he first heard rumors that the Cedar Hill Police Department was planning to apply for a grant from the Criminal Justice Division of the governor's office to fund undercover narcotics investigations. Wallace immediately went to his captain, Phil Hambrick, and asked to be considered. Most of the arrests he had made, Wallace explained, had been drug-related. As an undercover investigator, he felt he could help do something about this problem, though he didn't admit that the freedom and adventure promised by such a lone wolf–type assignment excited him just as much.

Captain Hambrick had already considered talking to Wallace about undercover work. He liked the officer's enthusiasm and had been pleased at how quickly he had learned to handle himself in difficult situations. Hambrick had not been at all surprised when the young patrolman was named the department's Officer of the Year in 1983. Jack Wallace, he had already decided, was the best candidate for the dangerous task of undercover work.

Hambrick advised him to let his marine-style flattop haircut grow out. He also suggested the addition of a beard, and he enrolled Wallace in the Dallas Police Department's undercover training school.

Finally, after a month of training, Wallace was sent out to make his first buy, entering a south Dallas apartment to purchase cocaine while two veteran narcotics investigators, his backups, waited across the street. Three times during his negotiation with the dealer, Wallace was accused of being a "fucking cop." Each time he responded with an angry curse and asked the dealer if he wanted to do business or not. The experience was the most frightening of his life. At one point his legs became so weak that he had to sit down on the couch in the dealer's living room.

He eventually managed to make the buy: five cocaine tablets—"coke tabs" as they were called—at twenty dollars apiece.

When the dealer was later arrested, officers confiscated over $20,000 worth of cocaine, heroin, marijuana, and stolen handguns from the apartment.

Jack Wallace had gotten off to a fast start—and had taken his first step into a dark side of society for which no amount of training could prepare him.

By the time he returned to Cedar Hill his sandy hair was creeping down past his collar and he was sporting an unkempt beard. His blue patrolman's uniform, which had been so carefully tailored by his wife, had been exchanged for faded jeans, tennis shoes, and a tattered T-shirt. Instead of a patrol car, he was driving a van badly in need of a paint job. He had adopted the quick, jerky mannerisms of one perpetually on uppers. Gone was the erect, authoritative carriage he had learned in the military. Now his shoulders slumped, and when he entered Captain Hambrick's office, he slouched into the chair.

"Damn," said Hambrick, "I don't know whether to shake your hand or throw your ass in jail."

The transformation was stunning.

It took Wallace little time to establish himself in the local drug community. With the help of an ex-con informant, he took on the identity of a part-time carpenter who moonlighted by running a booth at the Traders Village in nearby Grand Prairie on weekends, buying and selling stolen merchandise.

Soon the speed freaks, methamphetamine manufacturers, and coke heads who wandered aimlessly on the fringes of reality began to hang out with him. It was easy, he found, to quickly bring any conversation around to the subject of drugs. Dope, it seemed, was all anyone wanted to talk about.

Wallace began making cases in Cedar Hill almost immediately. And soon his investigations began taking him out of town, to the sources of the drugs coming into the community. It was not unusual for him to be in several cities during the course of a single day's work, making contacts and buys from a range of people that he found surprising. There were the "speed whores," young women eager to exchange sexual favors for drugs, brain-fried men barely past their teens whose only reason for existence was their next "bump," and family operations where young children, already robbed of their innocence, were used to make deliveries. They all had one thing in common: drugs ruled what was left of their miserable lives.

At a house in Waxahachie, Wallace waited while a father sent his six-year-old son to his toy box to get the plastic bags of marijuana he was there to buy. In an apartment in nearby Balch Springs he fought back a wave of nausea as he watched a man inject crank into the soft tissue beneath his tongue. The junkie looked him squarely in the eye, blood pouring from the wound made by the needle, and said, "Motherfucker, I don't know whether you're a narc or not. It doesn't matter, really. This shit's worth going to jail for. Hell, it's worth fucking dying for."

He watched as a twenty-year-old woman, several months pregnant, chewed crank, crystallized methamphetamine, her zombielike smile revealing rotted gums. She was afraid of needles, she explained, so had become an "eater."

Wallace quickly learned that the drug culture was highly mobile, constantly on the move from town to town. In just a few weeks, the boundaries of his undercover work had expanded to include a number of Dallas suburbs—DeSoto, Lancaster, Duncanville, Grand Prairie, Waxahachie, Glenn Heights, and Mesquite—and he began regularly working joint operations with police in those jurisdictions in addition to his duties in Cedar Hill.

With each new case he made, Wallace's reputation grew.

Police chiefs from throughout the Dallas area began calling Cedar Hill, asking if they could borrow him for short-term undercover operations.

Among those who called was Roy Vaughn.

In a meeting with Vaughn and Lieutenant Fowler, Wallace was told that his undercover investigation would focus on local residents and those bringing illegal narcotics into the city. Armed with names of several suspected Midlothian dealers, the Cedar Hill officer began making himself visible in yet another community.

He was stunned by what he found. Though Midlothian had 10,000 fewer people than Cedar Hill, the drug activity appeared far greater. In his first ten days on the streets he purchased cocaine, amphetamines, methamphetamine, and marijuana. He encountered dealers in private homes—even buying marijuana from a young businessman who lived in the same neighborhood as the police chief—and on the streets. He visited an abandoned mattress factory that was being used as a shooting gallery by a group of speed freaks. He bought crank from a woman whose addict husband had shot himself in the head in a suicide attempt. Wallace was taken to apartment houses, trailer parks, and even onto the grounds of Chaparral Steel, past uninterested security guards, where truck drivers openly bought and sold drugs.

He made buys on the town square, in front of the bank, in the parking lots of convenience stores, and at a truck stop. More than once high school students flagged down his rust-colored van and asked if he had anything to sell.

In a park on the edge of town he met a group of men in their twenties from nearby DeSoto who expressed interest in trading drugs for stolen merchandise.

And as he made his rounds, he repeatedly heard a warning that was on the one hand encouraging, on the other, troubling.

Sitting at the kitchen table in Fowler's house one evening, Wallace updated the lieutenant on his progress. "You've got drugs coming into town from every direction," he said, as he sipped at a cup of tea Fowler's wife had prepared. "Dealers are coming out of Dallas, Waxahachie, Maypearl . . . hell, all over Ellis County. But they're getting nervous."

"What do you mean?" Fowler asked.

"Every sonuvabitch I talk to warns me to be careful. Says things have really changed around here. They say that the old chief was a good dude, that he turned his head and didn't fuck with them. Apparently you guys aren't nearly as popular. The word on the street is that the new chief and his people will snatch your butt up in a sweet minute."

Fowler smiled. "Roy will be glad to hear that."

"No more than I am," Wallace said.

The news that Vaughn found most disturbing was that Wallace had encountered many students from the high school in his investigation. He reported that a man living in an apartment near the high school was selling pot and speed to kids. A sixteen-year-old had taken him to an address on the outskirts of town, assuring him he could purchase LSD. Numerous Midlothian parents and their school-age children were dealing together. "And," Wallace continued, "the kids who aren't able to score here in town are going over to south Dallas to buy nickle and dime bags."

The undercover officer told him of watching a sixteen-year-old lock himself in a car and roll up all the windows. When the heat inside became almost unbearable, the youngster, broke and unable to obtain the crank he generally favored, began sniffing typewriter correction fluid to get high. "If that little shit lives to be twenty years old," Wallace said, "it'll be a miracle."

On a hot August evening in 1987, Wallace's Midlothian operation ended with a raid that resulted in the arrest of seventeen suspects. In four months he had made twenty-eight cases. There was still work to be done, Wallace told Vaughn and Fowler during a private ceremony at the police station at which he was given a commendation, but his superiors in Cedar Hill had voiced concern that he had worked the area long enough. The Midlothian authorities had offered no argument. To continue beyond that point, it was agreed, might blow his cover.

Chief Vaughn expressed his gratitude, shook Wallace's hand, and assured him the battle would go on.

What he did not mention was that he had already begun laying plans to fight it on another front.

3

Dawn broke on Saturday under a thick layer of oyster gray clouds hanging so low they obscured the top of the old city water tower across the street from the police station. Roy Vaughn stood in the doorway, staring at its four steel girders, which rose skyward before disappearing into the fog. Though no longer in use, the tower had been allowed to stand, a favored landmark to those in town who found comfort in the preservation of history.

Vaughn squinted, trying to make out the peeling black-on-silver "Midlothian" lettered on the tower, then turned and walked back into the station.

Though he had already telephoned Al Castleman of the Dallas Police Department and requested help from his helicopter squad, an air search for the missing officer and his pickup, he realized, would have to wait until the cloud cover lifted.

The search would have to begin on the ground. Vaughn and Fowler began calling other agencies for help—the Ellis County Sheriff's office and nearby police departments—asking that any available men be sent to join the search for George Raffield.

Vaughn's mind raced with the organizing, briefly pushing aside the possibility that Raffield might be dead or injured. He contacted several local residents who owned four-wheel-drive vehicles, asking that they be loaned to the search party. He phoned home to tell his wife that a patrolman would be by to get his pickup.

Margie, who had not slept since her husband left, instinctively knew there had been no news. She also knew that the longer the young officer was missing, the greater the likelihood that something serious had happened.

"It doesn't look good," Roy told her, his voice already hoarse from lack of sleep and too many cigarettes.

"Is there anything I can do?" she asked.

"We've got a lot of people coming over to begin a foot search. If this goes on all day we're going to need to feed them."

Margie said she would begin making sandwiches. "Are you okay?" she asked.

"I've had better days," he replied. His weary voice sent a wave of concern through Margie Vaughn. She knew all too well that if something had, in fact, happened to George Raffield, her husband would be the target of those eager to place blame. It had happened before.

Vaughn had been in police work just five years when he became one of the central figures in the most intensive criminal investigation in the nation's history.

The son of a Depression-era farmer, Vaughn had returned from four years of naval duty in the spring of 1958 anxious to begin a career but uncertain what to do with his life. He worked briefly for a Dallas truck line but quickly saw that it offered little promise for the future. That summer he took the civil service examination and applied to the Dallas Police Department. On October 6, 1958, he was sworn in.

He was working as a patrol officer on November 22, 1963, the day President John F. Kennedy was shot while riding in a Dallas motorcade, the victim of sniper fire from the School Book Depository. Summoned to the scene, Vaughn had been among the first to enter the sixth floor of the building from which Lee Harvey Oswald had fired the fatal shots.

During the hectic hours following the assassination, Vaughn had participated in several arrests, including those of three men who were seen running from the area to hide in a railway boxcar.

And two days later, on the Sunday that Oswald, the prime suspect in the crime, was to be transported from the Dallas city jail to the county facility, it was Patrolman Vaughn who was assigned to guard the ramp leading to the underground garage where the transfer of the prisoner was to take place.

As millions watched on network television, the hand-cuffed Oswald was ushered into the basement by a group of officers. Suddenly from the crowd a Dallas nightclub owner named Jack Ruby stepped in front of Oswald and fired a single fatal shot.

The answers to all the questions surrounding Kennedy's assassination died that morning on the cold concrete floor of the basement parking garage, leaving only a morass of speculation and conspiracy theories.

Among the targets of those who felt certain that the murder of the President had not been the act of a lone, deranged communist sympathizer was Roy Vaughn.

Immediately he was singled out as the man who had allowed Ruby access to the basement. He not only became the focus of an internal investigation but was questioned by the FBI and eventually summoned to appear before the Warren Commission, which investigated the assassination.

In the carefully pieced together re-creation of the minutes preceding Oswald's death, it was generally concluded that Ruby had left a nearby Western Union office, walked directly to the police station, and entered the basement from the Main Street ramp where Vaughn stood guard.

Shortly, several accounts of what supposedly took place were being widely reported.

One witness told of seeing Vaughn step away from his post at the entrance to the ramp, to stop traffic so the police car that would transport Oswald might make a quick exit onto the one-way street. It was, the witness said, while Vaughn was away from his assigned post that Ruby had slipped into the basement to murder Oswald.

Another version was given by a fellow officer, N. J. Daniels, who reported he had seen a man walk quickly past Vaughn and down the basement ramp. He wondered at the time why the patrolman had not stopped him.

The truth was that Vaughn never left his assigned post, nor did he see Ruby—a man whom he knew on sight—enter the basement by way of the ramp.

It wasn't until later that Sunday that Vaughn became aware that he was suspected of allowing Oswald's assailant into the basement. Captain C. E. Talbert telephoned him at home, told him of the charges, and asked if he had seen Ruby come down the ramp. Vaughn said he had not.

The following day, however, he was summoned to the station and asked to write a detailed report. Included in Vaughn's report was the fact that he had telephoned Daniels that Sunday evening and asked point blank if he had seen anyone walk down the ramp. Daniels assured him that he had not.

As the days immediately following the horrifying sequence of events passed, Vaughn became convinced that the department, battered by nationwide criticism, was searching for a scapegoat. He agreed to take a polygraph test, and the results corroborated his insistence that he had not allowed Ruby entry.

Two days after passing the polygraph exam, Vaughn was summoned to Internal Affairs and again questioned. Yes, he said, he had known Jack Ruby. He'd answered disturbance calls at his nightclub several times. But, no, he had never socialized with him. And, no, he did not see Ruby walk past him that Sunday morning.

It was during the questioning that Vaughn's temper finally exploded. "I've done every goddam thing you people have asked me to," he said. "The answer to every question you've asked me is in the report I wrote. They asked me the same things when they put me on the polygraph. I'm sick and tired of you people fucking with me."

With that he got up, stormed out, and spent most of Thanksgiving afternoon in a bar, quietly getting drunk.

Though he insists to this day that Jack Ruby did not enter the basement by way of the ramp—in fact, he is convinced that Oswald's killer entered through an unwatched side door—Roy Vaughn was, in the minds of many assassination historians, the man who let Lee Oswald's murderer pass toward his moment of infamy.

For a while the investigation heavily weighed on him. He battled depression and dangerously high blood pressure. After testifying before the Warren Commission, however, Vaughn, firmly convinced he had done nothing wrong, made a concentrated effort to put the matter behind him. Still, his role in Dallas's most infamous days would never be forgotten.

He was at home one evening when his children returned from seeing a movie titled *Executive Action,* bringing with them a leaflet that had been passed out to everyone entering the theater. It was a "fact sheet" supporting the theme of the movie—that Kennedy's death was a part of an elaborate conspiracy.

Among the "facts" listed was that "Dallas police officer Roy Vaughn knowingly allowed Jack Ruby to enter the basement of the police department where he shot and killed Lee Harvey Oswald."

Enraged, Vaughn filed suit against the producers of the movie and its screenwriter, journalist Mark Lane, whose best-selling book, *Rush to Judgment,* had severely criticized the Warren Commission findings. The "fact sheet" was removed from circulation following an agreed settlement between General Cinema, Inc., and Vaughn. Vaughn got a default judgment against Lane which was later set aside.

Eventually, the stress of the event would subside, returning only when journalists appeared on the anniversary of the event, asking the same tired questions, each hoping to solve the conspiracy riddle that had so gripped the nation.

Vaughn, wanting to put the episode behind him, refused for years to be interviewed about that Sunday morning at the Main Street ramp.

By 1968 he had been promoted to sergeant, serving in Internal Affairs as one of the first officers assigned to the department's newly formed Metro Squad. By the mid-seventies, he was an administrative assistant to the chief.

Then, in March of 1980, at age forty-five, Vaughn retired, planning to devote his full attention to a glass and mirror business he had established in Midlothian.

Twenty-two years in law enforcement, he had decided, was enough. He was ready to disappear into the quiet comfort of civilian life. Novembers would finally come and go, free of requests from reporters that he again tell his side of the story.

Being the target of unwarranted public blame was not something he ever wanted to deal with again.

Now, though, a new nightmare had begun.

At the Dallas Police Department's southwest substation, patrolmen who had assembled for Saturday morning roll call were drinking coffee from Styrofoam cups and munching on sweet rolls and doughnuts. Day Sergeant Jim Aylor was addressing the gathering, passing out assignments, briefing those in attendance on the status of various investigations, and updating them on activities of the night shift.

He was nearing the end of the items listed on his clipboard when he came to the report left him by Sergeant Silva.

"Okay," Aylor said, "one other thing: Be on the lookout for a red 1986 GMC Sierra pickup, short wheel base, Texas license number 739 9JG. We got a call on it from the Midlothian P.D. They have a missing undercover officer who has been using the name George Moore. He apparently spent some time in our neighborhood, accompanying suspects who were making buys."

Among those in the room hearing the report was Tom Knighten.

After roll call ended, Knighten waited until the other

officers had left the briefing room, then approached Aylor. "I got a call last night from the Midlothian P.D. about George Moore," he said. "He's a friend of my kid. I'd like to know if you hear anything."

Aylor assured Knighten that he would keep him posted. Then, walking quickly to his office, he placed a call to Roy Vaughn.

"Does Tom Knighten know about your undercover man?" he asked.

"No," Vaughn replied.

"He does now. I just put the word out in roll call."

Vaughn was silent for several seconds. Neither he nor Fowler had remembered that Knighten was assigned to the southwest substation. "Shit," he finally said. "Make sure he doesn't call home. I need to talk to him right away."

If Raffield was okay, Vaughn did not want his cover blown.

Sergeant Aylor suggested they meet at a halfway point, the parking lot of Red Bird Mall.

It was still a couple of hours before the sprawling mall just off Highway 67 would open for business when Vaughn, accompanied by Fowler and Pinto, pulled into the vacant parking lot. They had been there only a few minutes when a Dallas police car turned off the access road and pulled up beside them.

Knighten was accompanied by his supervisor, Sergeant Fred Martin, and Aylor.

Briefly they all stood near the cars as Vaughn outlined the problem, recapping the night's unsuccessful search. While the chief spoke, Fowler motioned for Knighten to accompany him away from the group.

On the drive from Midlothian, Fowler had volunteered to be the bearer of the bad news. As they stepped out of earshot of the others, Fowler quietly explained that Raffield had been working for them since the school year had begun.

"I'm sorry, Tom," Fowler said, "but he's made some cases on your boy."

Knighten's face showed little expression as he slowly

shook his head. "George came to our house for Greg's birthday party. He was nice-looking, well mannered. I liked him. But I did tell Greg later that I thought his friend looked too old to be a high school student. I told him to be careful, that Dallas was putting people like that into the schools."

Staring out onto the empty parking lot, he continued shaking his head. Fowler felt sorry for Knighten, who, in his opinion, was in effect admitting that he knew—or at least strongly suspected—that his son was involved in drugs but was at a loss to do anything about it. Just for a moment Fowler found himself wondering if Tom Knighten had been the one responsible for blowing George's cover.

"Tom," Fowler said, "I'd appreciate it if you wouldn't say anything about this to your boy."

"I understand."

"Thanks," Fowler said, shaking Knighten's hand.

Before returning to Midlothian, Pinto drove Vaughn and Fowler to the Red Bird Airport, twelve miles north of Midlothian, where the Dallas police helicopter division was headquartered. Vaughn wanted to check with Al Castleman and see if there was any chance the cloud cover might lift soon.

Sitting in the small terminal's restaurant, the men drank coffee as Castleman briefed them on the weather conditions. It might be as late as noon before he could put a helicopter up, he told them.

Fowler had said little since leaving the shopping center.

"How did Tom take it?" Vaughn finally asked.

"He had George figured out," the lieutenant said. He then recounted his conversation with Knighten.

In Midlothian, Patrolman Steve Egan had reported for duty at 7:00 A.M., unaware of the problem that had developed during the night. It was just after eight when, making his regular route, he turned into the entrance of the Village South Trailer Park and was flagged down by a man driving a pickup.

As the pickup pulled up next to him, he saw that the

driver was J. W. Janson, whom the patrolman had known for some time. They had first met when Egan clocked Janson driving a hopped-up Chevy through the outskirts of Midlothian at 73 miles per hour and issued him a citation.

Surprisingly, from that initial encounter a friendship had developed. The men occasionally drank coffee together, and Janson had on several occasions sought advice from the policeman about problems he was having with his teenage son, Dale. Seeing the look of concern on J.W.'s face as he pulled up, the officer immediately assumed he wanted to talk about his boy.

"I was just coming to the station," Janson said. "I heard something that you might want to check out."

"What's that?"

"Dale was acting strange this morning, really nervous. Like he was scared about something. I finally asked him what was wrong. He said he had heard that some kids killed a narc last night."

"Where?"

"Out in a field somewhere. He didn't know for sure."

"You think he knows what he's talking about?" Egan asked.

"Considering the way he was acting, I'm afraid so."

"Did he say who did it?"

"A boy named Greg Knighten. All the kids call him Sparky."

Egan, unaware that the department had an undercover officer on the payroll, assumed that if, in fact, a murder had taken place, the victim was probably an informant, not a police officer.

Still, it was a serious matter. Egan told Janson that he wanted to talk with his son as soon as possible. First, however, he needed to report the information.

Pinto was driving in the direction of Midlothian when Egan was patched into his car radio, saying that he had information for Chief Vaughn. Aware that a number of private citizens amused themselves by listening to police scanners in their homes, Egan told the chief that he didn't think what he had to say should go out over the radio. He agreed to meet Pinto and Vaughn on the edge of town.

As the patrolman relayed the information given him by J. W. Janson, the blood drained from Roy Vaughn's face. His stomach knotted, and a wave of nausea swept over him.

"Billy," he said, turning to Fowler, "you go with Pinto and talk with the Janson boy. I'll go to the station with Steve. I'm going to get Tom Knighten down here. And I'm going to call the Rangers."

The chief wearily ran his fingers through his hair, as if momentarily lost in private thought. "I'm afraid we're going to need some help on this thing."

Fowler looked at Vaughn, saying nothing, trying to hold on to his last bit of hope that George Raffield might still be alive.

Soon, however, a long-distance telephone call would put that final shred of hope to rest.

It was a few minutes past 6:00 A.M. in Fredonia, Arizona, when Keith Judd, an Arizona Highway Patrol officer, answered the phone located on the bookshelf at the head of his bed.

He heard the cheery voice of a long-distance operator: "Collect call from Richard. Will you accept the charges?"

Awakened from a sound sleep, Judd tried without success to determine if he knew anyone named Richard. Then, just before refusing the call, he remembered a friend of his son's by that name. He told the operator he would accept the call.

"Can I talk with Tim?" the caller asked.

"He's asleep."

"Please . . . it's important."

"Okay, wait a minute. I'll get him."

Judd got out of bed and walked downstairs to his son's room, woke him, and told him he had a phone call.

Returning to the bedroom, Judd found his wife, Carol, sitting up in bed, a worried expression on her face. Looking at her husband, she nodded in the direction of the phone and, placing a fisted hand near her ear, indicated for him to listen in on the conversation.

The first voice the elder Judd heard was that of the caller. "I'm in deep shit, man. Can we talk?"

"Yeah," Tim Judd replied.

"You sure nobody's listening?"

"Wait a minute, and I'll check."

Keith Judd quickly placed the phone and receiver beneath his pillow and feigned sleep. When he heard his son walking back down the stairs, Judd sat up and gently put the receiver to his ear.

"Yeah, we can talk. Go ahead," his son said.

"I'm in real deep shit, man. Big trouble. We wasted a narc," Richard said. His voice was high-pitched and he was speaking so rapidly that his words were running together.

"What?"

"We shot a narc . . . a cop . . . a fucking pig, man."

Upstairs, Keith Judd was frantically signaling for his wife to get him a pencil and something to write on. He wasn't sure where Richard said he was calling from. It sounded like Middlerose or Midlow. The caller mentioned that it was somewhere near Dallas.

Judd heard his son talking again as he began to scribble notes.

"Oh, man," Tim said. "Who shot him?"

"We both did."

"Who was with you?"

"Jonathan, a friend of mine."

"Who was the guy you shot?"

"A narc from the school."

"When did it happen?"

"Last night, around midnight. We were at this party . . ."

Tim Judd's curiosity kept the rapid-fire questions and answers coming for several minutes. Richard said the weapon they had used was a .38 special, that they had shot the victim three times—in the back, the neck, and the head—and that they had hidden the body in a thicket next to an old house where a bunch of hippies hung out.

Richard said that he was no longer living with his parents, that he'd recently moved in with a group of people involved in Satan worship.

Occasionally the conversation was interrupted by traffic noises in the background. At one point the caller apparently turned from the phone and asked if there was someone walking in his direction. In the background another voice said, "No."

Keith Judd noted that the call was likely originating from an outdoor pay phone.

"What do you think I should do?" Richard asked, his voice now pleading. "I mean, what the fuck would you do?"

"You've got to turn yourself in," Tim replied.

"It's too late for that, man. We can't. What we need is to get the hell out of here and hide."

"Cut out for Mexico, then. Hit the road. You got a car?"

"Jonathan's got a truck. But we don't have any money. All we've got is twelve bucks between us."

"You still got your guitar?"

"Yeah, I've got two now."

"Hock 'em."

The caller was silent for a few seconds, as if contemplating the suggestion, then said, "Yeah, we could do that in Dallas. They've got hock shops out the ass over there. Look, is there someplace there where we could hide out?"

"I know a couple of caves near here," Tim said. "Maybe you could hide there. I don't know, man."

The conversation was beginning to make him uncomfortable. "Hey," he said, abruptly changing the subject, "are you calling collect?"

"Yeah."

"Shit, man, we'd better get off the phone or my folks will be all over me."

The next sound he heard was that of Richard hanging up.

Tim Judd sat on the edge of his bed for several minutes, replaying the conversation in his mind. For a moment he even considered that it had all been a dream. But it hadn't. The voice on the phone had been that of Richard Goeglein who had lived nearby in the town of Williams. The two boys had been friends until the Goeglein family had suddenly moved to Texas during the summer.

Though he had not heard from him since he left Arizona, Tim knew Richard well enough to believe he had been telling the truth about his involvement in a murder. Richard was a practical joker, but this didn't sound like one of his crazy games. There had been a very real tone of panic in his voice.

This was not something, Tim decided, that he could keep to himself.

Keith Judd was up and almost dressed when his son entered the upstairs bedroom. "Dad," he said, "there's something I need to talk to you about." The youngster's face was pale, and he was nervously biting on his lower lip.

Instead of admitting that he had been eavesdropping, Judd listened silently as Tim, sitting on the foot of the bed, reconstructed his conversation with Richard Goeglein. He was pleased that his son told him the entire story.

"Do you believe him?" Carol Judd asked, after Tim had finished.

Tim nodded. "Yeah, I do. He gets pretty crazy sometimes."

Still unsure where Goeglein had called from, Keith Judd decided to telephone the homicide division of the Dallas Police Department. He spoke with Detective Ed Hardy and told him of the conversation.

Hardy, having just come on duty, said he was unaware of any report of a missing Dallas officer and that he knew of no town in the Dallas area that sounded like Middlerose or Midlow.

"Let me do some checking," the detective said, "and I'll get back to you. It could be that the kid was talking about a street name instead of a town. I'll see what I can find out on this end."

A half-hour later, Hardy called back. "There's an undercover narcotics officer missing in Midlothian, a little town just south of here," he said. "I just talked to the chief down there, and he'll be calling you in a few minutes."

*　*　*

In his office, Roy Vaughn sat numbly staring down at notes he had hastily written on a legal pad as Keith Judd again told the story of the long-distance call.

The true pain, Vaughn knew, would come later, long after the rush of adrenaline had subsided and the fate of his young officer was a certainty.

Again he telephoned the southwest substation in Dallas and spoke with Sergeant Fred Martin, asking him to bring Tom Knighten to Midlothian as quickly as possible. "And," Vaughn said, "I'd appreciate it if you'd have Knighten bring his son along."

That done, the chief rose, shut his door, and returned to his desk. And for the first time in longer than Vaughn could remember, he made no effort to hold back tears.

Then, composing himself, he reached for his Rolodex and searched for the number of Texas Ranger George Turner, who lived in nearby Cleburne.

A few blocks away, at the Midlothian post office, mail carrier Fred Turner, younger brother of the Ranger whom Vaughn was about to call, walked into the mail room with a story to tell.

The night before he had traveled to Red Oak to watch his daughter April perform with the Midlothian High drill team. It began to rain shortly after the halftime performance, and Turner, disappointed that Midlothian was being soundly defeated, decided to leave the game early and return home.

When he walked into the parking lot adjacent to the football field, he found that his nearly new pickup truck had been stolen. It was the second time he had been forced to deal with such a problem. A year earlier, while he was visiting San Antonio, another pickup had been stolen from a motel parking lot.

After filing a report with Red Oak Police Chief John Gage, Turner was given a ride home by a Midlothian student.

As he entered the mail room, two women carriers, preparing for their morning routes, were sorting mail. "You're not going to believe what happened last night," Turner said.

It was Turner's perception that, on the other side of the room, Jackie Cadenhead, the mother of Greg Knighten's girlfriend, abruptly stopped sorting mail and turned to stare at Turner. She said nothing, but the stricken look she gave him puzzled the man who was there only to tell a story of his stolen pickup.

4

George Turner stood on the sidelines with a dozen other parents who had braved the morning drizzle to watch their children play soccer. The Texas Ranger was there despite a fever and the warnings from his wife, Dana, that standing in the cold, damp air would likely result in his spending the remainder of the weekend in bed with the flu. But it was his son's final game of the season, and since Dana, a registered nurse, was working the weekend shift at the hospital, Turner was determined that at least one parent would be on hand for Josh's last chance to score a goal that year.

The players, awkward and uncertain but bursting with youthful enthusiasm, had been racing up and down the field for almost a half-hour with neither side threatening to score when Turner noticed a Cleburne police officer walking in his direction.

He watched the officer stop and speak briefly with one of the fathers on the far side of the field. The man had pointed in his direction.

The policeman nodded and walked hurriedly toward the man wearing jeans, a windbreaker, and a cowboy hat pulled low over his eyes.

"You George Turner?" he asked, breathing heavily.

"Yes."

The officer quickly explained that he was there to deliver an emergency message from Roy Vaughn, who had called from the Midlothian Police Department. Turner sighed, watched the action for another minute or two, then arranged for one of the other parents to take his son home at game's end.

If Josh did manage to score a goal, he would have to hear about it later.

George Turner knew that the weekend he'd been so looking forward to had been ruined. Vaughn, whom he knew and respected, would not call—particularly at ten o'clock on a Saturday morning—unless it was something serious.

Turner drove home quickly to call Vaughn, then listened as his friend briefly detailed the situation.

"Under the circumstances," Vaughn said, "I'd feel better if the Rangers were in charge of the investigation."

Though neither mentioned it, there exists among law enforcement agencies a jurisdictional jealousy that often hinders investigations. Time is too often wasted determining whether the police or the sheriff's department should be in charge or whether the crime is legally the concern of local, state, or federal agencies. In an investigation that is likely to gain the attention of the media, egos sometimes get in the way.

Vaughn wanted to be sure that nothing hampered their efforts to find out what had happened to George Raffield. George Turner, he knew, was not only a first-class investigator; he was a man with a no-nonsense, take-charge personality. In his four years as a Texas Ranger, Turner had gained a great deal of experience as a "referee" in criminal investigations.

The summons to Midlothian filled Turner with mixed emotions. It marked the first time in his career that he was returning to his hometown in an official capacity.

The Midlothian of Turner's youth, where his father had farmed, had been different. George and his brothers had grown up with the responsibilities of daily chores, hunted and fished in the Ellis County pasturelands, and spent most of their Saturday nights hanging out at the local Freezette, then the only teenage hangout in the tiny downtown area.

On those rare weekends when finances allowed it, they would borrow the family car and drive into nearby Waxahachie or Dallas for a movie.

It was a time when the community had no strangers. Most of the forty students in his 1969 graduating class had attended Midlothian schools since the first grade. Turner, who was among the most popular boys in school, had played center and end on the football team until a knee operation ended his rather unspectacular athletic career. Those who asked him what he hoped to do eventually with his life were quickly told that he wanted to be an FBI agent.

The town in which Turner had grown up was quiet and conservative, comfortable with the fact it was ten years behind the times. Its one-man police department busied itself with the resolution of occasional family disagreements and keeping rein on teenage speeders.

After graduation Turner had left to spend two years in junior college, then joined the Texas Department of Public Safety as a highway patrolman. He stayed with the DPS for fourteen years before becoming the youngest of the ninety-four commissioned Texas Rangers in the spring of 1985. Following brief stays in Houston and Fort Worth, Turner was assigned to Company F and stationed in Cleburne.

The location was ideal for Turner and his family. The Johnson County community had the rural flavor he had missed and it was just a thirty-minute drive down Highway 67 to Midlothian, making more frequent visits to his parents and brothers possible.

The Midlothian Turner encountered upon his return, however, had drastically changed. No longer could he walk down the main street and greet the people he passed by their first names. His hometown had finally given way to progress. And, in a way, it saddened the Ranger.

Much of the isolated farmland he had roamed as a youngster had been sold to developers and was now dotted with new residential neighborhoods. The old high school he had attended had been retired, and a large modern building now stood on the edge of town. And the Freezette, locked nostalgically in his memory, had become a beauty shop.

Such were the thoughts wandering through George Turner's mind as he hurried toward his meeting with Roy Vaughn.

After entering the Midlothian Police Department, Turner went immediately to Vaughn's office and found him talking with a uniformed officer from the Dallas Police Department.

Vaughn excused himself and walked into the lobby to brief the Ranger on the events that had prompted his call. He quickly explained what Raffield had been doing in his undercover capacity, told him of the officer's relationship with Greg Knighten, then relayed the information that had been provided by Dale Janson's father.

"That's Tom Knighten in my office," the chief said. "He brought his son in so we could talk to him."

"Jesus, you mean the kid's daddy is a police officer?"

Vaughn nodded. "Tom's had his hands full with the boy for quite some time. We were just talking about it. I've already told him his son's a suspect. It hit him pretty hard. He just threw his hands up and started crying."

"Where's the kid?"

"Sitting in Billy's office. I tried to talk to him and couldn't get a damn thing out of him. He's a cold little sonuvabitch."

"Well, let's try some more," Turner said, walking in the direction of Fowler's office.

Entering the small corner room with Vaughn, the Ranger was taken aback by what he saw. Sitting there, arms folded over his chest, was a child, barely sixteen, sullenly staring at the floor.

He refused even to look at Turner as the Ranger began his questioning.

"George is my friend," the boy said. "I don't know why I'm here. I wouldn't hurt him. You're all crazy if you think I would do anything to him."

"Didn't you see him last night?"

Knighten nodded. "Yeah, he came out to my house. He

picked me and Richard up. We rode up to the gas station with him. When we got there, Jonathan Jobe was getting gas. I got in with Jonathan and he gave me a ride out to my girlfriend's house. The last time I saw George was at the gas station. Hey, if you think I did something to hurt my friend you can just go to hell," the teenager finished defiantly.

Turner, glancing in the direction of Vaughn, made no attempt to hide the immediate dislike he felt for the youngster.

Vaughn moved from his place against the wall and sat on the corner of the desk near Knighten. "Son, I think you killed him," the chief said in a firm, controlled voice. "In fact, I've already got information that you did. So why don't you just tell us about it?"

Knighten's expression did not change. "George is my friend," he repeated stubbornly.

Turner studied Knighten in silence for several seconds. "Look, little man," he finally said, "this person you call your friend was a police officer hired by this department. And something's happened to him. I don't know where he is or if he's dead or alive—but I damn sure think you do."

For the first time Greg Knighten looked the Ranger squarely in the eye. "Go to hell," he said.

"That's all you have to say?"

Knighten did not answer.

"Okay, you can go," Turner said. On the basis of the sketchy information Vaughn had given him, there was, he knew, not enough to keep the teenager in custody.

As Knighten stood, stuffing his T-shirt into his jeans, the Ranger glared at him. "I feel sure we'll be talking again."

While Turner and Vaughn were questioning Knighten, Billy Fowler and Chuck Pinto had been following up on the information J. W. Janson had provided Officer Egan.

Arriving at the Janson house, they were told that Dale Janson had left to visit his girlfriend, a fifteen-year-old eighth grader named Anna Roscoe.

At the Roscoes', Fowler did not find Dale but spoke briefly with Anna's father, explaining to him why they were there.

Reluctantly, Roscoe finally agreed to call his daughter to the front porch.

"It's just a rumor I heard," she told Fowler when asked about the story she had told her boyfriend. The girl nervously chewed at her fingernails as she answered the officer's questions.

"Who did you hear it from?" Fowler asked.

"I called Randy Marcott last night at around nine o'clock. We were just, you know, talking, and he told me that George was dead. He said that Greg and Richard had figured out that he was a narc and shot him. Randy said he had talked to them at Cynthia's apartment and they were bragging about it. They told him it happened out in a field. I didn't know whether to believe him or not."

"Who's Randy Marcott?"

"Just a friend."

Lieutenant Fowler felt a biting anger welling up inside him as he listened to the young girl talking almost nonchalantly about rumors of a cold-blooded murder. Already he had heard the names of three teenagers who had been told that George Raffield had been killed, yet none had so much as bothered to call the police.

He fought back the urge to ask Anna Roscoe why. "Where does Randy Marcott live?" he finally asked.

Back in the car, Fowler and Pinto sat in silence for several seconds, reflecting on what Anna had told them. "Every damn kid in town seems to know about this," Fowler observed.

Pinto rested his arms on the steering wheel and stared straight ahead, saying nothing.

"Let's check Knighten's story," Fowler suggested.

The Cadenhead home sits on a small hill five miles east of Midlothian, its yard a parking place for farm equipment and family automobiles. The two Cadenhead teenagers, Jim and Jamie, were outside when Pinto and Fowler pulled onto the gravel driveway.

Both quickly admitted that Greg Knighten had been there the night before. George Moore brought him, they said, dropping him off around seven-thirty or eight o'clock. Jamie said she and Greg had spent the evening watching television and making plans for a Halloween party that was scheduled at the Cadenhead house the following night. After midnight her parents had returned from an evening out, and her father had driven Greg home.

"Was there anyone with George and Greg when they got here?" Fowler asked.

"Yes," Jamie volunteered, "there was one other guy with them, but I didn't know him."

Fowler and Pinto were on their way back to town when they received word that the Dallas police helicopter was en route to Midlothian, the cloud ceiling having lifted enough to permit an air search. The dispatcher informed Pinto that the pilot would land on the parking lot adjacent to the community center and await instructions.

It had already been decided that Pinto would accompany the pilot, serving as the contact with the ground search.

"Got any suggestions?" the city manager asked Fowler as he pulled up near the helicopter.

"George mentioned that he went out to some field southwest of town with the kids a time or two to drink beer and smoke pot. I'm not sure exactly where. He never said. But you might try searching out that way first."

Pinto nodded, his long face already mirroring his dread of what he might find.

As Fowler pulled into a parking space in front of the police station, Tom Knighten and his son were walking out the front door, followed by George Turner.

"Where are you going to be today?" the Ranger asked Greg as he opened the door to his father's car.

"I'll be out at Jamie Cadenhead's, helping her get things ready for a Halloween party," the youngster answered.

Fowler approached Turner as the Knightens drove away. "Did he say anything about being out at the Cadenhead house last night?" the lieutenant asked.

"Yeah," Turner said, his eyes still following the car, which was turning onto Ninth Street. "He said a kid named Jonathan Jobe drove him out there."

"He was lying to you," Fowler said.

"Yeah, I know. That little shit's involved in this up to his stone-cold eyeballs."

In his regular reports to Fowler, Raffield had once mentioned someone named Jonathan. He had said he was a friend of Greg's and lived near the Knightens.

"I'm going to go see if I can locate him," Fowler told Turner.

At the Camelot Estates, the lieutenant easily found the Jobe residence but got no answer when he knocked at the front door.

A next-door neighbor, working in his front yard, yelled hello and said that there was no one at the Jobe house.

"Do you know Jonathan?" Fowler asked.

"Sure," the neighbor said. "I'm one of his teachers at the high school. I saw him and a friend of his—Richard Goeglein—leave early this morning. I think Richard must have spent the night with him."

By eleven o'clock, the search was under way in earnest. Trailers carrying horses from Dallas Police Department stables arrived, and mounted officers awaited orders. The vacant lot across from the Midlothian police station was filling with vehicles from agencies throughout the county.

In nearby Red Oak, Shirley Moore, mother of the missing officer, sat at the kitchen table with her older daughter, monitoring reports on a police scanner her son-in-law had purchased early that morning.

The rest of the family, including Raffield's stepfather, brothers-in-law, and younger sister, had already driven toward Midlothian to join the search.

Don Moore, a tall, balding man with the weathered face of one who had spent his working life outdoors, had married Shirley Raffield when George, her youngest child, was just six months old. The boy's father had left when Shirley was still pregnant, not to be heard from again after the divorce until six years later when word came from Houston that he had been shot and killed.

It had been Moore, who had four children of his own by a previous marriage, who nicknamed George "Tiger." He did so to avoid the confusion that he feared would arise from the fact that one of his own children was also named George. Too, the nickname fit the energetic child whom Moore had immediately embraced as his own. It didn't seem to matter if the kids were his or his second wife's; in the heart and mind of the gentle, soft-spoken Moore, they were all his. Though George had kept his real father's name—Raffield—it had been Fowler's suggestion that he use his stepfather's name as his undercover alias.

Don and his son-in-law, Mark Prine, had been driving the back roads between Red Oak and Midlothian since first light. They had spoken little, only occasionally offering some scenario of hope as they searched. Perhaps George had been drugged and taken somewhere as a captive, Mark had speculated. Or maybe he had been involved in a fight and was lying somewhere, injured and unconscious. As they drove, neither man spoke aloud the shared fear that the young man they were looking for might no longer be alive.

Nearing the city limits of Midlothian they saw several deputies from the Ellis County Sheriff's Department walking in fields along the highway. It was Don who spotted a group crouched some distance away, staring down into ankle-high grass. He told his son-in-law to pull over.

"They've found something," Don said, his voice hollow and apprehensive.

Mark Prine hurried from the driver's side of his pickup to help his shaken father-in-law from the cab. Don Moore was pale as he placed one foot on the gravel shoulder. Suddenly he felt as if his knees would buckle, and he steadied himself against the hood of the truck.

"You okay?" Mark asked.

"I can't go out there," Don said. "I'm too damn scared." For the first time he admitted his worst fear. "I'm afraid I'm going to see my boy lying there. God, Mark, I'm afraid he's dead."

Mark suggested that Don wait in the pickup while he walked into the field to talk with the officers. He, too, was afraid of what he might find and was relieved to discover that the searchers were examining the remains of a dead animal they had happened upon.

Having been unsuccessful in his attempt to locate Jobe, Fowler had returned to the station and picked up Turner. They were driving onto Sunlit Circle, approaching the address they had been given for Randy Marcott. Along the way they had passed several late risers who were making their first venture into the morning to retrieve newspapers or begin weekend chores. There was a slow-paced nonchalance about the neighborhood. For most Midlothian residents, unaware of the unfolding tragedy, it was still just another leisurely late fall Saturday morning.

Randy Marcott's father was sitting on his front porch, shirtless and drinking coffee, when the officers pulled into his driveway.

After being told the purpose of their visit, the elder Marcott called his sixteen-year-old son from inside the house. A freshman at Midlothian High School, he had only recently returned to classes after an automobile accident had forced him to spend several weeks in the hospital. Still pallid and frail-looking from the ordeal, Randy Marcott joined the men on the front porch.

"Do you know George Moore?" Turner asked.

Randy nodded.

"We've got reason to believe something's happened to him," Turner said, "and we've been told you have some information that might be helpful."

"I don't know what you're talking about," Randy said, glancing in the direction of his father. "I don't know nothing about George."

Lieutenant Fowler, who had been standing on the steps, walked onto the porch and stood directly in front of the youngster. "Your friend Anna tells a different story," he said. "She said you told her last night that somebody had shot George. Does that jog your memory?"

"She's lying," Randy said.

Fowler looked over at the youngster's father. "Mr. Marcott," he said, "do you mind if Randy and I go in the house for a minute and use your telephone?"

The elder Marcott just shrugged and continued to sip from his coffee cup.

"We don't have time to play games," Fowler said as he accompanied the teenager into the front room. "The best way to clear this up is to call Anna and let her tell us again what you were supposed to have said. I've got her number here if you don't know it."

Randy Marcott sighed and let his skinny shoulders slump. He began to cry. "You don't need to call her. Yeah, I talked to her. I told her what I heard—that Sparky and Richard did something to George. They found out he was a narc and took him out into a field someplace and shot him. Anna and I talked about it for a while, trying to figure what happened. You know, just guessing. We figured that Sparky probably did it, since his dad keeps a lot of guns around. We figured he probably got one of his old man's guns, you know, and . . ."

"Who's Richard?"

"Richard Goeglein. He moved here in the summer. I don't know him that well."

"Do you know where they took George?"

Randy shook his head. "All I heard was a field somewhere . . . somewhere nobody hardly ever goes."

"Who told you?"

"Man, they'll kill me if they find out I've talked to you," the young Marcott said, his voice high-pitched and pleading. "I just heard it, you know. I was over at a friend's apartment last night. I don't know if it's true or not. I swear. That's all I can tell you."

They returned to the front porch where Turner and the father were making small talk.

As the officers prepared to leave, Fowler turned to Randy.

"You ever go over to that old fat gal's apartment in Oxford Square?" he asked. The question was an afterthought, something Raffield had once told him about an overweight young woman whose home was a gathering place for many of the town's teenage drug users.

"You mean Cynthia Fedrick?"

"Yeah."

"Sometimes," Randy said. "She's my sister."

Back in the car, George Turner smiled for the first time since his arrival. "Billy," he said, "you've really got a way with words."

Fowler, embarrassed, shook his head. "How the hell was I supposed to know she was his sister?"

After driving back to the station, Turner placed a call to his brother, Fred. A postal employee, he knew, would likely have the address of everyone in town.

The Goegleins, Fred Turner said, lived in a yellow frame house at 303 North Fourth Street. "It's over next to the school bus barn."

"One other thing," George said. "Is Jonathan Jobe the son of Johnny and Sharrell Jobe?"

"I think so."

"Shit," the Ranger replied.

"What's going on?"

"I don't have time to explain right now," George said. "I'll call you later."

Turner hung up the phone and leaned forward, placing his hands on the desktop. The fever he had wakened with had broken into a cold sweat. He looked up at Vaughn who was standing near the door. "Johnny Jobe and I used to run around together in high school. Hell, we were best friends for a while. We played football together. And I've known Sharrell all my life. Their kid, Jonathan, and my nephew used to play with each other when they were little."

Fowler walked into the room as Turner was talking, not mentioning that he had been back in his office, also trying to locate the Goegleins address. Thumbing through the telephone directory, he had happened on a Goeglein listed in the nearby hamlet of Ovilla and immediately assumed that's where the boy named Richard lived. He had dialed the number and an elderly woman who identified herself as Richard Goeglein's grandmother had answered. Her grandson, she had told him, lived in Midlothian.

Careful not to alert her to his reason for wanting to locate the teenager, Fowler had invented a story about Richard's having spoken with him about a part-time job and needing to get in touch with him as quickly as possible about coming to work. The grandmother had provided him with the same address Turner had been given by his brother.

The Goeglein home, Fowler realized immediately, was less than a block from the small frame house he and his wife had briefly lived in when they first moved to Midlothian.

The lieutenant listened silently while Turner spoke of his relationship with the Jobes, then headed for the door, Turner following. Their next visit would be to the Goegleins'.

There, Frances Goeglein spoke to them from behind a screen door. Her son, she said, was not at home. He had spent the previous night with Jonathan. They had come by earlier in the morning to tell her they were going to pick up Richard's girlfriend and drive over to Waxahachie to a flea market. She didn't expect them home until midafternoon.

They had left, she said, in Jonathan's pickup. Pressed by Turner for a description of the truck, she said it was brown, had a tool box mounted behind the cab and a dented front fender—the right one, she thought, but couldn't be sure. She had no idea about the make or model.

"What's this all about?" she asked. "Is there some kind of problem?"

"We just need to locate the pickup," Turner said. "That's all I can tell you right now."

Back in the car, he radioed the dispatcher, requesting that the Waxahachie police be notified and asked to look for the vehicle.

At his rural home southwest of the city, Midlothian Patrolman Fran Ross was contemplating changing into a sweat suit and going for a run when the dispatcher called to tell him that Chief Vaughn had requested all off-duty officers to report to the station immediately.

Having worked the late shift the night before, Ross had napped briefly after getting home just before dawn and had been up less than an hour. He was surprised but relieved when the dispatcher told him to wear jeans rather than his uniform.

Even without asking, Ross immediately assumed he would be joining some kind of search. "Something serious has happened," he told his wife, Terry.

In minutes he was in his car, headed toward Farm-to-Market 875 on his way to town. It was the route he would have jogged—from his front yard down the winding gravel road that led to the little-traveled two-lane highway. Crossing the intersection he would have entered Weston Ramsey's pasture and followed a rutted dirt road that wound through the mesquite-dotted land toward an area the local kids referred to as Devil's Hill.

Ross paused briefly at the intersection and looked across at the entrance to the pasture. A carpet of yellow wildflowers glistened with the lingering morning dew. It would have been an ideal day for a run, he thought. Putting his disappointment aside, he turned onto the pavement and headed toward town.

One of the officers whom Vaughn had retained from the previous chief's staff, the thirty-six-year-old Ross was the most unlikely of all those assigned to keep the Midlothian peace. The son of an Italian father and a Yugoslavian mother, he had grown up on Chicago's tough South Side. The bucolic life-style of rural Texas had been foreign to him when he first arrived. His boyhood playgrounds had been the pool halls, back-alley dice games, and asphalt basketball courts of his Chicago neighborhood. His father, he recalls, was a close friend of the younger brother of famed mobster Al Capone.

He had been sixteen in 1966 when a deranged Chicago carpenter named Richard Speck entered the Jeffrey Manor apartment building just a few blocks from his house and brutally murdered eight young nursing students. On the evening of the tragedy, in fact, Ross had walked past the building on his way home from visiting a friend less than an hour before Speck's murderous rampage began. One of the young women who had been killed was the daughter of a man with whom his father had worked.

The event, which commanded headlines for weeks after, had played a major role in Ross's decision to become a police officer. As a high school senior, he enrolled in a cadet trainee program for teenagers interested in law enforcement.

Later, while in the Marine Corps, Ross had married. His wife, who favored life in the suburbs of Chicago, argued against moving into the city after her husband was honorably discharged. And since the Chicago police had a residency rule requiring all officers to live within the city limits, Ross pursued his law enforcement career in Calumet City, a boisterous southern Illinois town of 40,000 with 140 bars and a widespread reputation as a mecca for organized crime, illegal gambling, and political corruption.

It took Ross four years to get his fill of police work. Labeled a troublemaker because he refused payoffs and reported fellow officers and a couple of city councilmen who didn't, he was nicknamed Serpico. His outspoken opposition to the death penalty further alienated him from his colleagues. Other officers viewed his habit of providing some prisoners with cigarettes and seeing that they were allowed to make phone calls as a sign of weakness. When his wife began receiving threatening calls, Ross decided it was time to leave.

The prospect of opening an Italian restaurant in the Dallas–Fort Worth area with his brother and a cousin living in Texas had prompted his move to the Southwest. Plans for the restaurant failed to come together, however, and Ross, feeling the urge to return to law enforcement, applied to several small police departments in the area. He was hired by the Midlothian chief in January of 1984.

Friendly and handsome, Ross soon became a favorite of the young people in the community. Though unbending in his stance against lawbreaking, he enjoyed a rapport with teenagers that none of the other officers commanded. It was not unusual for him to spend a half-hour talking with a youngster after ticketing him for speeding. The muscular officer with the dark, wavy hair and eyes that sparkled with good humor willingly handed out his home telephone number and urged the local teenagers to call if they had problems, regardless of the hour.

Still a relative newcomer to the community, Ross saw Midlothian differently than his fellow officers did. Like them, he found the slower pace of rural life pleasant, almost hypnotic at times. On the other hand, there was a sameness from day to day that occasionally made him miss the hurried tempo of the big city.

One evening on patrol he counted sixteen churches within the city limits and was struck by the realization that the community offered little else in the way of social activity for adults or youngsters. Since the town was located in a dry part of the county, one could not even go out for a few beers in the evening. There was no movie theater, and the fare at the local restaurants ran from hamburgers to blue plate specials. In time he found that gossip was the primary source of entertainment and that people seemed to take a prurient delight in their neighbors' indiscretions yet would go to extremes to keep their own private. Divorce, drugs, and alcoholism were commonplace, Ross had quickly learned. He also knew they were discussed only in whispers. Like most small towns, Midlothian went to great lengths to keep its warts hidden. There were times, Ross told his wife, when he felt he had moved to another planet.

Eventually he found himself cast in the role of sounding board for a number of local parents whose children were becoming problems at home. Because he was an outsider, with different views and a fresh perspective, he was somehow easier to talk to.

Among those who sought his help was a Dallas police officer named Tom Knighten.

It had happened early in the fall of 1986 when Officer Ross, while on late night patrol, saw a car speed through a flashing red light. Ross's pursuit turned quickly into a high-speed chase out Highway 287 toward Waxahachie.

The patrolman had just turned on his siren when the driver ahead of him lost control of the car and ran into a culvert near a railroad bridge. At the wheel was Greg Knighten. He was semiconscious and had deep facial cuts and several missing teeth. His teenage companion, Tal South, had been knocked unconscious and had suffered cuts to his face and arms.

The car belonged to Knighten's father. As he checked the boys' injuries while awaiting the arrival of an ambulance, Ross comforted the young driver, who was in a state of shock. "Am I going to die?" Greg Knighten repeatedly asked.

Ross hugged the frightened, crying boy, assuring him he would be all right. That was how Officer Fran Ross and Greg Knighten became acquainted.

A year later Greg, accompanied by his father, arrived at the police station one afternoon. Tom Knighten explained that his son had become impossible to control and no longer wanted to attend school. Professional counseling had done little to resolve the problem. Frustrated, Knighten asked Ross to talk with his son.

For a half-hour Ross listened as Greg angrily described his parents as unreasonably strict. He explained that he was adopted and felt he wasn't really a part of the family.

Ross saw no indication that the teenager felt even the slightest remorse for the problems he had caused his parents. All he wanted was to drop out of school and be on his own, away from his parents' rules.

What Ross saw was an angry, unhappy youngster with no real sense of belonging. He empathized with Greg, even liked him, but was troubled by a message that had come through during their conversation: Greg Knighten appeared to have no feeling at all for his mother, father, or younger brother.

A rumor that had circulated among other teenagers whom Ross talked with was even more disturbing: on several occasions Greg had talked openly of wanting to kill his father.

Arriving at the police station, Ross was surprised by the amount of activity. Chief Vaughn was on the front steps of the building, organizing groups into search parties. Some of those gathered in the parking lot had obviously already been out looking and were back for further instructions.

As he stepped from his car, Ross was immediately taken aback by the wearied face of the chief. It was as if he had aged ten years since the last time the patrolman had seen him.

"If any of you get tired and need to take a break," Vaughn was saying, "feel free to come on back to the station and stretch out on one of the bunks in the jail. We'll have sandwiches and coffee here shortly."

Noticing Ross, Vaughn quickly explained why he had been called back to work and paired him with Travis Crump, the city building inspector, who had arrived with a four-wheel-drive Blazer.

For the next two hours Crump and Ross searched the fields south of town, finding nothing. Having covered the area, they returned to the station for additional instructions.

There they encountered DPS Officer Steve McKinney who relayed the information that they were looking for a brown pickup with three teenagers—two males and a female. Neither Crump nor Ross knew whether the youngsters were suspects or witnesses but left immediately in search of a brown truck with a dented front fender.

It took them less than thirty seconds to find it.

They had just driven away from the station and arrived at a stop sign on Tenth Street when they saw the truck coming into town. Behind the wheel was a blond young man. A girl sat in the middle, and another boy with dark shoulder-length hair rode near the passenger door.

"Damn, I think that's the truck we're looking for," Ross said. Crump then spotted the damaged right front fender as he turned to follow the pickup.

Ross radioed the license plate number into the station as Crump trailed the youngsters through the downtown area.

When the pickup pulled into the driveway at the side of the Goeglein house, Crump drove slowly past, stopping at the end of the block. "What do we do now?" he asked Ross.

"Turn around and let me out," the officer said. "I'll detain them until we get some help." He told the building inspector to remain in the Blazer and radio the station for backup.

By the time Ross got to the front yard, Richard Goeglein and his girlfriend, Gina McLemore, were walking toward the house. Jonathan Jobe was still in the pickup.

"Just a minute," the officer shouted. "I'd like to talk with you."

Jobe stepped out of the truck and walked in Ross's direction.

"Do you have some identification?"

The teenager, obviously nervous, pulled a driver's license from his wallet and handed it to the patrolman.

Ross then turned to Goeglein and was stunned when the youngster pulled a butterfly knife and took a defensive stance. The officer was relieved to hear the commotion of arriving squad cars behind him.

Goeglein looked apprehensively at the parade of uniformed men hurrying to join Ross and began to grind his teeth, glaring menacingly at the patrolman. "I can't deal with but one fucking pig at a time," he said defiantly.

Ross tried without success to persuade him to put the knife away. It was Richard Goeglein, Sr., who finally stepped from inside the house, took the knife from his son's hand, and gave it to the officer.

"What the hell is this all about?" the elder Goeglein asked.

His son said nothing, but continued to grind his teeth, his attention fixed on Ross. The young man's piercing blue eyes disturbed the officer more than the knife. They had a haunted, frightening quality he had never before seen.

Frances Goeglein emerged from the house and, surveying the scene in her front yard, frantically searched the still-growing crowd of officers for the men who had visited her earlier in the day. Seeing neither Fowler nor Turner, she called out to Patrol Sergeant Sonny Pfeifer who appeared to have taken charge upon his arrival.

"I want to know why it is necessary for so many policemen to be in my yard," she demanded. "Nobody here has done anything wrong. You have no business here. I want you to get out of here . . . right now."

Pfeifer, soft-spoken and polite, tried without success to calm the distraught mother. "Ma'am," he said, "we just need to ask the kids some questions. We're attempting to locate a missing officer and—"

"They don't know anything about that," she shot back. "They're just kids. Why don't you just leave them alone?"

"I'm afraid we'll need for them to come to the station," Pfeifer answered.

Frances Goeglein cursed and looked in the direction of her husband, her expression clearly urging him to defend Richard and his friends.

Instead, he tried to calm her. "It's okay," he said reassuringly. "Nobody's in trouble. They just want to talk to them." Then he turned to Pfeifer. "That's right, isn't it, officer? Nobody's under arrest or anything."

"No, sir," the relieved sergeant answered. "We just want to ask them some questions."

Richard Goeglein, standing at his father's side as if frozen in place, had never stopped grinding his teeth.

5

Roy Vaughn was sitting at the dispatcher's desk, awaiting reports from those involved in the search, when Richard and Frances Goeglein entered the police station, their son and his girlfriend following close behind in the company of Sergeant Pfeifer. Outside, Jonathan Jobe was pulling his pickup into the parking lot alongside the Blazer driven by Patrolman Ross.

The clock on the wall above the water fountain in the station showed twenty minutes to four as the three teenagers were escorted into Vaughn's office.

Fowler and Turner, returning from their afternoon visit to the Marcott home, watched the youngsters walk through the front entrance as they arrived at the station. Even before getting out of the car they were planning the next step in their investigation.

"Since I know the Jobe family," Turner said, "it might be better if you take Jonathan. I'll talk with the Goeglein boy." The girl, they decided, could wait. Since her name had not been mentioned by anyone whom they had spoken with, it was unlikely she could shed much light on the situation.

"We don't have time to beat around the bush with these

little punks," Turner added. "I don't think there's any doubt your officer has been shot. The only hope is that he might still be alive. What we've got to do is find out where he is as quickly as possible."

Inside, Turner spoke briefly with Sergeant Pfeifer, then turned to Fowler and smiled. "Looks like I got lucky," he said.

"How's that?"

"I picked the right one," Turner said. "Richard Goeglein turned seventeen last month."

Under Texas law, the murder of a police officer is a capital offense—punishable by death. The law, however, applies only to adults. A juvenile, even when certified by the courts to be tried as an adult, is exempt from the death sentence, regardless of his crime. In Texas, a person is considered a juvenile until the age of seventeen.

Goeglein, according to the Arizona driver's license he carried in his billfold, had celebrated his seventeenth birthday on September 14.

While Turner escorted the frightened youngster into a small office in the back of the station, Fowler, aware that the law required that a justice of the peace read a juvenile his rights, went in search of Glen Ayers. Ayers, the local J.P., had already been called to the station by the chief and was waiting in the lobby when the teenagers arrived. Fowler immediately told him to find a juvenile rights form and read it to Jobe.

Walking from the room, his official duties performed, the J.P. nodded to Fowler. "He's all yours," he said, then turned down the hall to where Goeglein waited.

The lieutenant hurried into the sparsely decorated room where the pale, wide-eyed Jobe sat, nervously shifting in his seat.

"Stand up," Fowler ordered. Though usually friendly and soft-spoken when interrogating a suspect, he made no attempt to reassure the young man.

Jobe rose quickly, moving across the small room until his back was against one of the gray metal filing cabinets.

Fowler arranged two wooden chairs back-to-back and settled into one of them. He motioned for Jobe to sit in the other.

The teenager straddled the chair, resting his arms on its back, as Fowler, no more than six inches away, stared at him for several seconds before slowly repeating the juvenile rights.

"What's going to happen to Richard?" the clearly frightened youth blurted out, surprising the lieutenant.

"Do you understand what capital murder is, boy?" Fowler responded. "We have information that it was you and your friend Richard who killed the officer last night. If you did, that's capital murder. Richard is seventeen, an adult. What that means is that he could get the death penalty. You, on the other hand, will get off easy. You'll get to spend the rest of your life in some crummy prison."

Jonathan, still apparently unconcerned about his own fate, began shaking his head. Tears rolled down his puffy cheeks. "That's not fair," he said. "It's not right for Richard to ride all the heat for this."

Jobe's observation amused Fowler. He wondered on what television cop show the youngster had heard the phrase "ride the heat."

"Well, you can bet he's going to ride the heat, as you put it, on this thing," the lieutenant said. "There's someone talking to him right now, and I guarantee you he'll wind up telling what he knows."

"Richard didn't do it," Jobe insisted. "Greg's the one who killed the guy."

"Greg Knighten?"

"Yeah."

"And you and Richard were with him."

"No, no," Jobe sobbed. His story came in short, quick sentences. He seemed to gasp for air as he spoke. "All I did was pick them up on the highway and bring them back into town. It was all Greg's idea. We were in his bedroom. He had a gun. I saw him put it down in his pants. He told Richard that he wanted him to go with him when George came by to pick him up. I was supposed to wait thirty minutes, then drive out and pick them up.

"I'm telling you, man, Richard didn't do it. Don't blame him for this. It was Greg's idea. He did it. He killed George."

Fowler was surprised that it had been so easy, but he was also saddened. Less than ten minutes had passed since he had entered the room to confront Jobe. Now, as he got up, he had a momentary concern that his legs wouldn't support him. For much of the day he had been resigned to the fact George Raffield was probably dead but had held to the faint hope that there might still be a miraculous ending to the nightmare. Now, though, the reality hammered at him and he felt nauseated.

"You're going to show me where you picked them up," he demanded, grabbing Jobe by the arm and directing him toward the door.

"It was dark."

"I think you can find it."

Jobe nodded, wiping the tears from his face with the back of his hand. "All right, I'll show you," he said, moving toward the door. Again he asked what was going to happen to his friend Richard.

"Frankly, I don't give a shit," Fowler spat, his temper exploding for the first time.

Jobe was silent, his head bowed, as he accompanied the officer through the crowded lobby toward the front door where Chief Vaughn was standing.

"He's going to take me out to where he picked the other kids up," Fowler said in a low voice. "You want to go with us?"

Vaughn stared wearily at the frightened teenager for several seconds. "I'd better stay here," he said. "Take Steve Egan and the judge with you."

Fowler escorted Jobe to his car, signaling for Patrolman Egan and Judge Ayers to get into the backseat.

Backing away from the station, the lieutenant looked over at the nervous youngster seated next to him. "Okay," he said, "where are we going?"

"Go out past my house," Jobe said. "All the way to where the road Ts."

"Boy, you better not be lying to me."

For the first time since they had left the office, Jobe looked squarely at the officer. "I'm not," he said. "I swear."

Back at the station, Richard's father approached George Turner before he entered the room where the teenager waited and asked if he felt his son needed a lawyer.

"I don't know," Turner said. "Until we've talked I won't know if he's involved in this or not." With that he entered the room and shut the door, leaving the anxious parents to wait in the lobby.

It didn't take long for the Ranger to satisfy himself that Richard Goeglein was, in fact, involved. The skinny young man with the piercing blue eyes, seated in a chair in front of Lieutenant Fowler's desk, appeared far too frightened to be innocent.

Unlike Fowler, Turner stood as he spoke, towering over the teenager. "I'm not going to play a lot of games with you," he began in a firm, measured voice. "You know something about the shooting of an officer last night, and I need to know what it is."

"I ain't a snitch," Goeglein said, straightening in the chair. "I'm not going to get my friends in trouble."

Turner leaned over, his face just inches from Richard's, and slapped his open hand against the top of the desk. "Look, dammit," he said, "I don't have time to discuss whether or not you're a snitch or what your friends are going to think. That's the least of my worries.

"My problem is that I've got a missing officer somewhere and I need to find him—right now. If he's not dead, I want to get him some help. Do you understand me?"

Goeglein, eyes downcast, nodded but said nothing.

Turner broke the silence with a question that vibrated against the monotonous gray walls. "What happened last night?"

"Greg shot him," Goeglein said, his voice barely audible. "He shot him three times."

"Where did it happen?"

"I don't know."

"Bullshit," Turner said. "I need to know where."

"I really don't know for sure," Richard insisted. "You go out past Camelot . . ."

"Where's that?"

"The same road the high school's on."

"Is Camelot a housing development?"

"Yeah, it's where Greg and Jonathan live. All I remember is we went out that road. We made a right turn; then a little later we turned left. That's all I know."

Turner burst out of the door and found Vaughn seated at the dispatcher's desk. "This shit's for real," he told the chief. "Greg Knighten killed him somewhere out near the high school."

The shaken Vaughn replied that Fowler had just left with Jobe, headed in that direction. "Their stories are tracking pretty damn close," the chief said, a new anger mounting in his voice.

"Then let's get the helicopter headed in that direction," Turner said, turning back to the room where Goeglein waited.

As the Ranger walked through the door he saw Richard reach into his pocket and lift a heart-shaped piece of black plastic to his lips. The youngster kissed it several more times before Turner, concerned that the amulet might be laced with some kind of drug, grabbed it away.

"What the hell is this?"

"It's something a girlfriend back in Arizona gave me," Goeglein said.

As Fowler sped south on Mountain Peak Road, past the high school and Camelot Estates, Jobe said little until they neared the intersection with Farm Road 575. "Turn right when you get to the stop sign," he said. "I picked them up somewhere down that way."

"How far?"

"I'm not sure," Jobe said. "It took me a while to find

them. I went too far the first time and had to turn around. They were walking along the road when I saw them."

Convinced that his passenger wasn't sure of the exact location, Fowler slowed the car, allowing Jobe to search for a landmark he might remember.

After less than a mile, they neared an abandoned gravel pit. "I'm not positive, but I think it was somewhere near here," Jobe said.

Fowler stopped the car, and Egan and Ayers got out to search the area on foot.

The patrolman and judge had just made their way through the barbed-wire fence when Jobe turned to Fowler. "I remember going across a concrete bridge," he said. The lieutenant knew there was a small creek another mile down the road. He put the car in gear and pulled back onto the blacktop, leaving Egan and Ayers behind.

As they passed a small country church and a cemetery, the bridge loomed ahead, at the beginning of a slight curve in the road.

"Is that it?" Fowler asked.

Jobe's body stiffened, his eyes focused straight ahead. "I think so," he said. For the next several minutes they rode in silence, Fowler's glance straying from the road to search the adjacent fields for Raffield's pickup.

Another mile down the road the lieutenant made a U-turn. Jobe had said he was traveling toward town when he picked Greg and Richard up. Perhaps, Fowler thought, he would more readily recognize the spot from the opposite side of the highway.

He hadn't gone far when Jobe told him to slow down. "It was right about here," the boy said.

Less than one hundred feet ahead was a turnoff leading into a pasture. Fowler slowed and abruptly swung onto the narrow dirt road.

Jobe began to cry, turning to face the driver. "No," he pleaded. "Take me back to town."

Fowler ignored him.

Jobe's sobbing became more hysterical. "You aren't going

to make me see this, are you? Oh, God, please don't. Take me back to town."

Fowler proceeded another hundred yards, then pulled to a stop. At that moment he had a strong feeling that he was very near the site of the murder. And he was convinced that the boy sitting beside him had already seen George Raffield's body.

Reaching the top of a slight incline, Fowler stopped the car and lit a cigarette. Jobe continued to beg him not to go any farther.

The officer considered the possibility that the youngster had, as he had said, only driven out here to give the others a ride into town. If so, it would be cruel to expose him to whatever awaited them. There was nothing, really, to be gained by going ahead.

Fowler, seeing the police helicopter off in the distance, reached for his car radio and spoke with Chief Vaughn. "Roy," he said, "tell the pilot to come farther south. If he'll follow 875 from the intersection and look off to the west, I think he'll find what we're looking for." Even on the two-way radio, the lieutenant's voice sounded hollow and exhausted.

Fowler turned the car around and headed back to the Farm-to-Market Road where he picked up Egan and Ayers. He wanted to return Jobe to the jail and get back to the area as quickly as possible. He was sure that Raffield's body would soon be located, and when it was, he would need to be there.

They were back on 663 en route to town when they were met by a caravan of patrol cars led by Sergeant Pfeifer. Trailing him were Midlothian Patrolman Jesus Chao and Red Oak Police Chief John Gage.

Pfeifer pulled his squad car alongside Fowler. "From the directions that Turner got from the Goeglein boy, it sounds like we need to be looking out on McAlpine Road," he said in an excited voice. "That's where we're headed now."

Fowler turned and looked over at Jonathan. "They're wasting their time," the boy said. "It's out there where I showed you."

Pfeifer was just about to pull away when a voice crackled over the radio: "Victim and vehicle located. Discontinue search. Notify family."

Pulling up to where Patrolman Chao was parked, Fowler quickly instructed him to take Jobe into custody and drive him back to the police station. Then he turned to follow the parade of cars screaming in the direction of the helicopter hovering in the distance.

In town, Vaughn walked slowly out into the parking lot where Fran Ross stood. In the chief's hand was a roll of bright yellow tape used for marking off a crime scene. "They'll need this," he said to the patrolman.

A dozen police and sheriff's cars were already parked alongside the road when Ross pulled onto the shoulder and approached a deputy. "I've got the crime scene tape," he explained. "Where do I need to go?"

"Right down that dirt road," the deputy said. "Back in the pasture a little ways."

Ross said nothing, then started walking down the same rutted dirt road he had planned to jog along earlier in the day.

Lieutenant Fowler stood on a small hill, staring down into an area of the pasture shielded from the highway by a thick stand of cedar and mesquite trees. Raffield's truck was parked in ankle-high weeds and wildflowers, which formed a bright yellow carpet. Nearby was a small stock tank, which Fowler did not immediately notice. His attention was focused on the body that lay face down near the driver's side of the pickup.

It would, Fowler knew, be his responsibility to protect the crime scene. But for a moment he was unable to move. He was still standing silently, unable to take his eyes off the prone body dressed in jeans, tennis shoes, and blue windbreaker, when Midlothian Officer David Bennett, who had arrived minutes before Fowler, walked back up the hill.

"I didn't get any pulse," Bennett said. "He's ⟨

Fowler bowed his head and began shaking it fr⟨
side. "Why?" he asked. "Why in God's name did⟨
to happen?"

It was a question that would haunt him in the n⟨
come.

Part
TWO

George W. Raffield, Jr.
(Died in Action)
1966–2001

As a soul once was within me, I had plans for being a policeman. I figured that's what I wanted to be when I was about 15 years old. I traveled on through my high school years and got in college at Southern Methodist University. I stayed there and graduated.

When I was on duty one day I was shot in the back, killed instantly.

I hope that people will take into consideration the things that could happen in one's lifetime and profession.

> *—An epitaph written by George Raffield when he was a high school student*

6

Had he not been caught shoplifting, George Raffield might never have considered a career in law enforcement.

He was fourteen then and had accompanied his sisters to the dime store near their Mesquite home. While Sherrie and Sheryl busied themselves along the aisles of lipsticks, finger-nail polish, and costume jewelry, George, his three-dollar allowance in his pocket, wandered alone among the model airplanes and baseball equipment. And, in a spontaneous act he had never before considered, he quietly slipped a couple of packets of BBs into his coat pocket.

The store clerk had witnessed the theft and immediately called the frightened youngster to the front. By the time Sherrie and Sheryl learned what had happened, a police officer had arrived and was preparing to take their brother to the station.

It was Sherrie who tearfully called home and reported to her father that George had been arrested.

Don Moore went immediately to the Balch Springs Police Department where the arresting officer met him in the foyer and explained the situation. While the offense was minor, the patrolman explained, a new "get tough" policy of the department required that youngsters caught in misdemeanors be brought in and their parents notified. No charges would be filed, of course, if the merchandise was returned or paid for. "Frankly," the officer explained, "it's a scare tactic, pure and simple. The chief feels if we can get a kid's attention the first time he messes up, maybe we won't have to deal with him again."

"I can promise you," Moore told the officer, "that you'll never have any trouble with my boy again."

In a stark interview room, Moore leaned against one of the rough cinder-block walls, his eyes fixed on his son as the officer dramatically outlined the consequences of being arrested for shoplifting.

George, his young mind ablaze with visions of jail cells and a ruined future, cried. But, to the relief of his father, he looked the officer squarely in the eye as he was being addressed. He made no excuses and told no lies to cover his offense. He did not know why he had stolen the BBs. He was sorry, and he would never do it again.

The stern-faced officer ended the lecture, then smiled for the first time since escorting the youngster to the police station. "Now," he said, "I'm going to do you a favor. If you'll go back to the store, apologize to the owner, and square your debt, we'll let you go this time." No formal charges would be filed, he assured the boy's father.

From the station, Don Moore, his son sitting silently beside him, drove straight to the store. He followed George inside and stood nearby as his son apologized to the store owner and returned the stolen merchandise.

They were almost home before Don finally spoke. Not taking his eyes off the road, he said, "Son, I hope you learned a lesson today." That was it. No lecture, no further punishment at home.

"I did," George said. Now safe in the company of his father, shame had replaced the fear he'd felt at the police station. "I'm really sorry," he said and began to sob again.

It was the last time Don Moore mentioned the incident. But to George Moore, it was a highly magnified event that he would never forget.

Two years later, when filling out an application for a job as a grocery sacker at a Minyard's Food Store, he came to a question: Have you ever been convicted of a crime?

In his boyish hand he had written "shoplifting" in the answer blank.

Shirley Moore, reviewing her son's application, had argued that it was not necessary for him to mention a forgotten incident for which he was never even formally charged.

"Yes, it is," George had told her. "I did it."

Neither Shirley nor Don was aware of the impact the young Balch Springs officer had on their son. Even in those fearful moments when imagining himself going to jail, maybe even to prison, George Raffield had been impressed by the man who arrested him. The uniform, the badge, the way the man had carried himself—all spoke of confidence and authority.

Whether his motives were redemptive or just a case of youthful admiration, George had made up his mind that one day he would be a police officer. His life's course was set.

Raffield was a sophomore at Mesquite High School when he enrolled in the Police Explorers, an organization cosponsored by the Department of Public Safety and the Boy Scouts. Students in the program were provided uniforms, given classroom lectures on police procedures, and occasionally allowed to accompany DPS officers on patrol. For the youngster, life offered no greater reward than wearing his uniform and riding alongside one of the DPS officers.

It was in August of 1984, just before the start of his senior year, that George's parents moved to a new, spacious home on the outskirts of the rural community of Red Oak. While he liked his new surroundings, enjoying the open spaces and country atmosphere, George was saddened at the thought of leaving so much behind. His friends, his school, and his job were still back in the Dallas suburb of Mesquite, a thirty-minute drive away.

All the other Moore children had graduated from Mesquite High School, and George pleaded that he be allowed to do the same. His parents finally agreed that he could commute daily to complete his senior year and continue his afternoon job at the grocery store.

By the time his final year of high school was drawing to a close, however, George was becoming more and more involved in the activities of his new home. Following his eighteenth birthday, he enlisted as a reserve officer with the Red Oak Police Department. He told the chief, John Gage, of his plans to go into a law enforcement career. Impressed by his maturity and enthusiasm, Gage offered to speed up the process by helping George enroll in an eleven-week law enforcement course at Fort Worth's Tarrant County Junior College as soon as he graduated from high school. It was there that Raffield earned his basic police certificate.

Her son's determination to become a police officer had troubled Shirley Moore from the start, but she had stopped short of voicing her concern about the dangers of the profession. She tried with little success to convince herself that she was only being an overprotective mother, guarding her youngest child too closely, fighting the maternal battle to prevent the last of her brood from growing up too quickly and leaving home as the others had done.

Though she loved all of their children, Shirley had a special feeling for her only son. Michael, George's older brother, had died at birth. Then George had been born prematurely, and for several long weeks the doctors had warned Shirley that his chances of survival were not good. She had visited the hospital daily after being released, looking in on her tiny son as he struggled to gain a firm hold on life. He remained there for three weeks before the doctors allowed him to go home.

George, then, had been her "miracle" baby, a fighter, a survivor, and Shirley Moore cherished his every accomplishment, each step toward manhood, in a special way. The idea of him in a dangerous line of work frightened her, and at the same time his determination filled her with a warm pride.

In September of 1986, her son entered the police academy after being offered his first full-time job as a policeman in the nearby community of Wilmer. And it was Shirley Moore who accompanied him to a police supply store to purchase the handgun he would be required to carry on the job. The irony of the shopping trip disturbed her. At nineteen, her son was old enough to enter the police academy, but not old enough under Texas law to purchase the nickel-plated Smith & Wesson .357 Magnum without parental consent.

Wilmer Police Chief Preston Parks was immediately impressed by the enthusiasm of his new patrolman. Raffield's eagerness to learn was apparent in the constant stream of questions he asked.

Three months later, however, Parks was forced to call the young rookie officer in and terminate him. Over a period of two days Patrolman Raffield had been involved in two high-speed chases: in each he had wrecked the patrol car he was driving. Raffield had been lucky to escape injury, particularly in the second accident in which the car he was driving was totaled.

Chief Parks explained that he could not risk a third accident.

Discouraged that his career had begun on such a negative note, Raffield returned to Red Oak where Chief Gage hired him as a relief dispatcher. George, not at all interested in a career sitting at a desk, monitoring calls from the field, began sending résumés to other departments.

After six months of unsuccessful job-hunting, he was considering looking for something outside law enforcement when Chief Gage stopped him one evening and told him that the police chief from Midlothian wanted to talk with him.

George was surprised when told that Roy Vaughn did not want him to come to Midlothian for an interview. Instead, the chief would travel to Red Oak.

From the moment Roy Vaughn took his oath of office, the drug problem of Midlothian's youth was an evil he was determined to fight. The battle, he knew, would not be easy, chiefly because of a troubling reluctance on the part of the school administration to accept the help of the police department.

What Vaughn faced was a stubborn refusal on the part of the school authorities to admit that they did, in fact, have a serious drug problem in the school. Despite several meetings with administrators at which he related the stories he was hearing—a fourteen-year-old selling marijuana to students in the middle school, a teenager snorting cocaine on a school bus, drug transactions taking place in the high school parking lot—Vaughn was unsuccessful in his efforts to convince them that the school needed the help of his department.

The Midlothian school system was, in effect, an island unto itself. The schools would, he was informed, police themselves, just as they had done in the years before he became police chief.

Initially puzzled, then angered by the school's reluctance to admit that the problem not only existed but was growing, Vaughn began formulating a plan. "There's absolutely no doubt in my mind that we've got a serious problem in the school," he told Chuck Pinto, "and ignoring it isn't going to make it go away. Hell, I put five kids of my own through the school system. I made it a point back then to find out what was going on."

Too, the information he had received from Jack Wallace during his summer of undercover work convinced Vaughn that the drug traffic among local teenagers was growing at an alarming rate.

If the school administrators didn't want to cooperate, he said, he was ready to attack the problem without their help. What he wanted to do was place an undercover officer in the high school, but he did not have the necessary budget.

The city manager, impressed with Wallace's accomplishments and concerned by the reports he had filed, had been surprised when many townspeople had continued to insist that Midlothian's drug problem was minor. He could, however, arrange to get the support the police needed and told Chief Vaughn to proceed.

It was in late June of 1987 that Pinto and Vaughn appeared before the city council requesting funding for what was described only as a "narcotics investigation." The council, after hearing Pinto speak passionately on drug trafficking and the image the community was attempting to create, voted to appropriate $10,000 for the project.

By big-city standards, the amount was paltry. To Vaughn, however, it represented the resources he needed. He was not, after all, going after drug kingpins. His primary target was fifteen- to seventeen-year-olds who were buying and selling ten- and twenty-five-dollar bags of pot and small amounts of crack, crank, and cocaine. What he hoped to accomplish with his proposed undercover operation was an awakening on the part of the community, parents, and young people to the growing problem.

The only way to get their attention, Vaughn had decided, was to provide proof that the problem existed. To do that, cases had to be made. In all likelihood, some of the kids who would eventually be arrested would be children of influential citizens in the community.

"Before all's said and done," Vaughn warned the city manager, "we'll get some heat on this thing."

"Taking a little heat goes with the job," Pinto said. It was an unnecessary reminder.

They had agreed that the operation would remain secret. Only Vaughn, Pinto, and Lieutenant Fowler, who would function as the undercover officer's contact, would know of the plan. Even the other officers in the department would not be informed. Nor would administrators or teachers in the school.

With the plan set and financing assured, Vaughn and Fowler quietly began searching for a young police officer who could convincingly play the role of a high school student.

The person Vaughn had in mind would have to be unique.

"We've got a different kind of situation here," the chief said as he sat in his office late one evening with Fowler. "In Dallas, you can put a really low-life-looking kid undercover and he'll fit in. Here he would stick out like a sore thumb. What I'm looking for is a kid who isn't going to come in and be branded a troublemaker right off the bat. I want him to be a good kid, no problem to the teachers. I don't want some outlaw who'll smoke a joint with the kids now and then or who'll pinch the ass of every girl in the school. That kind of behavior can come back to haunt you when you get ready to take the cases to court. This has to be done right if it's going to work."

Fowler agreed.

For weeks the search was fruitless. Fowler traveled to Dallas and spoke with several old friends in the Narcotics Division, asking if they knew of any likely candidates. Though he found a number of officers who were experienced in undercover work and interested in the job, they all looked too old to pass as high school students.

When it was suggested that female officers are generally more successful at passing as teenagers, Fowler and Vaughn quickly dismissed the idea, wary of the potential sexual problems a woman posing as a student might face.

On occasion Vaughn had heard one of his patrolmen, Jesus Chao, talk about a young dispatcher he had become friends with while serving on the force in nearby Red Oak. Chao had related the story of his friend's unfortunate auto accidents while working in Wilmer, pointing out that it was too bad he had been fired because he would have made an excellent officer. The only problem, Chao had remarked, was that his friend was so young-looking.

Vaughn telephoned Chief Gage in Red Oak but said only that he had an opening in his department. "What can you tell me about the young fellow you have working as a dispatcher?" Vaughn asked.

"He's a damn good kid," Gage said. "He's looking for something better, but I don't have anything for him right now."

"You mind if I talk with him?"

"Not at all. When do you want to come over?"

Vaughn suggested that Gage and Raffield meet him for coffee at a restaurant on the highway just outside of Red Oak later that afternoon. "I'll bring Billy Fowler with me," Vaughn said.

Gage, who had worked with both of the Midlothian

officers while with the Dallas Police Department, was mildly puzzled by the urgency in his friend's voice. "Three o'clock sound okay?"

"We'll be there," Vaughn said.

Seated in a booth at the café, Vaughn studied the youngster across from him. He listened as Raffield spoke of his enthusiasm for police work, admitted candidly the problems that had led to his dismissal in Wilmer, and talked of his eagerness to join a force on a full-time basis.

Raffield was confident, which Vaughn liked, but didn't come across, like many young would-be officers, as overbearing and macho. George Raffield also acknowledged that he had a great deal to learn and felt he could best accomplish that goal as a member of a small department.

Sipping his coffee, Vaughn made mental notes as Raffield talked. Though he had just turned twenty-one, he looked young enough to pass for a high school senior. His wavy black hair was cut shorter than the style most high school boys favored, but he could let it grow. His five-foot-six-inch frame was a bit stocky; Vaughn would urge him to lose a few pounds. He would also have to shave his neatly trimmed mustache.

"We'll be in touch," Vaughn said as he rose and shook Raffield's hand.

In the parking lot, Gage stayed behind with Vaughn and Fowler as George, thinking he had just been interviewed for a job as a patrolman with the Midlothian Police Department, drove away in the pickup he had purchased shortly after graduation.

"About that business over in Wilmer," Gage said. "I think if you call over there, you'll find that they thought the boy had what it takes to make a damn good police officer. He just had some bad luck."

"I'm not going to call them," Vaughn said. "In fact, I'd like to keep this as quiet as possible. What I'm looking for is someone to put into the high school."

George met with the Midlothian officers twice more

before he was told there would be a "special assignment" for him to work before coming into the department as a uniformed patrolman.

"We're looking for someone to work as an undercover narcotics officer in the high school for a few months," Vaughn explained. "If you're interested, we'll train you this summer, then enroll you when school starts in the fall. If all goes the way we hope it will, you'll be posing as a student for the first semester."

"I'm interested," Raffield said.

"It's important that this operation be secret," Vaughn said. "Lieutenant Fowler will work out a cover story for you and help you with any problems you run into. He'll be your only contact in the department."

Raffield nodded. "I understand."

Vaughn, pleased to have found his man, smiled. "Okay, then, if you start letting your hair grow a little longer, we'll get to work on things on our end."

John Gage had already established a cover story for his dispatcher's departure. George, he said, had decided to give up on his dream of a police career and join his machinist father on the assembly line at Dresser Industries, a supplier of oil and gas exploration tools.

Raffield was almost giddy with excitement as he outlined his new job at a family gathering the following day, at the same time warning them to keep his assignment secret.

"Damn! We've got a real-life 'Twenty-one Jump Street' on our hands," said his brother-in-law, Mark, referring to the popular TV show about young undercover narcotics officers posing as students in a big-city high school. George, a fan of the show, clearly enjoyed the comparison. The only subdued face in the celebration was that of Shirley Moore.

Even before he and Chief Vaughn had agreed to hire Raffield, Lieutenant Fowler had begun planning a cover story for the officer.

In late July Fowler and Raffield drove to Temple, a medium-sized city in central Texas, to establish the background story Midlothian students and teachers would be told when Raffield enrolled for the fall term.

Tom Vannoy, a former vice officer with the Dallas Police Department and a longtime friend of Fowler's, had become chief of police in Temple. Vannoy had also become something of a go-between in operations where the principal of Temple High School helped to establish records and backgrounds for undercover officers planning to work in Dallas schools.

With the help of a senior counselor, the principal would enter a fictitious scholastic history—grades, attendance and immunization records, parents' names, and a home address —into the Temple school system's computer. He had readily agreed to provide the same service to Fowler and the Midlothian Police Department.

"It's important that you use a name that you're going to be comfortable with," Fowler had explained on the drive to Temple. "It's been my experience that using your real first name is best."

George agreed, adding that he would like to reverse his first and middle names and use his stepfather's last name. To the Midlothian school officials, then, he would be known as William George Moore. He would tell his fellow students to call him George.

That afternoon his new persona was created, and his history—indicating he had attended public school in Temple from the first through the eleventh grades—was established. An average student, George Moore had completed most of the difficult courses necessary for graduation; thus his senior schedule would be relatively light and require little homework. The principal also gave him a Temple High School parking permit and suggested he attach it to the window of his pickup.

Then Raffield and Fowler were driven around town by one of Chief Vannoy's detectives, a Temple native, who pointed out popular teenage hangouts and discussed the things local youngsters did for entertainment.

By late afternoon, George Raffield/Moore felt sure he

could convincingly describe life in Temple to any new acquaintance who might quiz him about his former life.

On the way back to Red Oak, Fowler outlined additional details of the cover story: George was to say he was moving to Midlothian for his senior year because he and his father could not get along. An aunt and uncle who lived outside of town had invited him to live with them.

By saying that he lived several miles out of town, it would be easier for Raffield to continue living in the home of his parents in nearby Red Oak.

George would explain that he had left a girlfriend behind in Temple, where he would go every weekend for visits. He would buy drugs from Midlothian students, then sell them in Temple to help finance his weekend trips, he would tell the students. This, Fowler felt, would not only be convincing but would also assure the officer of having most weekends off.

"You're going to be putting in a lot of hours," Fowler explained. "In addition to being in school all day, you're going to have to hang around with the kids in the afternoons and evenings. There's no time clock in undercover work. But after this operation is over, we'll make it up to you. You'll get a month or so off before you go into uniform."

As George's only contact in the department, Fowler also emphasized the importance of staying in touch by phone, regularly telling him where he would be, whom he expected to be with, and what drug transactions were to take place. "I want you to call me before and immediately after any drug buys are made," Fowler instructed. "And when you get home in the evenings, your first order of business is to call and let me know you're there and safe," Fowler said.

"Sounds like I'm seventeen years old again," Raffield joked.

"That's the whole idea," the lieutenant said.

Raffield, fascinated by Fowler's attention to detail and his stories of the undercover operations he had orchestrated while working narcotics in Dallas, eagerly agreed to the plan.

The following day Fowler met Raffield at the regional

office of the Department of Public Safety in Garland where arrangements were made for a bogus driver's license bearing the name William George Moore and a Temple address.

Later that afternoon in the kitchen of Fowler's home, Chief Vaughn swore George Raffield in, officially making him a member of the Midlothian Police Department. He presented Raffield with a badge and an identification card and explained that he would go on the payroll as an "administrative special assistant" to the city manager. His bimonthly paycheck would go to Chuck Pinto, who would personally deliver it to the police station. Fowler would see that it got to Raffield.

George's next stop would be a month-long training session in the Narcotics Division of the Dallas Police Department.

Throughout the month of August, Raffield reported daily to the Dallas Police Department, working alongside experienced officers in the Narcotics Division. Just as Jack Wallace had, George learned to identify the various illegal drugs and to estimate their value. He was taught how they were prepared and weighed and what they were called on the street. He learned how to fill out reports and heard repeatedly how important it was for an undercover officer to develop a keen sense of observation.

"When you take the stand to testify about some deal that went down," one veteran undercover officer said, "you'd better be able to remember every little detail of the buy. The defense lawyers are going to do everything they can to trip you up any way they can. So be ready to describe what the person you were dealing with was wearing, what he was driving, what the weather was like. If the sonuvabitch had bad breath, make a note of it. Details are as important as the physical evidence you bring in. The defense attorney is always going to raise questions about your memory."

He accompanied officers on numerous raids and was amazed at the amount of drugs and money seized.

Twice a week he would place a call to Midlothian to inform Fowler of his progress. The lieutenant would listen as Raffield related his experiences, pleased with the enthusiasm he heard in the young officer's voice.

A tough-talking female officer who had recently completed an undercover assignment in a Dallas high school spent long hours with Raffield, going over the latest fads, hip phrases, and fashions. "Fitting in with whatever group you have to," she had said, "is important. You've got to stand out just enough to be noticed but be able to blend in at the same time. It's tricky. You're going to find yourself doing some things that you think are really silly. But you've got to think like you're seventeen and do some of the stupid shit a seventeen-year-old does.

"But the most important thing," she said, "is you've got to be a damn good liar. If you can't lie your ass off, don't get into this."

With each day's training, Raffield's eagerness to test his knowledge grew. The anticipation of what lay ahead was unlike any emotion he had ever felt. He began looking forward to September with an excitement he had never felt during his own school days.

7

A mile south of the downtown area, Midlothian High School, with its aggregate exterior, is the centerpiece of an academic complex that hardly looks its age. Built in 1969, it is flanked by tennis courts, administration buildings, and a football stadium named after lineman Don Floyd, the only former Panther ever to make it all the way to the National Football League.

In front of the high school an American flag waves.

The school complex is the pride of the community, its first monument to modern-day progress. Despite the daily traffic of 700 students, from freshmen to seniors, it shows little wear and tear from two decades of use. The wide halls that meander maze-like through the sprawling building are spotless. The bright blue metal lockers that line the walls are free of graffiti, unlike those of larger metropolitan schools.

No modern convenience was overlooked when the building was designed, and the science labs and band hall have the best equipment available. The hardwood floor of the spacious gymnasium is polished to a mirror sheen, and an auditorium in one corner of the building is the scene of assemblies, band concerts, and dramatic productions. The library, located in the northeast corner, is a unique combination of school and public facility.

During breaks and lunch periods, students gather in a manicured outdoor commons to sit on benches and at tables, enjoying a respite from the classrooms. The school mascot, a blue oversized fiberglass panther, its face frozen in a fierce growl, decorates one corner of the area—when it hasn't been stolen by pranksters from some rival school.

The classrooms are warm and bright, uncluttered and comfortable. The student–teacher ratio is an academic dream come true: seventeen to one.

At Midlothian High, extracurricular activities are enthusiastically encouraged. As in most rural Texas communities, football is the focus of a fall excitement that borders on mania. While the Panthers, coached by Bill Moore, have enjoyed only modest success in their District 7-AAAA battles, the home games are played before crowds ever optimistic that this just might be the year the team claims a district championship and advances into the state play-offs. On fall Friday nights, in fact, the community and student body come together in a unification no other social function provides. In addition to the young players clad in their blue and white uniforms, the cheerleaders, the band, and an all-girl drill team actively participate. Downtown businesses volunteer personnel to serve in the concession stand; members of the Panther Booster Club sit together, grown men and women proudly wearing the school colors. Local alumni serve as the sideline chain crew and operate the bank-donated scoreboard, and local doctors take turns standing in to treat any injuries that might occur.

Sports at Midlothian High are not, however, an all-male domain. Female students can choose cross-country, volleyball, basketball, tennis, golf, and track and field. And those—boys and girls alike—who are not interested in competitive athletics can enjoy activities ranging from debates to the school paper to one-act plays.

Principal Wilburn Roesler, however, places academic achievement above all else. He proudly notes that the

Midlothian Independent School District has fifty-three teachers with master's degrees and that his staff, while relatively young, can boast an average of ten years of teaching experience. With little prompting he can call off the growing list of graduates who have gone on to college in recent years.

There are strict scholastic eligibility requirements for participation in extracurricular activities, and the student handbook is thick with rules and regulations governing student behavior. In hard-line detail, students are advised about dress codes, parking regulations, school bus etiquette, class discipline, and attendance.

The Pregnant Homebound Program is outlined, detailing how female students can earn a diploma while awaiting the birth of a child. A dozen girls were enrolled in the program for the 1986–87 school year.

There is a Just Say No program manned by high school students who visit the middle and elementary schools to warn younger students of the hazards of drug use. The Student Assistance Program, led by a committee of teachers and administrators, tries to avert problems before they become unmanageable, monitoring any drastic changes in the behavior of a student and—if there is a problem like drug use, depression, truancy, or a dramatic fall-off in class participation—alerting the student's parents.

While the easygoing ideals of the rural school atmosphere have given way to modern academic procedures, Principal Roesler and the seven-member Midlothian school board worked hard to avoid the problems faced daily in the nearby Dallas school system. There, they knew, teachers were becoming disenchanted by the flood of daily problems. Youth gangs, sometimes armed, roamed the halls, terrorizing fellow students and teachers alike, and violence was common.

Roesler does not paint an idyllic picture of school life in Midlothian, but he is quick to point out that the academic process has not been hobbled by too much legislation, too little support from parents and school board members, or a lack of discipline among most students. He can count on one hand the number of times angry parents have threatened to bring in an attorney to resolve a discipline problem.

Midlothian, then, supported its school system above all else in the community. There had been precious little bickering back in 1969 when the plans for the new high school included far more space than was necessary. They had accepted the fact that the day would come, sooner than many liked to admit, when the enrollment would grow and the extra space would be filled.

When it came to education, the people of Midlothian put aside their small-town thinking and looked realistically to the future. It was for this reason that visiting business executives, researching new locations, generally left the town most impressed by the progressive school system.

Men like City Manager Chuck Pinto quickly recognized it as the best advertising Midlothian had.

While most youngsters were frantically completing last-minute vacation activities, enjoying group trips to the malls in Dallas, or shopping for school clothes in their final days of freedom before the beginning of another school year, George Raffield was putting the final touches on his new identity.

Accompanied by Billy Fowler, he had visited the country home of Bob Browning, a veteran Dallas police officer who, years earlier, had opted to live in the rural peace of Ellis County and commute daily to his job in the property room of the downtown Dallas police station.

A tall, powerfully built man with boyish freckles and sandy red hair, the forty-eight-year-old Browning had a reputation as a no-nonsense cop with little tolerance for those who violated the law. Some of his fellow workers thought he was stubborn to a fault, unbending once he had made up his mind on an issue. He chose his friends carefully and warmed slowly to new acquaintances.

His closest friends, in fact, were not fellow Dallas officers but Billy Fowler and Roy Vaughn. Only illness or some other family emergency interfered with their regular meeting at an all-you-can-eat seafood restaurant in Waxahachie every Friday. At 7:15 P.M. sharp, three cars would pull into the parking lot almost simultaneously. Fowler and his wife, Jeanie, would be in one, Roy and Margie Vaughn in another, and Browning and his wife, Martha, in another.

It was during one of those Friday night gatherings that Browning was told about the new officer Vaughn had hired and of the plan to enroll him as a student at the high school. "We're going to need someone to play the role of his aunt and uncle," Fowler explained. "He's going to continue to live at home, but we need someone here in Midlothian for the school to call if they need to, someone who can sign permission slips for field trips and notify the school if he's sick, things like that."

Bob and Martha Browning agreed to be a part of George's cover story without even meeting the young undercover officer, and Bob was convinced of the wisdom of his decision as they sat in the den talking during their initial meeting. Browning liked George's manners—the way he answered Martha with "yes, ma'am" and "no, ma'am"— and his youthful enthusiasm for the task at hand.

For Browning, who in recent months had found himself working for a department burdened by disenchantment as a result of a steady barrage of criticism from city council members and a public outcry for a police review board, the approach to law enforcement in Midlothian was a breath of fresh air. He privately envied the esprit de corps of Vaughn's department and the community backing it received. He liked the stubborn stance Roy Vaughn took against political pressures, his refusal to show favoritism to the town's influential citizens, and the way he supported his men. Browning, who viewed the Midlothian chief as something of a kindred spirit, had found himself talking with his wife often in recent months about leaving the Dallas Police Department. If the right opening occurred, he had told her, he might just submit his application to Roy Vaughn.

His willingness to help in the undercover operation, however, was nothing more than a simple act of friendship.

* * *

A bright September morning sun danced off the walls of the high school as George pulled his red pickup into the students' parking lot. Dressed in jeans, tennis shoes, and a polo shirt, he quickly blended into the crowd of teenagers making their way to the front entrance of the building for registration. A few students, recognizing that he was a new student, nodded a friendly hello before turning their attention to familiar classmates.

The lengthy discussions with the female Dallas officer who had worked undercover as a high school student had not prepared George for the unease in his stomach as he crossed the parking lot. The atmosphere of the first day of school was familiar enough to him: the excited tittering of young girls standing in groups, stealing glances at the horseplay of many of the boys; the smell of too much perfume and unnecessary after-shave; the fresh haircuts and new clothes. It brought back memories of similar times at Mesquite High School. Many of the young faces beamed with the anticipation of a new year, filled with the promise of football games, campaigns for class offices, dances, and romances; others mirrored the dread of homework and lost freedom. The carefree evenings of summer had become school nights once again.

George was concerned, for he shared none of the emotions swirling around him and would have to fake it. Not only would he have to lie successfully about his age, his name, and his background, but his actions would have to signal the emotions of those several years younger.

The prospect of the days ahead loomed more frighteningly than he had anticipated, and he felt a mild surge of anger that the self-confidence he had gained during his training period seemed suddenly to have disappeared.

Before entering the building he cast a quick glance back across the parking lot, out onto the street where Police Chief Roy Vaughn stood, directing traffic. George had not acknowledged the chief as he turned into the parking lot, and Vaughn had given no indication that he even recognized him.

George Moore took a deep breath, smiled at a fellow

student who was hurrying up the steps, and walked into the school to become a high school senior once again.

He didn't even make it past the administration desk before facing his first problem.

Lieutenant Fowler was in his office, having just returned from drinking a cup of coffee at Dee Tee's, when George called from a pay phone just a couple of blocks from the police station. "They won't let me enroll," he said, "unless I can provide documentation that my guardianship has been legally transferred to my aunt and uncle."

Fowler leaned back in his chair and sighed, angered that he had not anticipated such a detail. Why hadn't someone mentioned the necessity for such paperwork during George's training? Had the principal in Temple simply not known, or had he forgotten?

The lieutenant said nothing for several seconds.

"I told them I would go home and talk with my uncle about it," George said, breaking the silence.

Fowler quickly dismissed his frustration and set about to resolve the problem. "Meet me at the Waxahachie court-house at two this afternoon," he said. "We'll straighten it out and get you enrolled tomorrow."

The lieutenant hung up the phone and went directly to Vaughn's office. "Damn," said the chief as he crushed out a cigarette, "we're going to have to let the city attorney in on what we're doing." While the chief called Chuck Pinto to inform him of the problem that had developed, Fowler was on the phone to Bob Browning, hoping to catch him before he left for Dallas.

Later that morning Don Stout, an attorney retained by the city, drafted bogus transfer-of-guardianship papers requesting that Bob Browning be granted legal custody of the young man posing as his nephew. That afternoon, Stout, accompanied by Browning, Vaughn, Pinto, and George Raffield, met in the office of Ellis County Judge Al Scoggins, who would be required to sign the document, making the transfer official.

Before they entered the judge's chambers, Browning

called Stout aside. "Is the judge aware of what's going on here?" he asked.

Stout nodded. "Roy explained it to him and he fully supports what they're doing."

In less than an hour Browning was on his way to Dallas, officially the legal guardian of the young undercover officer.

The following morning George Moore enrolled for his senior year.

Fowler had repeatedly stressed to George that it was important he be in no rush to begin making cases. Go slow, he said, get a feel for the school and the students. Blend in, make friends, and listen. He urged him not to align himself immediately with any particular group, but instead to move among the well-established cliques.

In his frequent dealings with Midlothian teenagers, Fowler had become aware of a student class structure that had not existed during his long-ago school days in west Texas and Dallas.

There were the preppies, students from affluent backgrounds. They drove the nicest cars, wore the latest fashions, and campaigned vigorously to be head cheerleader, football captain, and student council president. The ropers were those whose parents operated the small ranches and dairy farms on the outskirts of town. They dressed in neatly starched Levi's jeans, western shirts, and cowboy boots, listened to country and western in their pickups, and thought winning blue ribbons at 4-H competitions more important than being elected to class office.

Then there were the dopers. Generally rebellious, they were routinely truant, had long hair, and spent considerable time in detention. They got poor grades and made little attempt to be friendly with those outside their group. Their uniform was scruffy faded jeans and T-shirts bought at recent rock concerts in Dallas. Pridefully blatant about their drug use, they often gathered at City Lake in the mornings to share a joint before school. They also made frequent trips into south Dallas to visit the Jamaican dealers who, day or night, could supply whatever drug they might want.

"Remember," Fowler had said, "you're a new kid in town. Let the others come to you at first. You'll learn soon enough who the dopers are. You won't have to ask. Hell, they stick out like a sore thumb. They'll be cautious of you at first. The best way to deal with that is to act like you're just as cautious as they are. The important thing is that you don't move too fast. We don't expect anything to happen for a while."

George had been fascinated by Lieutenant Fowler from the first time they talked. While training with the Dallas police, several vice officers had given him glowing reports on the man who would serve as his contact officer. "You're going to learn more from him in a year than most cops do in a career," one said.

Billy Fowler is a slightly built man with an energy level that belies the fact he is just three years shy of his sixtieth birthday. His coarse black hair is always neatly trimmed, and his deep-set brown eyes sparkle with a hint of mischief that makes it difficult for him to get away with many of the practical jokes he enjoys playing on friends.

He speaks with a thick, disarming Texas drawl, his soft voice gravelly from a three-pack-a-day smoking habit. A southern gentleman, he is quick to apologize if even the mildest profanity slips out in mixed company. An immaculate dresser who reports to work daily in a suit and spit-polished shoes, he looks more like a big-city banker than a member of a small-town police force.

Even before Roy Vaughn had been officially offered the job of Midlothian police chief, he had approached Fowler about serving as his second-in-command. While working together in the Dallas Police Department, Vaughn had been keenly aware of Fowler's efficiency and investigative skills. Billy, he knew, was a meticulous organizer, had a scholarly knowledge of the law, and approached his work with a genuine sensitivity that would be welcomed in a small town. "He's so damn polite and soft-spoken," a fellow officer had once observed, "that crooks wind up thanking him for busting them."

He had spent most of his adult life in police work as a result of happenstance. It was only after he married that Fowler began thinking seriously about a career. While working at a Dallas Safeway store, quickly advancing to the position of produce manager, he attended night-school drafting classes.

Ultimately, it was his wife who gently pushed him to put his drafting talents to use. She was the one who spotted a notice in the classified pages that an oil company in Midland, Texas, was looking for draftsmen. He got the job, and in the fall of 1956, Fowler and his wife made the move to west Texas. He worked for Honolulu Oil for three years before it was sold to a larger company that was already well staffed. As the newest employee in his department, Fowler was among those given notice.

Among the new friends he had made were a couple of patrolmen with the Midland Police Department who encouraged him to apply to the department. With a mortgage, a young son, and no other job prospects, Fowler took their suggestion and in 1959 was sworn in. It took him only a short while to recognize that he had found his calling. He liked working deep night patrol, the camaraderie, and the feeling that he was making a contribution to the well-being of the community. During his daily preparation to report for duty, he felt an excitement that he had never before experienced.

Midland, Texas, however, was another story. Fowler missed the lakes and trees and clear skies he had come to take for granted in Dallas. He wearied of the endless dust storms and the boredom of the barren, flat landscape.

He had completed his third year with the Midland force when he made the decision to apply to the Dallas Police Department. When offered a job, he immediately accepted and headed home. There he would stay for twenty years, working patrol, then vice and narcotics, and finally internal affairs investigations.

The intensity of big-city police work fascinated him from the beginning. It also brought him in closer touch with the grim realities, the madness, and the sorrow of the dark side of life, which law enforcement officers see daily.

Like Vaughn, Fowler had felt the impact of the Kennedy assassination even more keenly than most. He had been off duty that November day when Lee Harvey Oswald fired the shot that killed the President, but Fowler's partner, Officer J. D. Tippit, while working alone that afternoon, encountered the fleeing Oswald in a residential area. Tippit stopped his car and called out to the man fitting the description broadcast just minutes earlier. While Tippit stood near the front fender of his patrol car, Oswald pulled a pistol and shot him. Fowler's partner later died in the emergency room.

For months thereafter Fowler wrestled with the tragedy of Tippit's death, long after he had attended his funeral and the Dallas citizens' hostility toward the police had subsided. Could his partner's death have been averted if Fowler had been riding with him that November afternoon? Or would his own life have been cut short as well?

Questions about the assassination and its aftermath would continue to haunt him.

There was the night several months later, for instance, when Fowler routinely stopped a battered Volkswagen being driven with a headlight out. As he approached the car, Fowler saw that it was packed with personal belongings, as if the driver was in the process of moving.

At the officer's request, the obviously nervous driver handed over a license unlike any Fowler had ever seen. While it had been issued in Texas, the address it bore was Monterrey, Mexico.

When Fowler asked the driver to step from the car, he adamantly refused. Suspicious of the man's actions, Fowler and his new partner then demanded that he get out, and they proceeded to search the Volkswagen. In a piece of luggage in the trunk they found a number of travel visas, records of foreign bank transactions, and several letters in unsealed envelopes. One was addressed to Jack Rubenstein in care of the Dallas County Jail. Since few people knew that

Ruby, the man who was jailed for the murder of Oswald, had abbreviated his name from Rubenstein, Fowler wondered if he might have stumbled onto vital evidence related to the Kennedy assassination. His excitement soared when he opened the letter. In it the writer apologized profusely for the fact that Ruby was in jail, stating "we know you are there to protect the rest of us." It went on to thank him for killing Oswald "to keep him from talking."

In a time when conspiracy theories were flourishing, Fowler wondered if the "we" to whom the writer referred might include people who in some way had helped to orchestrate the murder of Oswald, possibly even that of the President.

The driver of the Volkswagen was quickly escorted to the police station, where he was turned over to investigators working the assassination. In his report, Fowler detailed the man's strange behavior and the contents of the correspondence addressed to Ruby.

For several days he waited anxiously to learn if the man had shed any light on the assassination. The days eventually turned into weeks. Finally, curiosity won out, and Fowler approached one of the investigators on the case.

"Aw, the guy was just some kook" was all he was ever told.

Like so many others who endured the lingering nightmare of Dallas's most infamous crime, Billy Fowler eventually vowed to put the Kennedy assassination from his mind and go on with his job. He had seen too many of his fellow officers, even those like himself who had never been directly involved, become obsessed with the event. Years later, even after he and Vaughn had become close friends, they rarely spoke of the scars left by that long-ago November day.

Only after two decades as a Dallas policeman did the job begin to wear on him. A climate of political infighting had developed, and there was a slow but noticeable erosion of the departmental unity he had so long been comfortable with. A man who had received numerous commendations and was the 1966 runner-up for Police Officer of the Year honors, Fowler agonized over the distractions. Too, the demands of the job had created mounting problems in his home life. The long hours, danger, and myriad other private miseries finally culminated in divorce. Having put in enough time to qualify for his retirement pension, Fowler began looking for something else.

For two years he worked as an investigator for the Dallas County District Attorney's Office and, in 1984, found himself involved in one of the most highly publicized and severely criticized investigations in the city's criminal history.

Lenell Geter, a young black engineer who worked for E-Systems in nearby Greenville, had been arrested for and convicted of the 1982 armed robbery of a Kentucky Fried Chicken restaurant in suburban Balch Springs. Suspected in a series of similar crimes, Geter received a life sentence and had been in prison for sixteen months when a "60 Minutes" segment raised serious questions about his guilt. The national media soon took up the cause, criticizing Dallas for its quick-draw justice and pointing out numerous problems with the case. In the minds of many, Geter, a young man with no previous criminal record, was innocent.

Finally, District Attorney Henry Wade, angered that his department's integrity had come under fire just months before his retirement, determined to end the criticism by ordering a new trial, even though he had publicly stated that he was confident Geter was guilty. Wade assigned a felony prosecutor, Norm Kinne, to the case. Kinne, in turn, requested Fowler's assistance in the reinvestigation. Since neither had been involved in the initial prosecution of Geter, they both approached the case as if it were new, interviewing witnesses and reviewing evidence.

What they found, they soon realized, would not please the district attorney. The volatile, pipe-smoking Kinne, a man with a reputation for aggressive prosecution, spoke with several E-Systems employees who had never been interviewed by defense attorneys. They convinced him that Geter had, in fact, been on the job at the time of the robbery. What the assistant D.A. found himself doing, in fact, was building a strong case for the defense.

Fowler, meanwhile, was gathering even more damaging

evidence. During the course of a frantic six-day investigation he was successful in obtaining evidence that a man named Curtis Mason, jailed in Houston for a series of Kentucky Fried Chicken robberies there, had, in fact, committed the crime for which Geter had been prosecuted. Ultimately, charges against Geter were dropped and he was released.

It was not the first time Fowler had proved that an innocent man had been wrongfully convicted or stepped in to solve cases abandoned by other officers.

Though Fowler is publicity-shy, word of his dogged investigative skills spread throughout the Dallas law community. Several defense attorneys, constantly in search of good investigators, began urging him to go into private practice.

In 1985 he decided to do so and in short order was earning a near six-figure income. He found the work exciting and challenging, but the nonstop pace was more demanding than he had bargained for. The travel, the all-night surveillances, and the constant battle with clients for payment took their toll. And there was a disconcerting matter he had not anticipated. As a rule, police officers hold private investigators in disdain and will go to extremes to avoid helping them with cases. Fowler suddenly found himself being treated as an adversary by men he had worked with for years. He realized quickly that private investigators, even those with lengthy law enforcement backgrounds, were not considered trustworthy. His new image ate at him.

By now Fowler had remarried, and he decided it was time to slow down, to spend more time with his new wife, Jeanie, and to tend to the new home they had recently purchased in a Midlothian subdivision.

When he heard that Ellis County District Attorney Mary Lou Shipley was looking for an investigator, he made the short drive to her office in the Waxahachie courthouse and applied.

Shipley made only one call before offering him the job. She contacted Norm Kinne in Dallas. "Billy Fowler," he told her, "is the best investigator the Dallas County D.A.'s office has ever had. If you don't hire him right away, I'm going to call him and do my damnedest to talk him into coming back to work here."

Fowler had been with Shipley less than six months when Roy Vaughn contacted him about returning to police work. Already bored with preparing hot-check warrants and doing paperwork on the trickle of petty crimes that crossed his desk, he was ready to get back to what he did best.

While discussing the possibility of his joining the Midlothian police force, Vaughn had told Fowler what he already knew. "I know you can make a helluva lot of money as a private investigator," he said. "Or you can stay with the D.A.'s office and work your own hours until you get ready to retire. But, dammit, Billy, you're a police officer. A good one. And we don't have enough of those."

The decision was easy. Fowler returned to police work with renewed energy. Soon he was again working sixty-hour weeks that seemed to fly by.

Such were the stories George Raffield had heard about the man who would direct him through his first assignment as an undercover police officer. Fowler never tired of Raffield's endless questions. George looked forward to those summer evenings sitting at the dining room table in the lieutenant's home, listening as Fowler repeatedly explained the procedures of making buys and tagging evidence and filling out reports. He watched intently as Fowler demonstrated the technique of "pinching off" a marijuana cigarette, showing him how to give the appearance of smoking the joint without actually inhaling. Fowler explained code phrases George could use when calling to check in. Just act as if you're talking to your aunt or uncle, the lieutenant told him, explaining why you're going to be late for dinner.

One evening, long after Raffield had left, Jeanie Fowler sat on the back porch with her husband, enjoying the relaxing night sounds and a rare cool breeze that floated across a small nearby lake. "You really like George, don't you?"

Billy nodded. "He's the kind of kid you would be proud to call your son."

8

At a time when each school year signaled the arrival of an increasing number of new families to Midlothian, the attitude of locals was generally welcoming to any new student with a willingness to fit in and make friends. Teachers eagerly assessed newcomers in the hope of finding another pupil with a genuine interest in academics; coaches looked to the new arrivals as potential added manpower for their teams; girls, quickly alerted to the new faces, evaluated their potential as boyfriends while the boys were doing the same.

For George Moore, easygoing but far from shy, the transition back to high school was easier than he had expected. For the first several days he said little as he went from class to class, reacquainting himself with the academic routine. He was polite to teachers and friendly to students who initiated conversation. In the first few days he established himself as an average student, neither a scholar nor a lazy nonparticipant. He grumbled along with the others about homework assignments but turned the required work in on time, helped a fellow student with answers to an English test when the teacher wasn't looking, and made certain that the fact he had already taken typing did not show when speed tests were given.

In short order he was welcomed among the other students during morning breaks and in the lunchroom. When asked where he was from, George told his well-rehearsed story of family problems back home in Temple that had resulted in his coming to live with his aunt and uncle. To avoid romantic entanglements with several female students who had already begun casual flirtations, he talked about the steady girlfriend he had back home and how he planned to return to Temple most weekends to visit her.

Though he had been warned, both by the Dallas instructors and by Fowler, that some of the more cautious students would be initially wary, suspicious that he was an undercover officer, George saw no evidence of such concern.

By the end of the first two weeks of classes, in fact, it was no longer necessary for him to continue repeating his cover story. Information had spread quickly about the background of the new kid with the shiny red pickup. As the routine of daily classes settled in, George Moore felt he was quickly becoming just another face in the Midlothian High School crowd.

Soon he was being invited to join a group of teenagers who went to the park after school for touch football. He began hanging out with others in the evenings in a downtown parking lot, passing time listening to music and honking at passersby before eventually winding up at the Pizza Inn, feeding quarters into the video games.

Following Lieutenant Fowler's instructions, he was taking it slow. Still, George watched and listened, mentally sorting out those he suspected to be drug users. It wasn't difficult. He was surprised, in fact, at the way they openly flaunted their habits. On several occasions he had seen students arrive at school high or hung over, only to be ignored by teachers.

Subtly, George began dropping hints that he, too, was in the market. He liked to smoke a little pot himself, he mentioned, and if he could get a good deal from local connections he could resell the drugs in Temple and finance his weekend visits to his girlfriend.

It didn't take long for word to spread. Neither did it hurt that he had transportation, the biggest problem faced by many of the school's younger students who were geographically isolated from their connections.

For all the drug activity in Midlothian, the city seemed to have no major local supplier. Most of what they bought came from the run-down apartment complexes in south Dallas, a predominately black area where spiraling crime statistics had frightened many of the residents into moving, leaving dope to fuel the economy.

On a Thursday afternoon, September 10, George got the opportunity to make his first buy.

As he was walking toward his pickup after school, a sophomore named Andy Lyle asked George for a ride home. George agreed, and they were about to get into his pickup when Andy asked if he had seen a fellow student named Dale Janson come into the parking lot.

"You mean the guy who drives the red Firebird?" George replied.

"Yeah, I need to see him before we leave. He's making a trip to Dallas to pick up some weed, and I've got to give him some money."

Fearful of appearing too anxious, George pointed out Janson's car on the other side of the parking lot. Dale, books in hand, was walking toward it.

"I'll be right back," Andy said.

George waited in his truck, watching as the two boys spoke briefly. When Andy Lyle had talked to him so casually about buying marijuana, his heart had begun to race. He had, he was confident, found an entrée into the group he wanted to infiltrate. It wasn't exactly "Miami Vice," he knew, but it was a start.

"He going to take care of you?" George asked when Andy returned.

"Yeah, but he can't go until tomorrow. He said to bring the money to him at school tomorrow."

"Is the stuff he buys pretty good?"

Andy grinned and nodded.

George did not pursue the conversation, changing the subject to the last-period typing class they shared and the next night's football game during the remainder of the short drive to the apartment where Andy lived.

The next day, during the morning break, Andy approached George. Smiling, he said he had given Dale fifteen dollars. "He said he'd have the stuff at his house about six."

"Look," George said, lowering his voice. "Do me a favor and ask him if he can pick up some pot for me. I'm going to Temple after the game tonight, and I need a couple of bags for a friend of mine there."

"I'll check it out," Andy said. "How much you need?"

George shrugged. "If he could get me a couple of quarter bags it would be great."

"You're talking fifty bucks," Andy said. George pulled his billfold from his pocket and gave the surprised youngster the money.

"I'll see him in the lunchroom during the pep rally," Andy said. "I'll ask him then."

As it had been when he was a student at Mesquite High School, those students not interested in attending pep rallies and awards programs were required to go to the lunchroom where they would remain while the rest of the student body was in the gymnasium. Though never good at athletics himself, George had enjoyed the excitement of the Friday football games. He had always felt that the pep rallies, with handmade banners, the band blaring, and the cheerleaders leading yells, were a big part of the buildup. It would have been fun, he thought, to see a pep rally again. But since the group he was hoping to join showed no interest, he, too, chose to report to the cafeteria.

He had been there only a few minutes when Andy found him and said that the deal was made. He would be able to pick up his marijuana later that afternoon.

For the remainder of the pep rally, George sat at one of the tables, watching as Dale Janson took orders for his after-school drug run. He couldn't wait for the opportunity to place a call to Lieutenant Fowler and tell him that he would soon make his first buy.

The excitement in Raffield's voice amused Fowler. Calling from a service station pay phone, George said he had just driven Andy home and would return later that evening to pick up the drugs. Then, he said, they were going to the game.

"This kid, Dale, has a real deal going," George said. "He was just sitting there in the damn cafeteria, cool as a cucumber, with a pencil and a notebook, writing down orders and taking money. It was like he was taking orders for the yearbook or something. I couldn't believe it. Hell, the assistant principal was standing no more than ten feet away. He even looked over at the kid a couple of times."

Fowler explained that his wife would be working in the concession stand at the game. "I'll be hanging around there somewhere," he said. "If the deal goes down, give me a signal when you see me. Run your fingers through your hair to let me know you made the buy. Then meet me in the men's room."

Fowler hung up and walked through the lobby to Chief Vaughn's office. "Our boy's about to make his first case," he said.

When George returned to the Lyle apartment shortly before eight, Andy and his father were standing in the small yard in front of their apartment. Once in the truck, Andy smiled and pulled a plastic bag of marijuana from the front of his pants.

"Great," George said. "Just put it in the glove compartment."

At the game, George and Andy mingled with a group of teenagers leaning against the fence that surrounded the playing field. Occasionally they shouted encouragement as the Panthers fought a losing battle against the larger, more polished team from nearby Cleburne.

The game was in the second quarter when Raffield

spotted Fowler standing near the concession stand and gave the signal before walking in the direction of the rest room.

As the two stood side by side at the urinals, the lieutenant did not look in George's direction when he whispered instructions: "Leave at the half and meet me at the house," he said, then zipped up his pants and walked away.

Even before the band marched onto the field for its halftime performance, the fate of the Panthers was obvious. Telling Andy he would need to catch another ride home, George said, "To hell with this. I'm going to Temple."

"See you Monday," Andy said.

"Yeah," George said. "And, hey, thanks for your help."

Thirty minutes later, Raffield had pulled his pickup into Fowler's garage and was sitting at the dining room table turning over the evidence and filling out his first case report.

Andy Lyle would, according to the report Raffield wrote, be charged with violation of Section 4.05 of the Texas Penal Code: unlawful delivery of a controlled substance—to wit, marijuana.

Later that night George called his fiancée to tell her of his first transaction. "The important thing about it all," he told her, "is that the word will get around really fast now that I'm in the market for the stuff. Believe me, there aren't any secrets in that little town."

Martha heard an excitement in George's voice that had never been there before. "Just promise me you'll be careful," she said.

"Hell, these are just kids," he replied.

George's prediction proved to be on target. In the next few weeks he drove two students to nearby Burleson, near Fort Worth, to purchase crank and found himself making regular trips to the Dallas apartment complex that apparently served as the supply house for most of the marijuana the kids were buying.

The dopers, aware that George was willing to provide transportation to and from the dealers, eagerly welcomed him into their group.

Among the new friends he made was a slight fifteen-year-old named Greg Knighten whom everyone called Sparky.

With his smooth olive complexion, his liquid brown eyes, and the thick black hair that covered his ears and hung down to the neckline of the T-shirts he wore, Knighten was considered "cute" by most female students in the school.

But there was about him an attitude that went beyond mischievous behavior carried out to gain the attention of his fellow students. His hostile behavior in class, designed to draw the ire of teachers, was rarely viewed as entertaining by classmates. With the new school year just days old, Knighten had already become a frequent visitor to Principal Roesler's office. "There's a difference between being the class clown and just acting like a punk," one student observed. "Greg is a punk."

In the two years he had been in the Midlothian school system, frustrated teachers had come to view him as his own worst enemy. He made no secret of his hatred for school and for those who wished to impose its rules and regulations on him. Greg was looked upon as one of the hopeless cases, a youngster whom teachers and administrators were forced to tolerate, a constant irritating distraction to their efforts to teach others.

Such had been his history since he first entered school at the private Christian academy in nearby Duncanville where his mother served as a physical education instructor. Hyperactive even as an elementary student, he was unruly and easily angered without apparent provocation, causing Nelda Knighten's colleagues to wonder privately why she was unable to exercise the same control over her own son that she did her other students.

One mother, arriving at the Christian school to take her son home early one afternoon, had sat in the parking lot watching as Nelda's class went through their routine of games and calisthenics on the playground. Only one student ignored her instructions, remaining off to the side, refusing to participate. He shouted back at Nelda when she ordered him to join the group. And when he did join, it was only to try to pick a fight with the other boys. The mother, looking closer, was surprised when she realized that the child was Greg. That night, as she told her husband what she had seen, she expressed concern about the school their child was attending. "There's something wrong," she said, "when a teacher has no control over her own child."

Tom and Nelda Knighten had wrestled with the problem for some time. They had adopted Greg when he was only a few weeks old. As an infant he had been bright-eyed, cheerful, and immediately responsive to his proud new parents.

But as he grew older, he withdrew. A constant stream of neighbors reported to the Knightens that Greg was provoking fights with their children or mistreating their pets or using abusive language. In time Nelda realized that several of her friends had instructed their children to stay away from her son.

It was such problems that prompted the Knightens' decision to move from one Duncanville neighborhood to another, leaving behind a house they had purchased only a year before. Friends who lived down the street were quick to welcome them to the neighborhood but admitted surprise that they had left the home they had obviously been so proud of. It was Tom Knighten, standing in the driveway at his new house, who explained the decision: "The kids in our old neighborhood wouldn't play with Greg," he said.

Less than a month had passed before the couple to whom he had made the observation told their own son that they would rather he didn't invite Greg to their home.

Nothing the Knightens tried seemed to work. Despite their strong religious convictions, their son showed no interest in church activities. There, his rebelliousness was even more dramatic than it had been in school. When they tried to talk with him about his problems he would reveal little except to insist that he wanted to attend a "normal school" like other kids. Nelda Knighten, disappointed that he had not adapted to the Christian academy, a place where she felt he would receive far more personal and academic attention from teachers, talked the matter over with her husband. They finally agreed to enroll him in the Duncanville public school system when he entered junior high.

The decision quickly turned into a nightmare. Greg's grades dropped even lower, his behavior became more erratic, and eventually school officials informed the Knightens that because of his constant troublemaking their son was being placed in an alternative school, isolated from the other students in an off-campus building where he and a handful of other problem youngsters would be monitored throughout the day by one teacher.

One afternoon a schoolmate returned home to tell his mother of an event few parents would have thought possible in the liberal Duncanville school system. "You're not going to believe this," the boy told his mother, "but Greg Knighten managed to get himself expelled from the alternative school."

It was probably then that Tom Knighten became concerned that the community's growing drug problem might well be one of the reasons for his son's disturbing behavior. He did not feel good about the few youngsters with whom Greg was associating. There was also the Knightens' younger son to worry about. Born a couple of years after Greg's adoption, he, too, would soon be facing the problems of what his parents viewed as a deteriorating society.

It was time, Tom told his wife, to get out of Duncanville, to escape to a smaller town more like the one in which he had grown up.

The Knightens then began searching for a more rural setting where life for young and old moved at a slower, more manageable pace. They wanted a place that had not been invaded by the insanity of adolescent drug pushers and crack fortresses, a place where kids were not shoved into adulthood before their time.

Eventually they decided on Midlothian, just fifteen miles away. All too soon they would find that the name of the development where they had purchased yet another home —Camelot Estates—was a misnomer. Though the setting was far more pastoral than the bedroom community from which they had moved, it would not be the idyllic hideaway they were searching for.

For a brief period, however, the Knightens felt they had solved their problems. They settled comfortably into the community, where the lives of Tom and Nelda revolved around the church, their jobs, and their children. They bought the boys go-carts and an off-road three-wheel motorcycle. The entire family joined the First Baptist Church and began to participate in its activities.

Tom taught Greg the mechanical skills he had learned from his own father as a boy. And, with future hunting trips in mind, he began to take his older son to the police firing range regularly, sharing the knowledge that had earned him a reputation as one of the finest marksmen in the Dallas Police Department. That Greg seemed to have a natural talent for target shooting pleased his father greatly.

In time, however, it was obvious to the frustrated Knightens that the new environment was not going to alter their son's destructive course. There was the late night joyride that ended in the accident Officer Ross had investigated, and there were frequent visits from teenagers who were hardly what Tom and Nelda would judge acceptable friends for their son. And there was the constant suspicion that Greg was becoming more deeply involved in drugs.

Tom Knighten began searching Greg's bedroom for drug paraphernalia. On at least one occasion he insisted on searching one of his son's visitors before allowing him in the house. Word of the incident spread quickly, and those few who had occasionally visited Greg in his home no longer came around.

The paranoia in the Knighten household grew to a point where the father demanded on several occasions that his son submit to urinalysis. And, according to one of Greg's friends, aware that, among marijuana users, eyedrops were a favorite remedy for bloodshot eyes, the Knightens would secretly empty the medication from the plastic bottle Greg kept in his room and replace the solution with tap water.

Teachers welcomed the first few visits from Tom Knighten, eager to make him aware of the problems his son was having in school. They were disappointed when it became clear that the primary purpose of his visits was to complain about the boys Greg was hanging around with and to request that their activities be monitored more closely.

When Greg returned home after having dyed a red streak in his hair, his father scheduled a visit with a Dallas police psychologist.

At home, Greg Knighten had begun to feel more like a closely watched prisoner than a member of the family. At school, things were not much better. Teachers, frustrated with unsuccessful efforts to modify his behavior and interest him in his studies, collectively decided that the best way to deal with his disruptions was simply not to respond. In those instances when Greg's misbehavior went beyond clowning and sarcastic remarks, teachers were instructed to send him to the principal's office or to see Perry Elkins, the school counselor.

Though neither administrators nor teachers said so publicly, the general belief was that Knighten would soon be one of the lost souls who dropped out of school and disappeared into the anonymity of some minimum-wage job. Unlike the growing number of students who had traveled a similar path in recent years, Knighten seemed somehow sadder to some of his teachers. He was, most felt, a young man with a sharp mind, a supportive family, and a personality that, at times, could be endearing. But there was something wrong, some inner problem behind the loud talk, boisterous behavior, and challenging attitude toward authority.

Though his actions were those of one constantly in desperate search of acceptance by his peers, he had difficulty maintaining friendships. The dopers would not go near his house, fearful of a confrontation with his father. Greg constantly begged rides and invited himself into discussions and activities where he was clearly not wanted. One classmate accused young Knighten of stealing his camera; another got into a fight with him over several tapes that had been stolen from his car. And among the group he most hoped to impress, even bragging of regularly stealing money from his parents, he committed the cardinal sin: more than once, Greg shortchanged people on drug deals.

Knighten could count as close friends only Jamie Cadenhead, the petite, doe-eyed sophomore with whom he was going steady, and Jonathan Jobe, a sixteen-year-old neighbor whom he had met just days after moving into the Camelot Estates.

He was, then, pleased when the new senior named George Moore began paying him some attention, waving as they passed on the school grounds or nodding a friendly hello in the halls. Word had filtered through the teenage drug community that Moore made frequent trips into Dallas to buy dope and was more than willing to take other customers along.

Greg had found a new means of transportation.

It was on a Wednesday in the third week of September that Knighten, accompanied by Jonathan, encountered George in the parking lot after school and told him of plans to drive to Dallas and "score some dope."

Picking up on the cue, George asked if he could accompany them, then suggested they go in his truck. "Can you get me a couple of quarter bags?" he asked.

When they arrived at the apartment complex on the corner of Morning Dew Trail and Bow and Arrow Drive, Greg told George to park in the corner of the parking lot; then he got out and disappeared into one of the apartments. When he returned, he told Raffield that his connection had had only one dime bag and returned the money he had given him. "He said to come back tomorrow," Greg said.

On the way home, Greg rolled a joint and shared it with Jobe. George, because he was on Highway 67 at rush hour, declined the offer of a hit. As he drove, Greg and Jonathan took turns bending down to take drags from the joint. Their conversation, punctuated with childish giggles, fascinated George.

Though he had made no buy and therefore no case, he was eager to get to a telephone and talk with Lieutenant Fowler. It was shortly after six when, having returned Jobe and

Knighten to the school parking lot and Jonathan's truck, he called Fowler.

"On the way back to town," he told the lieutenant, "Sparky suggested that we go by the apartment of some guy named Paul Jarbo and get high with him. We went to his place but he wasn't home."

The name rang no bell with Fowler. "Who's Paul Jarbo?" he asked.

"The sonuvabitch is a teacher," Raffield said. "A school teacher who, according to Sparky, gets high with the kids all the time."

"Jesus," Fowler replied. It was a development he had not anticipated. He was silent for a moment, thinking. "Don't press it," he said, "but see if you can talk them into going over there again. See what you can find out about this guy." The last thing the town needed, he thought to himself, was some asshole teacher doing dope with the kids.

The following Monday, after another trip into Dallas for dope, Greg, Jonathan, and George again drove by the teacher's residence. But since they didn't see his car, they decided not to stop. Yet, if what George had been told was true, it wouldn't be long before the kids made contact with him.

By the end of September, George had decided to make a move. Comfortable in his new job and optimistic about his future with the Midlothian Police Department, he told his parents that it was time for him to move into his own place. He had, he said, already made a deposit on a furnished apartment and would be moving in on October 1.

It was just off Highway 67, near the Red Bird Mall—a safe distance from his work but close enough to cut his commute substantially.

The news came as a great disappointment to Shirley Moore. Though she had often heard her son talk of his plans to get his own place once he settled into a permanent job, she had never really prepared herself for it. She and Don had both enjoyed having the last of their children at home and privately dreaded the day when they would be the only ones in the house.

Seeing Tiger regularly, even for the brief time in the evening after he had arrived home or while she shared a cup of coffee with him as he prepared to leave in the morning, had been reassuring. Though she no longer mentioned it, she still worried about the dangers of his new job. He had told her of the drug buys he had been making, but did his best to assure her that what he was doing in no way resembled the drug-fighting activities of Dallas police officers, seen almost nightly on the ten o'clock news, armed to the teeth and breaking down the doors of Jamaican-run crack houses and amphetamine labs, but she worried nonetheless. She had been able to sleep peacefully, however, knowing that her son had arrived home safely and was under the same roof. Now, with him living away, she would be robbed of that comfort.

"I want you to come over and look at the place," he said. Then he hesitated for a moment and added another bit of news he had been keeping secret for several days. "Martha's going to move in with me," he said almost shyly. "We've decided to get married."

For a moment his mother was speechless. She had known for some time that her son was serious about the pretty brunette he had met in high school. They had begun dating when they worked together at Minyard's Food Store. But Shirley Moore had seen no indication that her son was ready to take such a serious step. "Right away?" she finally asked.

"No, she wants the wedding in April," he said. "We talked to her boss, and it's been arranged for her to transfer to the Minyard's in Cedar Hill. She starts there the same day we move into the apartment."

Shirley Moore hugged her son. "Are you happy?" she asked.

"Things are great, Mom," he replied.

"Then I'm happy for you," she said, nodding her approval and kissing him on the cheek.

Sparky Knighten was soon referring to George Moore as his best friend, basking in the glow of the attention shown him by the senior. He sought George out during breaks and lunch periods at school, introduced him to his girlfriend, and could often be seen riding past the Dairy Queen or the Pizza Inn in his new companion's pickup.

And it was common knowledge that they were making frequent trips to Dallas to purchase pot. Making cases against Knighten, in fact, was even easier than George had anticipated.

On a Thursday afternoon in early October George and Greg left school for Dallas. As they passed the downtown washateria, they were flagged down by Kyle Royal and Eddie Friels. Kyle asked if they were going to Dallas to score and gave Greg ten dollars for a dime bag.

As they continued up Ninth Street toward the highway, George handed Greg forty dollars, explaining that he would need four bags for his weekend trip to Temple.

When they arrived at the Dallas apartments, the same Jamaican whom they had dealt with on previous trips approached the truck. When Greg told him he needed seven dime bags, the Jamaican said he had only four with him, got into the truck, and directed George to drive to the opposite end of the complex.

There he went inside and soon returned with two additional bags. Still one bag shy, they went to the end of the parking lot where another young black provided the seventh bag of marijuana. Greg then counted out the seventy dollars as the dealer stood silently, watching as each ten-dollar bill was placed in his outstretched palm.

As George drove away, the pleased youngster seated next to him carefully examined each of the plastic baggies for several minutes. Finally determining which seemed the smallest, Greg laughed and said it would be the one he gave to Kyle. He then handed George his four bags and began rolling a joint.

Back in Midlothian, they had difficulty finding Kyle, first going past the car wash, then by the restaurant where his girlfriend worked. At the restaurant they encountered Kyle's girlfriend, and she agreed to help them find Kyle. As they drove around town, Greg rolled another joint, took a deep drag from it, and passed it to the girl. The sweet smell of smoke filled the cab of the pickup as she, too, took a drag before passing the joint to George. As Fowler had taught him, he pretended to take a long hit.

Finally they located Kyle and Eddie at the Pizza Inn, playing video games, and Greg gave Royal the bag of marijuana he had purchased for him.

Later that evening, after George had taken the evidence to Fowler's home and filled out the now familiar case report forms, the lieutenant told him that the two cases he had made against Knighten were enough; he need not bother making any additional purchases from Greg unless it was necessary to protect his cover.

At the same time, Fowler and George agreed that mainte-nance of the friendship would be beneficial. It had become obvious that Greg was connected with virtually every student who was even remotely involved in drugs and therefore could help Raffield gain their confidence.

And, too, there was still the troubling matter of the drug-using teacher. Though George and Greg had stopped at his place on several occasions, they had yet to catch him at home.

Thus the friendship continued.

To some it seemed an unlikely pairing, the quiet-spoken senior and the widely disliked sophomore. Most, however, paid the two little mind. Those who did viewed Greg's relationship with George as something of a godsend. They were relieved that Knighten, his attention now focused on the new kid, had quit pestering them for rides or inviting himself along with them.

George, apparently looking for friends himself, seemed ready to take Knighten wherever he wanted to go, whether it was just an afternoon cruise around the teenage hangouts, over to the Cedar Hill Dairy Queen to visit his steady girlfriend, Jamie Cadenhead, on her evening break, or into the unsavory sections of Dallas to purchase drugs.

Among those who benefited from George's willingness to provide Greg with transportation was Jonathan Jobe.

Throughout the summer Jonathan had been Greg's con-stant companion. A stoutly built sixteen-year-old, he was one of the first people Greg met when the Knightens moved into their new home. Greg helped Jonathan keep his pickup tuned and running smoothly and installed a tape deck for him. In turn, Jobe gave Greg rides into town and out to Jamie's.

They, too, had seemed a strange pair. Jobe, a slow-talking youngster who wore his bushy blond hair shorter than most of the kids, was fascinated by the military and talked of attending one of the service academies.

While Greg wore faded jeans, rock T-shirts, and a dangling cross earring, Jobe rarely left home in anything less conventional than starched jeans and a freshly laundered cotton shirt. Though he had no interest in athletics, coaches at the school often remarked that he looked more like a football player than many they had on the team.

First thrown together as neighbors, Greg and Jonathan had developed an interdependent relationship. For Greg, Jobe represented a means of escape from home. For Jonathan, Greg, with his outrageous behavior and strange mannerisms, was a source of fascination. Too, Greg always had drugs, something Jonathan had begun experimenting with more frequently since they had met.

Shortly before the opening of the school year, however, the relationship cooled dramatically. At first Greg was puzzled. Jonathan was seldom home when he walked over to see him. And when he was, he was talking on the phone to a new girl he had met.

In time, Greg learned that Jonathan had begun dating a young girl named Becky Goeglein, who had just moved to town from somewhere in Arizona. And when he wasn't with Becky, he was running around with her brother, Richard.

Not only had Jonathan found a girlfriend; he had a new best friend whom even Greg found strange. Knighten did not meet Richard Goeglein until one evening in October when he and Jamie went to Dallas to attend the annual State Fair of Texas. Walking among the rides and games of chance along the midway, they encountered Jonathan and Becky. With them was a frail-looking kid with stringy hair, wearing a black sleeveless T-shirt with the word *Slayer* printed across the chest.

"Sparky," Jobe had said, "this is Richard Goeglein."

Knighten had seen Richard in the halls at school and had heard the strange stories of his fascination with Satanism and the occult.

Other students had talked of satanic activities Goeglein had boasted of participating in while living in Arizona. Several told of Richard's trying to get people to accompany him to the graveyard, his asking if anyone knew where he might steal a goat to use in some kind of ritualistic sacrifice, and the strange books on spells and witchcraft he was always reading.

And, word was, Richard and Jonathan had become blood brothers, each cutting his finger and then mixing their blood.

There was, however, a lot that Richard Goeglein had not told his new friends in Midlothian.

9

The longtime residents of Williams, Arizona, just a thirty-minute drive south of the Grand Canyon, can remember when it was a thriving community. Because it was a favored stopover spot for vacationing families, a dozen motels stayed filled and nightclubs, restaurants, and gift shops did a bustling business.

That, however, was when the legendary Route 66 ran through the heart of town, before the Arizona State Highway Department chose to speed travelers' progress and designed Interstate 40 to bypass Williams. Businesses began closing and people moved away to Flagstaff, the Coconino County seat, or to Phoenix in search of new ways to make a living. In just two years, the population dwindled from almost 10,000 to just over 3,000. Enrollment at the school dropped from 450 students to 150.

Such was the state of affairs when Carolyn Loftis and her husband moved to town in the fall of 1986 to serve as principal and shop teacher at Williams High School. What they encountered was an age-old problem shared by small, isolated communities. For the youngsters of the town there was little in the way of social activities—not even a movie theater or a bowling alley. For those without transportation or financial resources for Saturday night trips east to Flagstaff, cruising the main drag or hanging out at the truck stop on the edge of town was the chief form of entertainment.

The restlessness of the teenagers troubled Carolyn. Teachers and parents she spoke with alerted her to widespread drug use among the high school students and warned that she would be shocked at the number of junior high and high school girls who became pregnant. It was not at all uncommon, she was told, for girls as young as thirteen and fourteen to leave town with a passing truck driver and be gone for several weeks.

And there were whispered stories of occult rituals in which small animals were stolen and sacrificed. The recent disappearance of a number of family pets in town had newly fueled the rumors.

The community, she was told, was a dead end for any kid whose life didn't revolve around academics, the church, or sports.

In Williams, the youngsters' complaint that there was nothing to do was more than an idle whine.

To combat the problem and get the kids off the streets on weekends, Carolyn turned the high school gymnasium into a Saturday night social center, offering supervised dancing, movies, video games, and refreshments provided by civic-minded parents. The turnout was disappointing.

Among those who showed no interest in the new principal's efforts was a skinny sophomore named Richard Goeglein. A constant truant and one of the poorest students in the high school, he became one of her immediate concerns.

For reasons she could not put her finger on at first, the youngster frightened her. He often arrived at school wearing sleeveless black T-shirts bearing rock band logos, a denim jacket with a pentagram sketched on the back, and leather-studded wrist bands. There was, she would later confide to her husband, a coldness in Richard's eyes that she found unnerving.

Carolyn had long ago learned to deal with rebellious

children and had an impressive track record of turning them into productive students. Richard Goeglein, however, was unlike any problem pupil she had ever faced. She heard rumors that he was deeply into drugs, but the only evidence she saw was in his behavior: he often came to school exhausted and slept through most of his classes; when he did turn in assignments, which was rare, the margins of his papers were generally cluttered with doodles of pentagrams, inverted crosses, and the logo of his favorite heavy metal rock group, Slayer.

But it was not Richard's lack of interest in school or his apparent fascination with the occult that most troubled the principal. What worried Mrs. Loftis most was the unexplained allegiance a small group of her students had to this strange young man. She saw in him none of the qualities of leadership, yet all Richard had to do was suggest skipping school to any of a half-dozen other high school boys and they would be gone. Too, he would stop by the junior high and elementary campuses during a recess break and lure several of the younger students away. Without exception, the youngsters over whom Richard exercised his strange power were those with low self-esteem. Most had been loners until Richard welcomed them into his group.

Regularly, the principal would get into her car after morning roll call and drive around town until she found Richard and his wandering band of followers. When she demanded that they get in and accompany her back to school, Richard was always the first into the car, urging the others to follow. The principal sensed that he knew just how far he could go before getting into real trouble.

The principal judged his fascination with the macabre unhealthy and potentially dangerous. One afternoon an English teacher approached her after school and showed Carolyn a poem Richard had written in response to a classroom assignment. "Read this," the teacher said, clearly shaken. He had underlined a stanza in which Richard graphically described the rape and murder of the teacher's wife.

Finally Mrs. Loftis spoke to the superintendent about her

concerns. "He's never done anything serious," she explained, "but he scares me. I have no real basis for my feelings, but this kid is really bad news. I'm afraid he's going to wind up killing someone or killing himself and taking someone with him." When she questioned Richard about his satanic interests he only answered with a cold stare. "He never admitted it," she said, "but he never denied it, either."

She was also worried about an incident in which a Molotov cocktail was tossed into the car of a high school teacher. The explosion occurred when the car was parked in the teacher's driveway, just a few feet from the room occupied by the woman's month-old baby. The boys who ultimately confessed to the bombing were among Goeglein's followers. And while none of them implicated Richard in the incident, Mrs. Loftis could not help but wonder if he had planted the idea in their heads.

"There are boys in this school," she insisted, "who would walk off a cliff if he told them to."

The superintendent's only suggestion was that she discuss the matter with Richard's parents. She had already tried that, setting up several school meetings that neither Frances nor Richard Goeglein, Sr., had shown up for. Mrs. Loftis went to Buckle's Restaurant, where Richard's mother waited on tables, to tell her that her son had asked the school librarian to order books about the occult and Satanism from the local community college. Mrs. Goeglein quickly dismissed the principal as meddlesome. The other parents Mrs. Loftis spoke to had asked that their children not be allowed to check out such books, but Mrs. Goeglein issued a belligerent speech about freedom of religion and said that she had no concerns about her son's choice of reading material.

Convinced that she would get no help from the Goeglein parents and determined to protect the rest of her students from Richard's influence, Carolyn quietly began doing a background check on the young man who had been in the Williams school system since the first grade.

It was an almost forgotten file kept by the principal of the elementary school that provided her with the first tangible evidence that her concerns were justified. When he was in the third grade, Richard, she learned, had been recommended for special classes for the learning disabled and emotionally disturbed. His parents, however, had refused to have their son removed from the school's mainstream classes.

Mrs. Loftis spent much of one afternoon in the elementary school office, reading and rereading that file.

What she had found was frightening.

There was a copy of a letter sent to Richard's parents, suggesting their child needed special academic attention and recommending psychological counseling. With it were several pictures Richard had drawn as a third grader. The childish drawings, done in crayon on notebook paper, looked like something from the pages of a horror comic. In one, Richard had drawn himself standing over his younger sister, Becky, a knife in his hand. Becky's body was washed in blood, her head and hands severed. In the background, Richard's mother was crying while his father clapped his hands. In another, the father was throwing Richard against the wall while the mother laughed.

Carolyn Loftis's hands began to shake as she studied the pictures. Something, she knew, had to be done. A telephone call from a distraught mother just a few days later convinced her it had to be done soon.

Chuck French had moved to Williams with his family the previous summer. A friendly, handsome seventeen-year-old, he had immediately become involved in school activities and was doing well in class. After he struck up a friendship with Richard Goeglein and his thirteen-year-old sister, however, Chuck began to change.

Soon he was going steady with Becky, and Richard had become his constant companion. Chuck's parents were alarmed at the sudden change in their son. He began dressing like Richard and spent hours listening to heavy metal music and poring over books on Satanism and witchcraft loaned him by his new friend. His grades dipped dramatically. Unknown to his parents, Chuck and Richard had cut themselves and used a heated cigarette lighter to burn a series of parallel lines into their shoulders, signifying they were blood brothers. His attitude toward his parents became hostile, and his behavior bordered on violence. Chuck's mother, Dotty, was particularly concerned with her son's fascination for an ornamental dagger Richard had given him. Chuck constantly sharpened it and carried it with him everywhere he went. When she began to suspect that her son was smoking marijuana, she launched a concerted effort to prevent Chuck from associating with Richard and his sister.

Her effort backfired in a strange way. Chuck began running away from home, spending more and more time with Richard and Becky. The Goegleins apparently encouraged Chuck's relationship with their daughter; Becky, it seemed, loved him and they were going to do everything they could to see that the two were allowed to stay together.

Richard Goeglein, Sr., who was out of work, became a regular visitor to the high school campus. He would make almost daily trips to visit with his son and Chuck during the lunch break or when they were outside for physical education classes.

One afternoon the principal received a call from a distraught Dotty French, asking if her son was at school. Battling flu, she had left work early and returned home to find a suicide note left by her son. The note, which Chuck had not expected his parents to find until later in the day, ended with a brief, dispassionate good-bye and a plea for them not to worry about him. "Satan is looking after me," he wrote.

When Chuck's mother told Carolyn Loftis about the note, the principal urged her to come to the school immediately. She would have Chuck and the school counselor waiting in her office.

After hanging up, Mrs. Loftis thought back to a conversation she had overheard just a few weeks earlier. She had been standing in the hall, talking with several students, when Chuck approached with the news that a student had attempted suicide the night before.

139

Richard had grinned and asked, "Did he make it?"

"Naw," Chuck said, "he's in the hospital, but he's going to be okay."

Goeglein shrugged. "I guess I'll have to help him plan it better the next time," he said, then walked away.

The flippant remark had chilled Mrs. Loftis. That evening she told her husband what she had heard. She mentioned that there had, in recent months, been several suicide attempts by Williams youngsters.

"And every one of them has been a kid who runs around with the Goeglein boy," her husband had responded.

Sitting in the principal's office, Chuck at first insisted that the note he had left was nothing more than a joke, another way of getting back at his parents. He was angry, he said, because they had called the police after finding marijuana in his room.

Mrs. Loftis questioned Chuck about his relationship with Richard, and he finally admitted to her that his friend had persuaded him to enter into a suicide pact. Richard, he said, had explained that death was the ultimate gift one could offer to the devil.

When confronted by the principal, Richard Goeglein laughed. He and Chuck, Richard said, had just been kidding around.

In January of 1987 Carolyn Loftis drove out Spring Valley Road to the Goeglein mobile home in the Red Lakes area north of town and informed them of the course of action she had decided upon. The bylaws set forth by the school board provided for dismissal of any student with a lengthy history of disruptive behavior and failing grades. Mrs. Loftis explained to the Goegleins that if Richard wasn't passing at least four subjects by midterm—just four weeks away—she would recommend to the school board that he be expelled.

Frances Goeglein informed the principal that the family was contemplating a move to Texas in the summer. Rather than have expulsion on her son's record, she said, she would simply withdraw him from school immediately.

When they did move, Mrs. Goeglein added, they were

going to take Chuck French with them. However, it was Carolyn Loftis's remarks to a judge in Flagstaff in early June which blocked the Goegleins' efforts. She told of the drawings by Richard and of his parents' lack of interest in their own son's academic and psychological well-being.

The judge, having heard Chuck French emphatically state that he no longer wished to live with his parents, and fearing that the boy would only run away if forced to stay at home, suggested a compromise. He would not allow the teenager to reside with the Goegleins but agreed to let Chuck go to live with relatives out of state. The distance, he felt, would prevent Chuck from staying in touch with the Goegleins and would offer him a new start.

Drained by the experience, Mrs. Loftis and her husband left the following afternoon for a two-week vacation. Though neither mentioned it to any of their friends or fellow teachers, the real purpose of their trip was to search for new teaching jobs. Williams, they had decided, was not a place where they wanted to raise their own children. With any luck, they would have to return only to pack their belongings.

What transpired during their absence convinced them that their decision had been a good one.

On the evening of Monday, June 15, Richard Goeglein and a friend named Frank Ross were driving around Williams in a five-year-old Datsun that belonged to Richard's mother.

Ross, a nineteen-year-old ninth grade dropout, had moved to Williams eight months earlier with his mother and two younger brothers. A troubled youngster who had been described by school counselors as a slow learner, he struck up a friendship with Richard shortly after moving to town. After Goeglein had withdrawn from school, the two became even closer. Ross regularly spent the night with Richard in his small travel trailer. Located behind the Goegleins' mobile home, Richard's twelve-by-six-foot living quarters provided a privacy that Frank Ross did not have in the small apartment he shared with his mother and brothers in town. There he and Richard would spend evenings listening to heavy metal music, poring over Richard's collection of occult books, and talking late into the night.

Richard would listen sympathetically as Frank reminisced of life in Santa Fe, New Mexico, and Tuba City, Arizona, where he had lived before with his mother and father. When Frank and his mother moved to Williams, his father remained in Tuba City. It was not, however, Frank's family troubles that sparked Richard's interest. What fascinated him was the wildness he detected in Ross. Slow-talking, almost docile at times, Frank would change in an instant, often without warning. One minute he might be talking lovingly about his pet cat, Prowler; then suddenly he would begin to laugh menacingly and brag of getting drunk at the Sultana Bar in downtown Williams and standing in the middle of the street, shooting the finger and yelling "fuck you" to passing cars.

One night they went to the long-deserted Harvey Building near the Santa Fe railroad tracks on the edge of town. Local residents called the condemned building the White House because of its bleached stucco walls. Said to be haunted, it had become a gathering place for devil-worshiping ceremonies. Richard had started going there long before he met Frank. Sometimes he went alone; sometimes he dared other teenagers to accompany him. Much of the graffiti on the walls inside the spacious old building was Richard's handiwork.

Several months earlier, a Williams teenager named Elliott Smith confided to several friends that he had followed Goeglein to the building one evening. Smith had watched through a dirty window as Richard drew an encircled pentagram in the middle of the floor of one of the rooms, placed lighted candles at each point of the pentagram, then knelt and read aloud from a book. The spellbound Smith then saw Richard take out a butterfly knife and cut the throat of a stray cat.

Elliott Smith ran all the way home that night, frightened by what he had seen. He did not sleep at all. Neither did he ever mention the incident to Richard.

There were times, however, when Frank Ross scared Richard. The two boys entered the White House one night, hoping to conjure up evil spirits in the building. After sitting silently in one of the darkened rooms for some time, Frank moved close to Goeglein and said, "Richard, I think the devil wants you dead." At first, Richard thought his friend was joking. But a few minutes later Frank repeated himself. "I'm sure of it," he said in a voice that was almost a growl. "The devil wants you dead."

Frightened, Richard rose to his feet quickly and pulled his knife, pointing it at Ross. "You fucking better leave me alone," he yelled.

Frank began to laugh. "Hey, man, I was just kidding," he said. It was then that he lifted his shirt to show Richard the inverted cross he had recently burned into his stomach. "I ain't gonna hurt you. Shit, you and me, we're brothers. We're disciples of the devil."

Richard Goeglein and Frank Ross had much in common. Both liked heavy metal music, both had rebelled against the authority of school officials, and both were fascinated by the occult and by Satan worship.

While neither would have admitted it, they had another common bond.

Though he had never mentioned it to Richard, Frank Ross, like his new friend, had his own problems. A year earlier, his parents had admitted him to the Flagstaff Medical Center following a suicide attempt. A staff psychiatrist who treated the teenager had diagnosed him as seriously emotionally disturbed.

That night, the last traces of summer daylight were disappearing as Richard drove the white Datsun along the six-mile stretch of Highway 64 leading from Red Lake into Williams. Ross, who had spent the previous night with him and had remained at the Goegleins' all day, rode in the passenger seat. They had no particular plan except to cruise until Richard's 11:00 P.M. curfew.

Neither mentioned the fact that Frank had brought along a baseball bat he had taken from Richard's trailer.

Excitement is difficult for kids to find on Monday nights

in Williams, even during the summer vacation. Teenagers gather in parking lots to sit on the hoods of cars or in the beds of their pickups, listening to music and talking among themselves, watching their slow-moving world pass by along the main drag. When that becomes boring, they drive. Their routes are predictable and tedious: out to the truck stop, past Denny's, and through the park; sometimes out the highway toward the Havasupai Indian settlement of Supai, located in an area so rugged that the mail is delivered on horseback; or maybe over to the nearby community of Fredonia where teenagers are doing basically the same thing. The most coveted commodity in the social life of small-town teenagers, then, is a full tank of gas.

It was a few minutes after six when Richard and Frank drove past the Pinecrest Apartments and saw Elliott Smith sitting on the curb, listening to his radio.

The sixteen-year-old Smith had been one of the first youngsters called to the attention of principal Carolyn Loftis when she arrived in Williams. Slow in school, Elliott had spent most of his frustrating academic life with younger children. Finally, after falling back yet another grade in junior high, he quit school and worked at odd jobs—hauling firewood, washing dishes for Virgil Curry at his restaurant and helping him with his after-hours carpet-cleaning business.

Carolyn Loftis had sought Elliott out and spent long hours trying to persuade him to return to school. What she saw was a gentle, lonely youngster who was embarrassed by the fact he was forced to attend school with twelve- and thirteen-year-olds instead of those his own age. He was constantly ridiculed for voicing the strong religious beliefs passed on to him by his mother, and he seldom went anywhere without his Bible in hand. And while other youngsters listened to rock music, his taste was for the music played by a Christian radio station in Flagstaff. He was once caught stealing a soda from a grocery store, but that was the closest he ever came to getting into trouble.

Mrs. Loftis won Elliott over when she informed him that the Williams superintendent had agreed to allow him to move up to the high school with students his own age if he would come back to school. And while the classwork was difficult and his grades were poor, Elliott had emerged from his shell, made new friends, and gained self-esteem.

There were those, however, who feared the influence of some of Elliott's new friends, for there was a disconcerting change in the boy. Members of the church he had faithfully attended saw him less frequently. He no longer carried his Bible to school. It was, in the minds of some, as if Elliott was trying to make up for lost time, to achieve a level of maturity for which he was not really prepared.

Among the new friends he had begun spending time with were Richard Goeglein, Frank Ross, and Chuck French. Starved for acceptance, Elliott chose to overlook the fact they often made him the butt of their jokes. They regularly tried to urge him into fights and made fun of his religious commitment.

Richard had given Elliott books on Satan worship, demanding that he read them if he wanted to be his friend. After reading the books, Elliott was told it would be necessary for him to make vows to the devil. Part of the ceremony would require that Elliott cut himself and let his blood mix with that of the others. When he refused, Richard and Frank ignored him for several weeks.

When they did finally allow Elliott to accompany them again, they often tried to frighten him. One winter afternoon he was riding with Richard along a gravel road into a wooded area outside town. Goeglein, laughing and driving erratically, finally came to an abrupt stop when they reached a wide spot on the isolated road. There Richard drove the car in a tight circle for several minutes. Then he got out and drew a huge pentagram inside the circle made by the tire tracks. That done, he took candles from the trunk and placed them around the perimeter of the circle, one at each of the five points of the pentagram, and began praying to Satan. Elliott, recalling the scene he had witnessed in the old Harvey Building, refused to get out of the car while Richard went through the bizarre ceremony.

On another occasion he accompanied Richard and Frank

to a graveyard late one night. Richard told frightening stories of his power to raise the dead and communicate with spirits. When they were convinced that Elliott was properly terrified, Goeglein and Ross ran away, leaving him alone in the dark cemetery. Elliott waited several hours for them to return, then finally walked home.

Another time when Smith was riding with Goeglein and Ross, Richard pulled into the driveway of a convenience store, jumped from the car, put a knife to the throat of an elderly man, and demanded his money. The victim, far stronger and more agile than he looked, slapped the knife from Richard's grasp and told him to leave before he called the sheriff.

Richard quickly returned to the car, cursing. "I didn't want the old bastard's money," he said. "I just wanted to hassle the old fucker a little."

While such activities went against everything Elliott Smith had been taught, the lonely youngster continued to look on Richard and Frank as his friends.

On that Monday evening in June when he saw the white Datsun approaching, Elliott Smith flagged Richard down and asked where he and Ross were going. When told they were just cruising, Elliott asked if he could go along. Richard told him to climb into the back seat.

A few minutes later they picked up another youngster named Buddy Lester, then stopped by the home of a girl named Wanda Leslie. Wanda and Patty Ware, friends of Richard's sister, eagerly accepted the invitation to go riding.

The addition of the two teenage girls necessitated a shuffle in the seating arrangements. Wanda took Frank's place in the front seat next to Richard while Frank got into the back seat with Lester and Patty. Frank told Elliott Smith if he was going with them he would have to ride in the cramped quarters of the car's hatchback.

Elliott was surprised by the demanding, almost angry tone of Frank's voice, but he complied, climbing over the back of the rear seat and crouching behind the others. Frank laughed and asked Elliott if he was comfortable in his "coffin."

For a couple of hours they drove around town, then out the highway into the picturesque countryside to the north. When it began to get dark, the girls asked to be taken home. Both had babies they had left with Wanda's mother. Buddy Lester said he also needed to get home since his parents, angry with him for having stayed out too late the night before, had instructed him to be in before nightfall.

Back in town, Richard let Buddy and Elliott out, then took the girls home. Wanda and Patty suggested he and Frank stop by later. If they could locate baby-sitters for their infants, they would rejoin them.

To that point it had been a typical, uneventful Monday evening in Williams.

Later, shortly after nine o'clock, Richard and Frank drove past the Circle K Grocery on their way to see if the girls had found someone to watch their children.

Standing at the corner of the store, leaning against his bicycle, was Elliott. In one hand was a half-empty bottle of Jack Daniel's whiskey. He waved, and Richard pulled up alongside him. "You getting shit-faced?" Goeglein asked.

Elliott's only response was a nod and a crooked grin. "Let me go with you guys," he finally said, "and I'll share."

"Get in," Frank said.

"I've got to take my bike home and put it up first." The bicycle, everyone in town knew, was Elliott's prized possession.

"I'll race you," Richard said, backing out of the parking lot.

He was waiting at the Pinecrest Apartments when Elliott, pumping as hard as he could, turned into the covered parking area where he kept his bicycle.

When Elliott approached the car, Richard and Frank took long drinks from the whiskey bottle, then handed it back to him.

"If you're going with us," Frank said, "you've got to get your ass back into your coffin." Disappointed, Elliott went to the rear of the Datsun, lifted the hatchback, and climbed in.

* * *

In truth, neither seventeen-year-old Wanda Leslie nor sixteen-year-old Patty Ware liked the boys who arrived to pick them up. Both were aware of the boys' reputation as troublemakers and considered their behavior strange and often crude. Additionally, neither Richard nor Frank was all that good-looking. Normally the girls would have been embarrassed to be with them, but summer boredom had already begun to weigh heavily. Any opportunity to get out of the house, to escape even for a few hours the responsibilities of motherhood, sounded good.

Even at that, Wanda had to persuade Patty to call around for a baby-sitter so they could go out. Frank Ross, Patty said, gave her the creeps. His younger brother had once told her that Frank very nearly killed two young Indian boys during a fight when they lived in Tuba City prior to moving to Williams.

"Hey, it's not like a date," Wanda had argued. "We're just going to ride around for a while."

It was a few minutes past nine when the white Datsun pulled up in front of the house. Only Wanda saw Patty grimace when she realized that she was expected to sit in the back seat with Frank Ross.

Both girls, holding their babies in their laps, were surprised to see Elliott lying in the cramped hatchback, sipping from a bottle of whiskey.

Almost immediately they began to doubt the wisdom of their decision. On the way to the baby-sitter's house, Richard drove crazily, speeding up and then braking suddenly, tossing Elliott against the back window repeatedly. Each time Elliott complained, Frank turned and glared. "Shut up, nerd," he said.

When Elliott asked that he be allowed to sit in the back seat with Frank and Patty, he was told to stay in his "coffin." Ross, holding the baseball bat he had carried from Richard's trailer, pounded it against his palm every time he turned to look at Elliott.

"Why don't you just leave him alone?" Patty demanded. She liked Elliott. Her brother had sold him his bicycle and taught him many of the riding tricks that Elliott performed for the younger children in town.

"Aw, he's drunk," Richard said. "Don't worry about him. We're going to take care of him."

"Damn right," Frank said, then turned again to Elliott, slapping the bat harder against his palm. "You want it now, or do you want to wait until you're really shit-faced?" he asked.

During the two hours they rode aimlessly around town, the girls became increasingly apprehensive about the situation they had gotten themselves into. Richard tuned the radio to a heavy metal station at maximum volume, and Frank beat his head against the side window to the rhythm of the blaring music.

"You guys are acting crazy," Wanda said, for the first time wondering if they, too, were drunk. "Cut it out."

"We're just having a good time," Richard said, pulling a knife from his hip pocket and pointing it at Elliott. "Now or later?" he said, then laughed and speeded up.

When Wanda voiced her displeasure at the threat, Richard reached over and flipped the small gold cross she wore around her neck. "Why are you wearing that damn thing?" he chided. "People who believe in that junk are just afraid. Are you afraid to die?"

Wanda put her hand on the cross and turned away, ignoring the question.

Later, as they neared the almost deserted downtown area, Frank saw a kid named Ross Ortiz riding his bicycle along the street. "Run over the little motherfucker," he said to Richard.

When Richard refused to acknowledge his demand, Frank leaned forward. "I'm serious. Get him."

The girls were relieved when Richard drove on past Ortiz without incident. "You're chickenshit," Frank said, then laughed.

In the back, Elliott Smith had fallen asleep.

It was a few minutes before eleven when Richard returned the girls and their children to Patty Ware's home. Elliott awoke when the car stopped and raised himself up on one elbow. "I've got to take a leak," he said, his voice slurred by the booze. "Somebody let me out."

Richard and Frank got out with the girls and watched as Elliott staggered away into the darkness to relieve himself. Standing at the back of the car, Patty idly traced her name in the dust on the back window. Suddenly realizing that she didn't want anyone to see the car later and think she had been out alone with Richard, she began adding the names of the others. After she had printed Elliott's name with her finger, Frank added a final touch.

Before and after Elliott's name he wrote the word *die.*

The boys were back in the car, preparing to leave, when Patty's mother appeared at the front door and waved. She hurried out to the car and explained that she needed to pick up some groceries, asking Richard if he would give her a ride down to the Circle K.

As they made the short trip to the all-night grocery, the woman asked about the youngster who was again sleeping in the hatchback.

"That's Elliott Smith," Richard said. "We saw him downtown and picked him up. He's pretty drunk, so we're going to take him to my house and let him sleep it off. I don't want him to get into any trouble with his mother."

The woman nodded approvingly. "That's very thoughtful," she said.

Red Lake, north of Williams, is not so much a lake as a shallow basin of volcanic cinder that catches and retains water. Only the most optimistic fishermen are drawn to its banks, and most return home empty-handed, nor is it deep enough to attract boat owners and water-skiers.

Still, it is regarded as scenic and served as the centerpiece for an investment group that parceled off twenty-acre plots with a grand plan for a bucolic residential development. That, however, was before the economy of Williams spiraled downward.

Most of those who did buy acreage never got around to

building their lakeside dream homes. Some, like the mother of Frances Goeglein, simply turned the land over to their children, providing them a rent-free place to call home.

Richard Goeglein, Sr., thrilled by his mother-in-law's generosity, bought a mobile home for the property. As part of the agreement, the dealer anchored the home on a concrete foundation, built a wide redwood deck that served as the front porch, and helped Goeglein put in a gravel driveway that ran from the gate marking the entrance to the property, then circled in front of the porch.

Since the mobile home had only two bedrooms, it was agreed that Richard, Jr., could live in a small travel trailer parked on the west corner of the lot. Though only twenty feet from his parents' mobile home, the travel trailer gave the youngster privacy and independence, which he relished.

He could play his music as loud as he liked and entertain guests away from the rest of the family. Directly behind his living quarters was a stand of trees leading into a thick forest, which Richard often disappeared into late at night, long after everyone else was asleep. The woods, with its solitary quiet and spooky shadows, fascinated him almost as much as the dusty, deserted rooms of the old Harvey Building downtown.

After Richard had parked the Datsun at the side of the mobile home, he and Frank shook Elliott awake and helped him out of the car and into the trailer. Inside, they placed him, wobbly-legged and sick, on the bunk bed that occupied one end of the small trailer. Elliott immediately fell asleep again. Richard then walked over to the mobile home to tell his parents he was home.

While inside he drank a glass of milk and watched a few minutes of a late movie with his mother. She asked if Frank was spending the night again and Richard told her he was. He did not, however, mention that another visitor was already asleep in his trailer.

In truth, Richard was already regretting not having taken Elliott back to the Pinecrest Apartments before returning home.

"'Night," he said as he walked toward the front door.

"You boys, don't stay up too late," Mrs. Goeglein said, then turned her attention back to the TV set.

For the next hour Richard and Frank did what they usually did when Frank stayed over.

Sitting at the small table in the trailer, Richard opened the leather case containing his collection of heavy metal tapes and selected one titled "Hell Awaits" by Slayer. For a while the two boys sat in silence, eyes closed, heads frantically swaying to the pounding electronic beat of songs with titles like "Angel of Death," "Raining Blood," "Altar of Sacrifice," and "Necrophobic."

Frank's favorite was "Piece by Piece." Its lyrics told of bones and blood, decapitated heads and rotting limbs.

"Awright," he said as the group's lead vocalist, Tom Araya, shouted the hellish lyrics above the thunder of drums and guitars. "Man, that makes me fucking crazy. I love it."

After a while the teenagers began thumbing through Richard's books on the occult as they continued listening to the music, chain-smoking, and discussing the various satanic rites and rituals the books outlined for communicating with spirits of the dead.

Neither was aware that Elliott had awakened until he rose from the bed and joined them at the table. "I've got to get home," he said. Though his stomach still churned, the brief rest had helped to clear his head.

"Go back to bed and sleep it off," Frank replied.

"You've got to take me home," Elliott pleaded.

"Sit down and jam with us," Richard said.

"I don't like that kind of music. It stinks. I need to go home." Suddenly Elliott was angry and on his feet. As he stood, the table toppled and books and tapes spilled onto the floor.

Richard, momentarily knocked off balance by the overturned table, cursed and lunged at Elliott, shoving him against the wall.

No longer drunk, Elliott grabbed an old army sword that was mounted among the rock group posters on the wall near the trailer door. He pointed it at Richard. "You believe in what that T-shirt you're wearing says?" Elliott asked. Goeglein's sleeveless black shirt, purchased at a Slayer concert, had the words "Do You Want to Die?" printed beneath the band's logo.

Richard did not answer. Instead, he rushed toward Elliott and shoved him, knocking Elliott out the door of the trailer. He fell to his knees in the dirt yard, and Goeglein followed him out. The sword lay several feet away near a clothesline.

The two angry teenagers stood, glaring defensively, each waiting for the other to make the first move. Frank stood watching from the doorway of the trailer. "Get it on," he urged.

Elliott, his back to the door, turned briefly to look at Ross, then returned his attention to Richard. The last thing he heard was Frank saying, "Give yourself to the devil."

Ross, wielding the baseball bat he had been carrying all evening, stepped from the trailer and delivered a full-swing blow to the back of Elliott's head. The teenager again fell to the ground, this time moaning in pain as blood began to trickle from both ears.

Frank, his teeth clenched and a maniacal look in his eyes, swung the bloodied bat again. When it connected with the side of Elliott's head, the defenseless youngster went limp.

"I had to shut him up," Ross said, looking over at Richard.

In his semiconscious state, Elliott thought he heard Richard tell Frank to "hit him again."

Ross struck Elliott a third time. Then a fourth. His last swing glanced off Elliott's head and slammed against the trailer door, leaving a large dent. "Damn it, I had to shut him up," Frank repeated.

Richard stood speechless, looking down at the still body. Elliott's head rested in a square of dim light that shone from the trailer window. His eyes were open, and his fractured skull was exposed by a large gash from Frank's blows.

"He's dead," Frank said. "We've got to bury him." Still gripping the bat, he was tense and rigid, as if an electric current were running through him. "Let's get rid of him."

Shaking, Richard bent over Elliott. As he did he noticed a

small puff of dust rising from where Elliott's nose rested against the ground. "He's still breathing. We've got to get him some help."

"Shit, it's too late," Frank said, as tears began to well in his eyes. "He's already messed up pretty bad. I'm going to get the fucking electric chair for this anyway. I've got to finish him off."

"Put the goddam bat down," Richard said. His voice was calm but authoritative.

Frank, suddenly drained of emotion, let the bat fall to the ground. "What are we going to do?"

They decided to drag Elliott Smith's body into the nearby trees and leave it while they planned their next step.

It was Richard who suggested they put Elliott in the trunk of the car and take him to the Williams Medical Center in town. "We could leave him there, ring the emergency room bell, and get the hell out," he offered. "They'll take care of him."

"Hell, no," Frank said. "Somebody might see us." After pacing the area in front of the trailer frantically, he finally stopped and looked at Richard for several seconds without speaking, then said, "We've got to have a story."

Richard nodded. "The crazy shit threatened me with the sword," he said. "He was drunk and was going to kill me. You had to hit him to keep him from stabbing me. That's our story."

In his bedroom, Richard Goeglein, Sr., had been jolted awake by the sound of what he thought was his son and Frank lifting weights and dropping them onto the floor of the camper. Angered that his sleep had been interrupted, he dressed quickly and went outside.

In the moonlight he could see the two boys standing in the shadows of the trees near the camper.

As Richard, Sr., approached, Frank suddenly retrieved the sword Elliott had dropped. "You come any closer," the youngster screamed in a crazed, high-pitched voice, "and I'll kill you. I swear I'll cut your goddam head off."

The elder Goeglein, stunned by the threat, moved no

closer. His son raced to Frank's side and grabbed him by the shoulder and began shaking him. "Frank," Richard said, "that's my dad."

Ross lowered the sword and looked at his friend's father. "Oh, God," he said, "I don't know what's wrong with me."

Richard Goeglein, Sr., hurried to the stand of trees where Elliott lay unconscious. Saying nothing, he then went over to where the baseball bat lay, picked it up, and tossed it under the trailer. "Put him in my car," the father said. "We've got to get him to the hospital." The elder Goeglein then went into the house to wake his wife.

For the next nine days Elliott Smith lay in a coma. Doctors at the Williams Medical Center, who estimated that his skull was fractured in as many as six places, later had him transported to the Barrows Neurological Institute in Phoenix.

Summoned to the hospital in Williams by doctors shortly after Elliott was admitted, two deputies from the Coconino County Sheriff's Department arrived to find the Goegleins, their son, Richard, and Frank Ross seated in the waiting area adjacent to the emergency room.

In a report submitted to Detective Jeffrey Greene, who had been assigned to investigate the offense, Deputy Diane Christian noted that the parents seemed upset and concerned about the condition of Elliott Smith. Richard Goeglein seemed nervous, staring at the floor the entire time Christian was in his presence. Frank Ross, on the other hand, displayed no emotion.

Deputy Christian wrote her report in the pre-dawn hours of Tuesday. At the same time, Richard Goeglein, Sr., having returned home from the hospital, was in his son's trailer. After instructing Richard, Jr., to remain in the mobile home, he ripped the rock group posters from the wall and collected the books and tapes that had spilled onto the floor when Elliott upset the small table. He carried the items to a trash barrel on the edge of the yard and burned them. He found Richard's jacket with the pentagram on the back and tossed it into the fire along with Elliott's whiskey bottle.

That done, he repaired the hinges that anchored the broken table to the wall.

It was near dawn when he completed his cleanup. He did not, however, retrieve the baseball bat from beneath the camper.

Returning to the mobile home, he found his son asleep on the living room couch.

A veteran investigator, Detective Greene wasted little time putting the case together. By midday Tuesday word had spread throughout Williams that something terrible had happened at the Goegleins' the night before. Wanda Leslie and Patty Ware voluntarily visited the Williams substation and gave statements about the way Richard and Frank had treated Elliott while they were with them. Several callers reported having seen the youngster in the hatchback of Richard's car the previous evening. No one seemed surprised to hear that Goeglein or Ross might be capable of such violence.

In their initial statements the teenagers stuck to the story that Richard had suggested: Elliott, drunk and acting crazy, had attacked Richard, threatening to kill him with the sword; Frank, fearing for his friend's life, had hit Elliott with the baseball bat. He couldn't remember how many times.

It was Richard who finally wavered. On Wednesday Detective Greene went out to Red Lake to review the crime scene and to talk with the youngster about the brief written statement he had given the day before.

They were standing in front of the travel trailer after the obviously nervous Goeglein had again described the sequence of events. "Richard," the detective said, "you aren't telling me everything. There's a kid lying in the hospital who might not make it. Think about that. I want you to tell me the truth so we can get this thing settled."

Richard, his shoulders slumped, looked up at Greene. "How much trouble will I get into?"

"I can't tell you that until I know what happened. Why don't we go inside and sit down and talk about it?"

Seated at the same table he had shared with Frank on

Monday evening, Richard Goeglein told Greene everything, beginning when they first picked Elliott up at the Pinecrest Apartments and ending with the frantic ride to the hospital with his parents.

"I had a feeling all along that Frank was going to do something bad, that he was going to hurt somebody. I shouldn't have brought Elliott home with us. Frank was acting too crazy."

With that he broke into tears and reached out for the detective. For several minutes Jeffrey Greene held the sobbing youngster in his arms, for the first time feeling a tinge of sympathy for Richard.

Though it would be all but impossible to make a strong enough case against him to satisfy the district attorney or a grand jury, the young man crying on Greene's shoulder would serve well as a witness.

That afternoon, Frank Ross was arrested, charged with aggravated assault, and taken to the county jail in Flagstaff. Justice of the Peace Joanne Everidge placed bond at $50,000. Two days later charges of attempted first-degree homicide were added after the judge read Richard's statement. Ross's bond was increased to $77,400.

David Ross, having learned of his son's arrest, drove from Tuba City immediately. Sitting in the visiting room of the jail, he listened as Frank described what he had done. There was little passion in the youngster's voice, and he never asked how Elliott, still comatose, was doing.

The elder Ross, at a loss for words, shook his head and stared into the eyes of his troubled son. "Why?" he finally asked.

For the first time since their visit had begun, Frank Ross showed signs of emotion. For a moment it appeared that he might cry. "Satan has my soul," the boy said, "and he won't give it back."

For Detective Greene, the case was one of the most unsettling he had ever investigated. That Elliott Smith had been brutally beaten with apparently no provocation troubled him. So did Frank Ross's total lack of remorse.

At times, though, it was the mystery surrounding Richard Goeglein that bothered him most. The girls who had been riding with the boys had both said they felt that Richard had subtly egged Frank on that night, encouraging the threats and aggressive behavior.

And there had been anonymous phone calls from local youngsters that made Greene wonder whether the attack on Elliott might have had something to do with Richard and Frank's involvement in devil worship. One teenager said he had attended several satanic gatherings. He told stories of a stolen goat that had been killed and its blood consumed by the self-styled devil-worshipers, who called themselves the Fans of Slayer. At the meetings, generally attended by ten to twelve people from thirteen to twenty years old, prayers for power and money were offered up to Satan. Once, a curse was placed on the pet of an elderly Williams woman whom the youngsters disliked. A few days later she found her dog lying dead in her front yard, apparently poisoned.

Another caller, who also admitted having attended several ritualistic meetings, gave Greene directions to a wooded location where he said animals had been sacrificed. Following the directions, the detective found a clearing. In it was a metal frame filled with branches. The caller had said this was possibly part of a sacrificial altar. Affixed to the limb of an overturned tree were the skulls of a dog and a cow. The strong odor of putrefying flesh assaulted the detective's nostrils, but he found no animal remains.

The wooded area that sheltered the altar abutted the eastern property line of the Goeglein residence.

Jeffrey Greene would not have an opportunity to look further into Richard Goeglein's involvement in occult practices, for the boy and his family moved to Texas shortly after Richard testified at Frank Ross's preliminary hearing.

The young Goeglein was several hundred miles away when Ross agreed to a plea of guilty in exchange for an eight-year sentence in the Arizona State Prison for the assault on Elliott Smith.

Miraculously, Smith was well enough after a month-long

stay in the hospital to return home to Williams. Doctors told his mother that she could expect him to recover fully in time. Though his speech was still slightly slurred, he returned to Williams High School. He was absent only to testify at Frank Ross's trial. And he was again able to ride his beloved bicycle around town, performing tricks for young admirers.

Such were the details that Richard Goeglein failed to mention to his new friends in Midlothian, Texas. Most of them viewed his infatuation with the occult as little more than a harmless offshoot of his taste for heavy metal music. The pentagram he wore around his neck, the satanic doodles he was constantly drawing on the covers of his school books—these were nothing most students hadn't seen on dozens of album covers at record stores in the Red Bird Mall.

Richard seemed strange, but he was friendly enough.

Though he had seen the boy at school, George Raffield did not meet Richard Goeglein until one Monday afternoon in early October when he and Greg were driving around town. They ran into Jonathan and Richard in the parking lot of Del's Drive-in and stopped to talk for a few minutes. Over the pounding beat of the music playing on the tape deck in Jobe's pickup, George introduced himself to Richard.

10

Making drug cases against the Midlothian teenagers was easier than George Raffield had expected. As soon as word spread that he was willing to drive to Dallas for drugs, he found himself being approached several times a week. One afternoon, in fact, he made two trips with different people, buying marijuana on each occasion. If that kept up, he told Lieutenant Fowler as he turned over the evidence, he would need to start drawing more buy money at the beginning of each week.

The work had also become more exciting. On a visit to the apartment complex in Dallas with Kyle Royal he encountered a new routine. On his trips with Greg, dealers had simply walked up to the truck and begun the transaction. On the trip with Kyle, however, a black man appeared on a second-floor balcony when they pulled into the parking lot. He stared at them for several minutes before putting his fingers to his lips as if smoking a cigarette. Royal responded to the signal with a nod, and the man on the balcony pointed at Kyle and waved for him to come inside. The dealer, whom George had not seen before, obviously wanted to deal only with Royal.

Kyle had been gone less than ten minutes when he returned with six plastic bags of marijuana and handed five of them to George. "Let's get the fuck out of here," he said.

"What happened?"

"Nothing. But they're getting jumpy as hell. There was a dude in the apartment holding a fucking shotgun on me while the other guy got the stuff."

Nightly drug raids by the Dallas Police Department had obviously spooked the dealers, who were no longer willing to sell to customers on the street.

"Screw that," George replied, feigning fear. "I'm damn sure not going into one of those places." One of the rules the safety-conscious Fowler had insisted on was that Raffield never go into any enclosed area to buy drugs. Since his undercover role prohibited his carrying a weapon, Fowler had explained, he would have no way to defend himself if the need arose. "Let them bring the stuff to you," the lieutenant had instructed.

George, however, had chosen to ignore one of Fowler's rules. He had been told not to front any money unless he went along on the buy. But one Friday afternoon George overheard Dale Janson mention that he was going to Dallas to score some pot, and he asked the teenager to bring some back for him.

Janson agreed, took George's fifty dollars, and told him to meet him at the car wash later that afternoon. George waited, but Janson failed to return with the dope. Raffield drove around town looking for him for several hours before he learned that Janson and his girlfriend had gone to a movie in Dallas.

Reluctantly, George reported to Fowler that he had been ripped off.

The incident, Fowler knew, would provide the first real test of the young officer's cover. "You can't let him get away with it," Fowler said. "Monday, when you go back to school, find him and raise hell with him. Demand that he give you the weed or your money back. If you just let it pass, people are going to wonder."

Raffield listened to the nearest thing to a chewing-out he had heard from Fowler since they had begun working together.

"One other thing," the lieutenant said.

"What's that?"

"It wouldn't hurt to spread the word to some of the other kids that you're really pissed off about being ripped off."

Solemn-faced, George looked across the dining room table at Fowler. "That won't be hard," he said, "because I am. I'm pissed off at myself."

As the officers discussed the situation, Dale Janson sat with friends in the parking lot of one of the movie theaters adjacent to the Red Bird Mall. Rolling a joint from the marijuana he had purchased earlier that afternoon, he bragged of ripping off the new kid for fifty dollars.

"Man, he's not going to go for that kind of shit," one of the others said.

"Fuck him," Dale said, taking a drag on the joint. He didn't mention it, but he doubted seriously that George Moore would say anything about his lost money. Suspicious of anyone he didn't know well, Janson had watched as George moved quickly into the drug crowd after enrolling at the school. Though most of his friends seemed to like the new kid, Dale had kept his distance. To him, George Moore seemed too eager, had too much money, and looked too old to be in high school. Hell, even Randy Marcott had noticed that he seemed to have a five o'clock shadow by the time school was out every day. He'd kidded George about it, calling him Grandpa.

There was a good chance, Dale had decided, that the new kid in school was an undercover cop. It was that suspicion, more than any brazen decision to steal his fifty dollars, that had prompted his decision not to deliver the drugs he had bought for George.

Still, all day Monday, Dale made a concentrated effort to avoid George, even though several students passed along the message that George wanted to see him.

Toward the end of the school day, however, Dale entered

the boys' bathroom and turned to find that George had followed him in.

"Where's my stuff, asshole?" George demanded, pleased to see that Janson was frightened.

"I ain't got it, man."

"Then give me my money."

"I ain't got that, either. Things got fucked up and—"

"And you thought you would just rip my ass off, right?" George gritted his teeth as he finished the sentence.

Dale backed against the sink, his arms raised as if fearful that George might attack him. "Look, man," he said, "I'm sorry. Okay, okay, I fucked the deal up. It won't happen again, I swear. Give me until Friday and I'll have the stuff for you. Just wait until Friday, okay? I promise."

George stared away for several seconds, then shook his head. "Okay, Friday," he said, then turned and left the bathroom.

When Friday came, however, Janson again successfully dodged George throughout the school day. When Raffield went into the parking lot after school, Dale was nowhere to be found. It was obvious he had no intention of making good his promise, and George knew he would have to confront him.

Just before six o'clock that afternoon George caught a glimpse of Janson walking toward a shopping center. Dale, waiting there for his mother, did not see George until he had pulled into the parking lot, climbed out of his truck, and yelled at him.

Dale walked over to George, a belligerent look on his face. "What the fuck do you want?" he asked.

"You know what I want," George replied. "I want my money or the stuff you were supposed to bring me. And I want it right now."

He was not prepared for Janson's response. "Well, I ain't giving it to you," Dale said, "because I think you're a fucking narc."

"That's bullshit and you know it. How do I know you aren't one?"

From inside a store in the shopping center, Dale's mother

had been watching the confrontation. She walked to the front door and called her son inside.

"Isn't that great," George said. "You've got Mama watching over you."

Dale bristled. "Fuck you," he said, then slapped George. The open-handed blow had been hard and stinging, but George did not respond. It caught him off guard, and for a second he just looked at Dale, fighting to keep his anger in check.

Janson then turned and ran toward the store entrance.

That night George sat in the living room of his brother-in-law's trailer, replaying the incident. He was not happy with the way he had handled it, he said, and now dreaded having to tell Lieutenant Fowler that his cover had been blown.

Mark Prine listened as George explained what had happened. Finally, after hearing the story, he rose to his feet and walked across the room. "Dammit, Tiger, why didn't you just haul off and knock the crap out of him?"

"I just couldn't. He's just a kid, a punk little kid. I'm a police officer. I never felt so damn helpless in my life. It's hard to explain, but I can't go around beating up on some kid every time I get mad. Dammit, I just can't!"

"Your problem," Mark replied angrily, "is you're being too nice to these little bastards. You've got to act like you're just as sorry as they are. Quit being such a nice person. If you don't, you're going to get yourself in trouble."

Billy Fowler had been anticipating just such a situation even before George told him of the confrontation. He had repeatedly warned George that some of the kids would be suspicious and test him. The real trick was to prove those suspicions wrong.

Fowler had already begun planning to use an old undercover dodge, something that had worked successfully more times than he could remember. He would arrange for George to be arrested.

The lieutenant had suggested to Chief Vaughn that they put a set of old tires on the patrol car that was usually parked in front of the station late at night. When George was out cruising with his buddies he was to mention that he was in a hell-raising mood, and then he was to slash the tires.

"It'll be easy enough to arrest him at school and bring him down here. We'll book him, throw his ass in jail, and make him handle his own bail. You can count on word of his arrest getting around pretty quickly," Fowler promised.

In the next few days, however, the urgent need to bolster George's reputation waned. Those who had heard about his run-in with Dale Janson seemed genuinely sympathetic. Dale, several said, was just a two-bit thief, a chickenshit. No one trusted him. George wasn't the first person he'd ripped off.

"I guarantee you," George vowed, "that I'll get him before it's all over with."

Relieved that there apparently was no widespread concern that he might, in fact, be an undercover police officer, George tried to put the incident out of his mind.

He was pleased when Greg Knighten approached him in the hall and invited him to dinner. Greg would be celebrating his sixteenth birthday and had asked his mother if he could ask George and Jamie Cadenhead over.

That Thursday, October 15, was a busy day for the young officer.

After school he drove Kyle Royal into Dallas to make a buy, returned him to Midlothian, then drove to Red Oak where his grandparents had just arrived from Georgia for a surprise visit. On a cross-country vacation, they would only be there overnight, so George wanted at least to say hello.

He was particularly fond of his grandfather, a retired fire chief. George still had the badge his granddad had given him after his retirement. His grandfather, in fact, had been one of the first to encourage his interest in law enforcement. George, then, was anxious to tell him about the new job he had taken.

He was also disappointed that he had to leave after only a short visit. "Can't you just stay for dinner?" his mother asked.

"I can't. I promised to go to Sparky's birthday party."

Shirley Moore, who had heard the youngster's name often

in recent weeks as George discussed his work in Midlothian, returned to the kitchen.

George's grandfather walked with him to his pickup, his arm draped over the young man's shoulder. "I'm sorry I have to run," George apologized.

His grandfather waved his free hand as a sign of understanding. "I'm just glad we got to see you," he said. George was in the pickup and had started the engine when his grandfather approached and signaled for him to roll his window down. "I just want you to know," he said, "that I'm proud of what you're doing."

A broad smile spread across his grandson's face. "Thanks."

"Take care of yourself."

"I will."

Tom Knighten was openly pleased that Greg had invited George to the birthday celebration. He liked the young man's manners and the fact that he dressed neatly. Too, George looked directly at him when they talked. That, more than anything else, impressed Tom Knighten. Most of Greg's friends were obviously uncomfortable in his presence, avoiding him as much as possible on their visits. When he tried to talk with them, they answered his questions in monosyllables, often while staring at their feet.

George, however, was different. He was relaxed and seemed confident in himself, mature for his age. He joked with Greg's younger brother, complimented Nelda on the inviting aromas coming from her kitchen, and acted generally pleased to have been invited into their home. And, most important to Tom Knighten, he seemed to like Greg.

As they sat down to dinner they all joined hands and bowed their heads as Tom Knighten gave thanks, expressing his gratitude for the friends who had come to share the meal and his son's birthday with them.

After the cake had been eaten, the gifts opened, and some pictures snapped, Greg asked his father if he could go riding around with George and Jamie for a while. Pleased with the way the evening had gone, Tom agreed but reminded his son that it was a school night.

"We won't be gone long," George said. Weary from his afternoon of traveling first to Dallas, then to Red Oak, he was ready for the long day to end.

No sooner had they gotten into his pickup, however, than Greg suggested they make a quick run to Polk Street, referring to the exit off Highway 67 that led to his drug connection.

Once they had driven away from the house, Greg's mood quickly turned sullen. Even Jamie was unable to cheer him. He cursed Tom Knighten repeatedly, angry that his father's birthday gift had only been a ten-dollar bill. On the trip to and from Dallas he continued berating his father. He had expected something more than the money, which he had just used to purchase a dime bag of marijuana.

As they returned to Midlothian Greg asked that George drive him to the Oxford Square Apartments. "Cynthia's got my water pipe," he said. "I want to pick it up."

George and Jamie waited in the gravel parking lot while Greg disappeared into apartment 31. In a few minutes Greg returned, his pipe in hand.

"Now where?" George asked.

"I guess I'd better go home," Greg said. There was a hollow note of dread in his voice.

After driving Greg home, George turned the truck around to take Jamie to her house. They were well into the isolated countryside when Jamie, trying to make conversation, asked how he liked living in Midlothian.

"It's okay," George said.

"Greg hates it," she said. "He wants us to get away from here as soon as we can after we get married."

As George slowed at the intersection of the road that led to the Cadenhead house, Jamie asked about his aunt and uncle. "Where do they live?"

Not taking his eyes off the road as he made the right-hand turn, George said, "It's down this same road. About five miles back the other way, out in the boonies."

As he spoke, they drove past the house of Bob and Martha Browning. For a second he silently pondered the irony of it all. The people who had volunteered to pose as his aunt and uncle had been chosen, in part, because of the isolated area in which they lived. Yet now George's destination was less than a mile down the road from their driveway.

"Jamie," George said, "who's Cynthia?"

"Cynthia Fedrick. She's just a friend of Greg's," she said.

In truth, she was a friend to a number of Midlothian teenagers. She had moved to Midlothian in July of 1987, looking for a fresh start. Twice divorced and constantly in and out of trouble with the authorities, twenty-three-year-old Cynthia Fedrick seemed always to be looking for a new beginning. For a while she thought maybe she had found it in a new job as a waitress at the Road Runner truck stop.

She and her four-year-old daughter had moved into the Oxford Apartments, she had managed to buy an old Valiant for fifty dollars, and she was back near her family—her mother, stepfather, and stepbrother—who had moved to Midlothian two years earlier.

Her mother, also named Cynthia, was candid with those who asked about the family's move. She explained that they had left nearby Cedar Hill because the drug problem there had grown out of control. She and her husband didn't want to see Cynthia's brother, Randy Marcott, mess his life up as their daughter had.

The mother's frank assessment of Cynthia's past was hardly an exaggeration. As a young girl, Cynthia had been headstrong and quick-tempered. Once she had been sent home from junior high school for throwing a chair through the window of a classroom. By age fourteen she was smoking marijuana and selling Black Mollies—speed—to classmates. Pregnant at sixteen, she had a child and dropped out of school. She and the child's father had married but separated after a few stormy months, and the father assumed custody of the baby. A second marriage at age eighteen produced Ashley but lasted less than three years.

Cedar Hill police officers soon came to know the overweight young woman with the blue eyes and bleached blond hair by her first name. A lengthy list of unpaid fines for a variety of traffic violations had resulted in her first arrest. Since she was unable to pay the fines, the judge ordered her to jail. Then there had been a series of disorderly conduct calls from neighbors who wearied of the fighting between the volatile Cynthia and her husband. One evening her father-in-law called the station to report that Cynthia was in his front yard threatening to "kick the shit" out of his son who had returned home to escape her harassment.

When she was arrested and charged with possession of drug paraphernalia, she began to think seriously of getting out of Cedar Hill. On several occasions Officer Jack Wallace had questioned Cynthia at length about her involvement in drug activity. At one point, in fact, she had offered to work for him as a snitch, providing information on suspected dealers. Wallace did not need time to think about the offer. "I wouldn't trust that speed whore as far as I could throw her," he told his captain, Phil Hambrick.

She had left Cedar Hill and moved to Dallas, where she lived with friends for a time before deciding to reestablish her relationship with her family. It was her stepbrother who told her of an opening at the Road Runner, where he worked.

And it was Randy who introduced her to Greg Knighten. One afternoon at work she asked if he knew anyone who could get her some marijuana. Randy called Greg.

After being introduced, Cynthia gave Knighten fifty dollars and some strong advice. "Don't fuck me around," she told the youngster. Assuring her that she could trust him, Greg returned later that day with the pot. Pleased to have found a new connection, Cynthia invited him to her apartment after work to share the dope he had bought for her. She even suggested that he bring some of his friends along if he liked.

Thus it was that Cynthia established herself in Midlothian's youthful drug community. Apartment 31 in Oxford Square quickly became a gathering place for a growing stream of teenagers looking for a safe place to meet and get high.

Of all the kids who visited her, Cynthia liked Sparky Knighten best. He seemed shy and lonely, badly in need of a friend, someone he could talk to. Cynthia saw much of herself in Greg. He was being strangled by the rules of his teenage world, just as she had been at his age.

By the end of the summer a strong bond had developed between the rebellious policeman's son and the woman living in apartment 31. Many of the kids who visited Cynthia feared her and were careful not to invite her sudden displays of temper, but Greg felt comfortable in her presence. He dropped in on her at the Road Runner just to say hello. And he began spending more and more time at her apartment, sharing his problems, smoking pot, and occasionally dropping acid.

Cynthia was someone with whom Sparky Knighten could share private thoughts he did not even feel comfortable confiding in Jamie. Cynthia listened sympathetically as he talked of the cruelty imposed on him by his "paranoid" father, and she offered no discouragement when he outlined his plans to quit school, get a job as an auto mechanic, and marry Jamie. "Her parents have already told us we can live in the trailer they have out behind their house," he told her.

In the meantime, though, Cynthia's apartment would have to suffice as Greg's home away from home. For the first time in his life he had found a place where he felt comfortable.

There were others, however, who wished Cynthia Fedrick had never moved to Midlothian.

Among those whom Greg had introduced to Cynthia was Tal South. Eager to be welcomed to her apartment, he had agreed to purchase fifty dollars' worth of marijuana for her in late August. When he did not deliver the drugs or return the money, he learned firsthand how explosive Cynthia's temper could be.

When she began asking where Tal could be found, Jonathan Jobe told her that he had taken Tal to make the buy. They had smoked a couple of joints after their trip to Dallas, Jobe said, and South had told him that he had no intention

Martha Asbury and George Raffield as they posed for their engagement picture. *(photo courtesy of Sherri Prine)*

Midlothian Police Chief Roy Vaughn. *(photo by Pat Stowers)*

Texas Ranger George Turner. *(photo by Pat Stowers)*

Midlothian Police
Lieutenant Billy
Fowler. *(photo by
Pat Stowers)*

Jonathan Jobe.
*(Midlothian High
annual photo)*

Greg Knighten.
*(Midlothian High
annual photo)*

Texas Ranger George Turner *(far right)* instructs searchers outside the Midlothian Police Department. *(photo by Gabe Smith,* Midlothian Reporter)

Richard Goeglein. *(Midlothian High annual photo)*

Tom Knighten, Greg's father. *(Dallas Police Department photo)*

Satanic graffiti on the walls inside the abandoned house. *(photo by Pat Stowers)*

Texas Ranger John Aycock re-enacts Raffield's murder during a blood-splatter experiment. *(photo courtesy of George Turner)*

Cynthia Fedrick.
(Cedar Hill Police Department photo)

Richard Goeglein is returned to jail after a pre-trial hearing. *(photo by Richard Michael Pruitt,* Dallas Morning News)

Greg Knighten, escorted by deputies Jim Underwood *(center)* and Mike Torrigiano, arrives at the Ellis County Courthouse as jury selection gets under way. *(photo by Richard Michael Pruitt,* Dallas Morning News)

Assistant D.A. Kevin Chester. *(photo by Pat Stowers)*

Headstone at grave of George Raffield. *(photo by Pat Stowers)*

of making the promised delivery to Cynthia. "Fuck the bitch," he had said. "She'll never see me again."

Upon hearing the story, Cynthia flew into a rage and threw a chair against the wall of her apartment. A few days later she happened upon Jonathan and Tal at a car wash near the Road Runner. She approached South, screaming. "Look, motherfucker, you either get me my weed or give me my money back, or your ass won't be worth two cents."

It pleased her that both boys seemed genuinely frightened by her tirade.

A rumor began to spread that Cynthia had said she was going to get someone from east Dallas to come to Midlothian and "take care of" South.

Just three days before the opening of school, Tal's parents, aware that their son had been unusually agitated and nervous, demanded an explanation for his behavior. Finally, he broke down, pacing the living room and crying, and said that a woman in town had threatened to kill him because he had kept fifty dollars that belonged to her.

Robert South listened to his son's story and insisted that he was overreacting to the situation. He suggested that the police be notified. At that Tal began shouting wildly, claiming that the entire family would be killed. "She's crazy," he said. "Her brother told me she was after me. I'm afraid to go to school. There's going to be somebody waiting there to kill me."

The following afternoon, a Sunday, Lana South answered the door to find a young woman standing on her porch. Dressed in a wrinkled shift that failed to hide her 170-pound weight, Cynthia introduced herself. "I'm sorry to have to involve you in this," she said in a polite voice, "but your son owes me some money." Robert South joined his wife at the front door and listened to the woman's story.

Cynthia had given Tal fifty dollars to buy drugs, she explained, and he had ripped her off. "My daughter is about to start school," she went on, "and I need the money to buy her some new clothes."

Robert South told her that he and his wife would discuss the matter and get in touch with her. "I'm on my way to work. You can call me at the Road Runner," Cynthia said as she turned and walked from the porch.

There had been nothing threatening about her, no promise of violence. In fact, the elder South had thought her on the verge of tears as she mentioned her daughter's need for new school clothes. Tal, however, was still convinced that she would have him killed and pleaded with his father to pay her the money.

That night Robert South drove to the truck stop, gave Cynthia fifty dollars, and told her not to have any further contact with his son.

One evening just a week after the confrontation on the South porch, a group of teenagers arrived at Cynthia's infamous apartment 31. They had been out cruising, they said, and had just stopped by to say hello. Dale Janson mentioned that Tal was outside in the pickup, afraid to come in.

Cynthia laughed, left the apartment, and walked into the parking lot. Approaching the terrified youngster, who slouched in the darkened truck, she asked, "What in the hell are you doing, sitting out here?"

"I didn't think you would want to see me," Tal said meekly. "They didn't tell me they were coming over here."

"I think the best thing for you to do," Cynthia said, the trace of a smile crossing her face, "is to come on in. Hey, everything's cool now that I have my money back."

Relieved, Tal also smiled. "You scared the shit out of me," he said.

"I intended to," Cynthia replied.

She had hit on an effective method of maintaining control over her growing circle of young friends. The message she had sent out about Tal was the same she had given Greg Knighten that first time they had met: Don't fuck me around.

Cynthia enjoyed the fact that they all seemed even more eager to please her following the Tal South incident. And, she thought, if they needed an occasional reminder that she was the boss, so be it.

In time, even Greg Knighten would be the target of one of her angry outbursts.

On the afternoon of Tuesday, October 20, Cynthia had just returned from picking her daughter up at school when Kyle Royal appeared at her door. Excitedly he entered the apartment and told her he had something he knew she'd been wanting.

Sitting in her living room, he said he had stolen a stereo system and needed to sell it as quickly as possible.

"How much?"

"Five hundred dollars. It's worth a helluva lot more."

"Where in the hell am I going to get five hundred dollars?" Cynthia asked sarcastically.

"You can pay it out," Kyle said.

"Do you have it with you?"

At the same time, Royal's mother was on the phone to the Midlothian Police Department, reporting the theft of a stereo system she had recently leased.

By nightfall, rumor was on the street that Kyle had stolen his own mother's stereo and sold it to Cynthia.

Among those who heard the rumor was George Raffield. He passed it on to Lieutenant Fowler when he reported in that evening. George volunteered to try to find out if the stolen merchandise was, in fact, in Cynthia's apartment.

His chance came the following afternoon.

He was returning from Dallas where Greg had purchased a dime bag of marijuana when Greg suggested they drop by Cynthia's. He was in a bad mood, he explained, and wanted to smoke a joint before going home.

As punishment for having skipped school on Monday, Greg had been sent to detention and had remained all day in a small room not much wider than a hallway. Late in the afternoon a school secretary came in and instructed him to report to the office of the school counselor, Perry Elkins.

It would be Knighten's third visit to Elkins since school opened. And, as in their previous sessions, it was Elkins who did most of the talking. He asked why Greg had skipped school, reminded him again of the importance of an education, and encouraged him to talk about his plans for the future.

During most of their twenty-minute visit Greg was unresponsive, slumped in his chair with a bored look on his face. Finally, after several minutes of silence, he looked across the desk at the counselor. "I'm tired of other people telling me what to do and when to do it," Greg said. "All I want to do is get a job and get married. I'm going to quit school at the end of this semester."

"How are you going to support yourself?"

"I'm going to be a mechanic."

The counselor nodded, and maintained his practiced, even tone of voice. "Being a mechanic takes a good deal of training," he observed.

Greg made no response.

"Look," Elkins continued, "if you decide you want to make some changes in your life, come back and see me before you do anything. Let's talk about it. I'd like to help you if I can."

Knighten rose from his chair and began walking toward the door. "I don't need your help," he said.

When Greg and George arrived at apartment 31, they found Anna Roscoe sitting at the kitchen table talking with Cynthia. "Party time," Greg said as he waved the plastic bag and sat down on the couch to roll a joint. He did not seem to notice that Anna appeared less than pleased to see him and George. Nor did he pay any attention when she followed Cynthia back to the bedroom.

"Do you know that guy out there with Sparky?" Anna asked.

"Not really," Cynthia admitted. "I met him once when he came by here to pick Sparky up. They're evidently good friends. Why?"

Keeping her voice to a whisper, Anna told Cynthia about the slapping incident George had been involved in with her boyfriend, Dale Janson. "Dale says the guy's a narc," Anna said. "He's sure of it."

Cynthia stared at the girl for several seconds but said nothing. She had heard the same unfounded accusations made about a lot of her friends. It was just part of the dopers' paranoia. Still, she decided, it would be a good idea to get to know this kid named George Moore a little better.

From the living room she heard Greg's voice. "You guys are missing out," he yelled.

Anna took only one quick hit off the joint Greg held out to her before abruptly announcing that she had to go home. She did not even bother to say good-bye to George as she hurried out the door.

For the next half-hour Cynthia sat in her living room studying Greg's friend, watching his movements, his reactions to the conversation, and how he handled the joint when it was passed to him. He seemed friendly enough, asking her questions about her daughter and talking about how much he liked kids. And he joined in the laughter as Greg, feeling the effects of the pot, began to clown around. Still, there was something that troubled Cynthia. He did look a little older than most of the senior students she knew. And his pickup was nicer than most of the kids' trucks. Maybe, she thought, Anna's warning had alerted her own suspicions.

Proof or not, she had no intention of taking any risks. Already her mother had hinted that if Cynthia got into any more trouble with the law, particularly if it involved drugs, she would take action to gain custody of her daughter.

When George excused himself to go to the bathroom, Cynthia had Greg follow her into her bedroom and closed the door. "You need to watch out for that guy," she said.

"What do you mean?"

"Anna told me he's a narc. And, dammit, he looks like one to me."

"Aw, bullshit," Greg argued. "He's cool. Hell, he smokes dope with me all the time."

"That doesn't make him cool, you dumb little shit. I'm

not even sure he inhales when he smokes a joint." Cynthia was getting angry. "No eighteen-year-old needs a shave by late in the afternoon. And look at his truck; what kid can afford one that new?"

"You're wrong. I know the dude. He's a friend of mine. Anna's all fucked up, just like Dale Janson. I don't like people spreading crap about my friends."

Seeing that she was getting nowhere trying to reason with Greg, Cynthia grabbed the teenager by the shoulders and shoved him against the wall. "Now listen to me," she said, her voice turning to a low growl. "You do whatever you fucking want to do. I don't care. But keep me out of it. Don't ever bring him back to my house again, understand?"

"You're full of shit," Greg said, recovering from the shock of being pushed.

"I don't want you here anymore, either," Cynthia answered. "Don't come back here . . . ever."

With that she turned and walked out of the bedroom, leaving Greg to regain his composure. Cynthia entered the living room to find George leaning over her new stereo, looking at something on the back side of the turntable.

"Hey, this is really nice," he said.

Goddammit, Cynthia thought, Anna was right. Dale was right. The sonuvabitch was checking the stereo for a serial number.

She smiled. "Yeah, I just got it."

Behind her, Greg emerged from the bedroom and looked at George. "We've got to go," he said. "I told Jamie we'd come by the Dairy Queen before I went home."

As he followed George out the door of the apartment, Greg turned and shot an angry look at Cynthia. She wasn't certain if he was mad at her or at himself.

11

Long before the population growth created the demand for fast-food pizzas and microwaved hamburgers, the Dairy Queen reigned as the social center of Cedar Hill. In the morning it is still a gathering place for retired older men who come to swap stories over coffee and sweet rolls. In the evening it is the lone option for families with kids who want to give Mom a respite from the kitchen.

Most afternoons, however, it takes on the loud, boisterous character of the community's teenage hangout. Located just across Highway 67 from the junior high and high schools, it is the first stop for youngsters free from another day's classwork. It is then, while the high-pitched teenage voices beat a steady drum of noise, that adults stay away.

Since the 5:00 to 9:00 P.M. shift is the busiest, owner Jerry Reeves usually has at least five employees—most of them high school students—behind the counter.

Just a month earlier Jackie Cadenhead, looking for a job for her fifteen-year-old daughter, had stopped in and asked if he had any openings. A few days later she was back with her daughter, Jamie, who filled out an application and talked with the assistant manager. Before they left that afternoon, Reeves had agreed to hire her.

Now, though, he was questioning that decision. While Jamie was personable and a good worker, Reeves disliked the dark-haired youth who regularly came in the early evening to visit with her during her break. Jerry Reeves had developed a near fanatical attitude toward the drug problem and had made it clear that dopers were not welcome in his restaurant. Certain that the boy who stopped in to see Jamie was often high, the owner was angered by his presence.

Unhappy with this situation, Reeves had told Steve Womack, his assistant manager, that he was planning to let Jamie go.

Womack had persuaded his boss to think it over for a few days before making a final decision. Reeves had reluctantly agreed to wait until after he and his wife returned from a weekend trip to the horse races in Hot Springs, Arkansas. In truth, however, Jerry Reeves's mind was already made up. When Jamie Cadenhead reported to work the following Monday afternoon, he would tell her she was no longer needed.

Though Womack had to admit that his boss's decision was, in all likelihood, justified, he liked Jamie personally. At twenty-three, he demanded a no-nonsense approach from the youngsters who worked for him but also felt it important to temper the demands of the job with understanding and friendship.

Jamie, like several other teenagers who worked at the Dairy Queen, felt comfortable confiding her problems to Womack. She told him about constant conflicts with her mother and of the difficulties her boyfriend was having with his parents.

Steve, too, had noticed on several occasions that Greg Knighten appeared to be high when he came into the restaurant. When he finally asked Jamie about it, she expressed concern that Greg's problem might be out of control and that he needed help. She insisted that she had done everything she could to persuade him to quit using.

Womack, then, was someone the youngsters trusted, and he seemed to understand the things that were important to teenagers. When, for instance, Jamie explained that the lone earring that dangled beneath her hair was a gift from her boyfriend, symbolizing that they were going steady, he had made no issue of the rule that employees were not allowed to wear dangling earrings or loose bracelets.

Jamie was waiting on a customer at the drive-through window when Greg and George entered the restaurant that Wednesday evening, ordered soft drinks at the counter, and went to a booth to wait for her. A few minutes later, after informing Womack that she was taking her break, Jamie joined them.

Normally, Steve Womack would have paid them no mind, continuing with his business between the counter and the kitchen. Since he had promised the owner that he would keep an eye on Jamie, however, he occasionally glanced in the direction of the booth where the three youngsters sat, talking and sipping soft drinks.

When he made rounds of the restaurant to make sure the tables had been cleared, Womack stopped at the booth and asked Jamie if she was keeping track of the time. She looked at her watch and told him she still had a few minutes remaining on her fifteen-minute break.

Steve nodded at Greg and George, then returned to work. A few minutes later he saw George head out the door, walking through the parking lot toward his pickup. Jamie and Greg, however, were standing in the small hallway leading to the telephone and rest rooms.

Womack had returned to the kitchen when Jamie entered, crying.

"What's wrong?" he asked.

"I can't talk about it."

"And I can't have you waiting on customers while you're upset like this," Womack said. "Did you and Greg have a fight?"

She shook her head and walked toward him. "You know that I smoke pot sometimes," she said.

"So?"

"Well, Sparky just told me that he's found out that guy he was in here with is a narc."

"What do you mean?"

"A narc, an undercover policeman who goes to our high school," she said, the tears coming more freely. "He's gone over to Dallas a bunch of times with us to buy marijuana. And he's seen me smoking pot."

Though they had never been introduced, Steve had seen George Moore in the Dairy Queen with Knighten on several occasions and had never considered the possibility that he might be anything other than just another student. "Hey," he said, trying to make light of the situation, "he seems to be your friend. What's the problem?"

"I'm afraid I'm going to get busted."

"What are you going to do about it?"

"I don't know what to do. And I don't know what Sparky's going to do," she said, "but I'm scared."

After George dropped him off in front of his house, Greg went straight to his room and shut the door. The composure he had maintained on the drive back to Midlothian was gone. He turned on the radio but paid the music little mind. He paced the room, mentally replaying the earlier conversation with Cynthia. It had upset him far more than he let on. Then there had been the frightened reaction from Jamie when he confided his suspicions about George. Suddenly Greg was locked in a nightmare, feeling angry and betrayed.

Needing someone to talk with, he desperately wished that Cynthia had a telephone. Instead, he dialed Jonathan Jobe's number and cursed to himself when Jobe's younger sister answered and said Jonathan wasn't at home.

After putting his finger on the button to break the connection, he called Randy Marcott. He would see if Cynthia's brother shared her concerns about George Moore.

By the time Randy answered, Greg had composed himself. "What are you doing?" he asked casually.

For several minutes they talked about the auto accident Randy had been involved in just ten days earlier.

"Jamie and I were going to come see you in the hospital," Greg said, "but we couldn't get a ride. You okay?"

"Yeah."

"When are you coming back to school?"

"The doctor says it'll be another month."

"Lucky you," Greg said, then shifted the conversation to the real purpose of his call. "You know George, don't you?"

"Yeah, the dude with the red pickup."

"The motherfucker's a narc." When Randy did not immediately reply, Greg knew that he was unaware of Cynthia's suspicions.

"I've got to do something about it," Knighten added.

"How the hell do you know he's a narc?"

"Just look at him," Greg replied. "Fuck, you've seen him." Then he began to parrot Cynthia's observations. "Man, I've got to do something," he said.

"Like what?" Randy asked.

Before Knighten could answer, Randy's mother stuck her head into his room and told him to get off the phone. He argued that it was only nine o'clock, but she insisted.

At the same time, Jamie, off work and waiting for her father to pick her up, was talking with JoAnne Dupree from a pay phone at the edge of the restaurant parking lot. Still upset, she related to her friend what Greg had said. "He says George Moore is a narc. They were over at Cynthia's before they came by here," she said, "and she took Sparky into the bedroom and told him. She was really pissed. She slammed him against the wall and called him all kinds of names."

Although she was aware that Jamie was scared and upset, JoAnne could not help but smile at the mental picture of Cynthia taking out her anger on her friend's boyfriend, whom she considered a smart-mouthed bore.

The following day Cynthia would be even more upset.

On Thursday morning she answered a knock at her door to find Lieutenant Fowler, accompanied by patrolmen Don Blanton and Jesus Chao, standing on the porch. "Ma'am,"

Fowler said, "we're investigating the theft of a stereo, which we have reason to believe is in your possession.

"We've had a young man named Kyle Royal under surveillance for the past several days, and he was seen entering your apartment with a stereo yesterday." Reaching into his coat pocket, he produced a waiver-to-search form.

"What's this?" Cynthia asked.

"It authorizes us to search your apartment for the stolen merchandise," Fowler explained. From the doorway he could already see the stereo.

"I didn't know it was stolen," Cynthia said. "He just said he would sell it to me. I don't want to get in any trouble."

"Ma'am, all we want to do is return the stereo to the owner," Fowler said. He explained that if she would sign the waiver to search they would take the stereo and be on their way.

"Why do you want to search my apartment?" she asked.

"We don't," Fowler said. "The consent form is just procedure. All we want is the stereo."

Cynthia studied the lieutenant's face for several seconds, signed the form, then backed from the doorway. "That's it over there," she said. "I swear I didn't know it was stolen."

"We understand," Fowler said.

Standing in the living room, Cynthia watched silently as Blanton and Chao carried the stolen merchandise from the apartment.

As she stood at the window, watching the patrol car pull out of the parking lot, Cynthia lit a cigarette with shaking hands and began to curse. She didn't believe for a minute that Kyle Royal had been seen entering her apartment with the stereo. Hell, she wasn't stupid. It was that goddam George Moore. That fucking narc. Now she was sure.

Looking at her watch as she angrily paced about the apartment, she began counting the hours until Sparky Knighten would be home from school.

At the high school, Jimmy Lee Parish, a fifteen-year-old freshman, stood near the soft drink machine drinking a

Coke during the morning break. Less than ten feet away, Greg Knighten was talking with Jonathan Jobe and Richard Goeglein. Their girlfriends were with them, listening as Greg spoke in hurried sentences punctuated by wild gestures.

The fact that Knighten was so animated gained Parish's attention. Instead of wandering among the crowd, his normal routine during break periods, Parish remained near the vending machines, pretending to study the selections. Although he wore a hearing aid, he was able to pick up pieces of the conversation.

". . . I'm telling you, the sonuvabitch is a narc," Greg was saying. "I'm going to kill him."

Parish drained his Coke, tossed the can into a trash basket, and turned away. Greg Knighten, as usual, was trying to stir up something, he thought.

After Parish walked away, Greg began pleading for Jobe and Goeglein to come to his house that evening to talk about what to do about George Moore.

"I'll tell you one fucking thing," Goeglein said just before the bell rang, summoning students back to class. "I'm not going to risk my life by getting involved in killing some cop."

"Yeah, well, I don't want to get my ass in trouble for drugs," Greg shot back.

For the remainder of the school day, Greg was less disruptive than usual. The class clown was not in the mood to entertain; he sat through his classes in a daze. When the final bell rang, he did not even bother to go by Jamie's locker and tell her good-bye. Instead, he hurried directly to the school bus. He needed to get home, to be alone, to think.

He had been in his room, stretched out on his bed, only a few minutes when the phone rang.

Cynthia, after picking up her daughter at school, had driven to the Road Runner to make the call. As soon as Greg answered, she launched into a tirade about her visit from the police earlier in the day.

"If that doesn't tell you that your asshole friend is a

fucking cop," she screamed, "you're a real dumb shit. He's got to be the one who told them about the stereo, goddammit. And now he's going to get us all in trouble. I ought to kick your ass."

The curses and threats stung Knighten. On top of everything else, the valued trust Cynthia had once had in him had been destroyed. Suddenly the person he had felt most comfortable confiding in was talking to him like just another one of the kids who dropped by her apartment. Now he, too, was afraid of her, and it was all George's fault. George Moore had ruined everything. Greg wished he had never met the bastard.

It was several seconds before Greg spoke, his voice weak and barely audible. Cynthia sensed he had begun to cry. "I just can't believe it," he said.

"Jesus, Sparky," she said in disgust, "you better quit messing around and do something about the guy."

"I will," he replied. "I'm damn sure not going to let him bust me and Jamie. I'll take care of it. Don't worry about it."

"By God, if you don't," Cynthia yelled, "I'm going to." Then she slammed the phone back into its cradle.

Nelda Knighten had just begun clearing the dinner dishes from the table when Jonathan and Richard arrived and asked to see Greg. "I think he's in his room," she said as she walked toward the kitchen. She failed to notice that Richard was carrying something beneath his jacket.

At the end of the hallway, Greg, having heard them arrive, stood, and waved them toward his bedroom.

As soon as they entered, he shut the door and turned up the radio to muffle their conversation. Though Greg rarely smoked at home, he puffed on a Marlboro. Immediately, he began to describe the phone call he had received from Cynthia.

Pacing about in the small room, Greg was like a lawyer frantically arguing his case in front of a two-man jury. The fact that the police had taken the stereo from Cynthia's apartment, he said, was the final proof of George's guilt. George had used him. Hell, he was probably responsible for some of the guys over on Polk Street getting busted. And soon George would be busting him and his friends.

"If I don't do something about it," Greg said, "he's going to fuck us all."

"What are you going to do?" Jobe asked.

"I'm going to kill the sonuvabitch," Greg said.

Jonathan glanced over at Richard. This wasn't Sparky Knighten playing big shot with wild talk and outrageous ideas; Sparky was scared. And he was serious.

"How are you going to do it?" Jonathan asked.

"Shit, I don't know," Greg said, then launched into a jumbled story he had heard about how mercury was immediately fatal if swallowed. There was mercury in the science lab at school, wasn't there? Maybe they could steal some and put it in George's food. It would look like an accident.

"Why not put a bomb in his pickup?" Richard suggested.

"The best thing to do," Jonathan said, "is to take him over to Polk Street and stab him. Leave him there and let the cops think some of the dope dealers killed him."

"Maybe I can get a gun," Greg added.

"Where?" Richard asked.

"I can get one," Greg said, sitting down on the corner of his bed. "I can get one easy."

Jobe silently studied Knighten for several seconds. Across the room, Richard, who had said little since their arrival, pulled a Ouija board from beneath his jacket and placed it on Greg's weightlifting bench.

"What the fuck are you doing?" Greg asked.

"I'm going to see what Terry thinks about this," Richard said as he removed a small black heart-shaped amulet from his pocket.

Richard had told Jobe about Terry's heart shortly after they had become blood brothers, how it allowed him to communicate with the spirit of the girl who had given it to him; how she could predict the future for up to three days and answer his questions. One day, he said—after he learned more about the techniques—he hoped to use it to raise Terry from the dead.

Placing the heart in the middle of the board, just below

the stylized alphabet, Richard knelt, barely resting his fingers on the amulet, and closed his eyes. Jonathan and Greg looked on in silence as the amulet began to move in a figure-eight pattern, slowly at first, then more rapidly.

When it slowed, finally returning to its original position, Richard waited several seconds, then posed his first question.

"Is George Moore a cop?" he asked.

The plastic heart slowly slid several inches to the left, coming to rest on the letter C. Richard's fingers then followed as it made a weaving trail across the board, stopping on the letter O. And, finally, the amulet found its way to the letter P.: COP.

"Should Greg kill him?" Richard asked.

His arms jerked slightly, as if an electrical current had suddenly surged through them. Slowly, the heart began to move. It slid to the right, then seemed to weave aimlessly about on the board before it began spelling out its answer: TROUBLE.

Richard stood and looked at Greg. "This," he said, "is some heavy shit."

"I know," Knighten answered.

As Jobe drove Goeglein home, the music of Slayer blared from the tape deck that Greg had installed for him. Away from Knighten, their mood had immediately lifted. They had crossed the railroad tracks and entered the downtown area before either even mentioned the conversation that had taken place in Greg's bedroom.

"What if the dude's not really a cop?" Goeglein said.

"Didn't Terry say he was?"

Richard shrugged. "Yeah."

Jonathan reached over and turned the music up even louder. "Hey, fuck him, he's a nerd and deserves to die anyway," he shouted.

"'Scream till you like it,'" Richard yelled back at him, borrowing the words from one of his favorite heavy metal videos.

"Damn right," Jobe answered, holding up his right index finger and pinky in the satanic salute his friend had taught him. "Scream till you fucking like it."

Whether Greg ever carried out his threat against George Moore or not, the talk of actually plotting someone's death had a dark, arousing effect on the youngsters.

Jonathan was still feeling a rush of excitement as he headed back toward the Camelot Estates after dropping Richard off. The mood was spoiled, however, by the sight of the flashing lights of a Midlothian police car in his rearview mirror as he turned from the downtown area onto Mountain Peak Road.

By the time he arrived home, Jobe was no longer concerned with Greg Knighten's talk of committing murder. His greatest worry was that his parents would find out that he had gotten another speeding ticket.

In town, teenager Grant Donley walked into the parking lot of a local restaurant to see if his mother had arrived to pick him up. He had been working since five o'clock, and though his mother had not yet arrived, he decided to wait for her outside, enjoying the cool night air.

Walking to the corner of the building, he saw Cynthia Fedrick standing near a car talking with two men.

Earlier in the evening, she had come into the restaurant with her daughter, looking for Kyle Royal. Since Kyle and Grant often spent time together, she thought Grant might know where he was. "I haven't seen him today," Grant said.

Cynthia was turning to leave when she saw George Moore standing alone in front of one of the video games in the back of the restaurant. "See that guy," she said, pointing at George. "The asshole's a narc. Because of him I damn near got busted today over that stereo Kyle sold me."

Now, at ten o'clock, she was still upset. Seeing Grant standing in the parking lot, she called him over. As he neared the car, he saw that the men she was talking with were Jay Little and Don Castle. He had seen them a couple of times when he and Kyle visited Cynthia's apartment.

"You know where George Moore is?" Cynthia asked.

Grant shook his head. "He left around eight," he said. "I haven't seen him since then. What's up?"

"We're going to get him," Cynthia said.

12

On Friday morning, October 23, the students in Brenda Carrigan's first-period biology class were, like most of those arriving at Midlothian High School, in a festive mood, already anticipating the excitement of a trip to Red Oak for that evening's football game. In those final minutes before the bell rang to signal the beginning of the period, the roomful of freshmen and sophomores chatted enthusiastically about the upcoming pep rally. Several of the girls were discussing dates they had made for the game and what they would wear. A few of the boys were busily making frantic last-minute arrangements to get to the game.

Freshman Guy Grigson, a member of the B-team who looked forward to the day when he would earn a spot on the varsity, was one of the late arrivals, settling into his desk just a few minutes before the bell. Greg Knighten, who sat near to him, was blankly staring down at his books. Generally one of the most boisterous in the class, today he was sullen.

Though they were not close friends, Guy had known Knighten since they were both youngsters living in Duncanville. While he liked Greg, secretly admiring his talent for drawing laughter with his classroom clowning,

Guy had made no real effort to become close friends. Greg openly admitted that he was a doper—once even asking if Guy wanted to go with him to Dallas to buy marijuana—and Grigson was determined that his coaches not get the impression he associated with anyone suspected of being involved with drugs. Being friendly with Greg Knighten, the only person he knew who had ever received a failing grade in P.E. class, would not help him one day make the varsity football team. And, too, his parents, aware of the problems Tom and Nelda Knighten had had with their son in Duncanville, had quietly warned him against associating with Greg.

That, however, didn't prevent Guy from being friendly in class.

"You going to the game?" he asked, leaning over toward Greg.

"I've got something else to do," Knighten replied. Guy immediately sensed anger in Greg's voice.

"What's the matter?"

"There's an undercover cop in school," Greg said, not even bothering to look up. "A guy I thought was my friend."

Guy was aware that Greg had developed a friendship with a senior who had recently moved to town and, though he had not met him and didn't know his name, he assumed Knighten was referring to the new student who drove the red pickup.

"How do you know?"

"Dammit, I just know," Greg said sharply. "And I'm going to do something about it."

Feeling a sudden rush of discomfort, Guy Grigson decided not to pursue the conversation further. He was relieved when the teacher entered the room and called the class to order.

During the morning break, Greg joined Jamie, Jonathan, and Richard at one of the circular tables in the school alcove. While Richard sipped on a Dr Pepper, the foursome was unusually subdued. Jamie, still upset over the Wednesday night incident in Cedar Hill, held Greg's hand and said little except to mention that she was going to call her boss at the Dairy Queen after school and tell him she was sick. She needed to get to work on the decorations for Saturday's party.

It wasn't until the bell rang, signaling students back to classes, that Greg spoke. As he looked across the table at Jobe and Goeglein, his eyes were cold and flat.

"I've got a plan," he said.

Goeglein's only response was to nod, then drain what remained of his soft drink as he rose. Jonathan gathered his books. "Later," he said.

Greg and Jamie were still seated at the table when the others hurried away toward their next class.

Across town, Cynthia Fedrick also had a plan. It had been a lousy week—she had lost her job at the Road Runner, there was the incident with the stereo, then her confrontation with Knighten—and she was determined to do something to lift her spirits. She had a final paycheck coming and was going to use every penny of it to escape from her miseries.

She had wakened early, prepared breakfast for her daughter, dressed her, dropped her off at school, and arranged for her mother to pick her up in the afternoon. That done, Cynthia returned to the apartment, telephoned her mother to ask that she pick her daughter up after school, then went back to bed. Jay Little and Don Castle, two twenty-one-year-old construction workers she had met at the Road Runner and had talked with the night before, wouldn't be arriving until the middle of the afternoon. They had, in recent weeks, begun to visit her apartment regularly to smoke pot and listen to music. Jay had told her he knew a place where they could score some crank.

Cynthia had been awake, dressed, and anxiously pacing the apartment for over an hour when the men finally arrived. "I had to wait to get my fucking paycheck," Jay said apologetically.

Having recently moved to Midlothian from Quinlan, Texas, Little had previously purchased crank from a dealer in the small community of Cash, just six miles north of his hometown. "The guy's got good shit and his price is right," he had promised.

"Let's get going," Cynthia said, making no attempt to hide her impatience. "I've been cooped up here all day, waiting on you assholes."

Jay slid behind the wheel of Cynthia's battered Valiant and drove to the truck stop where they cashed their paychecks.

It was just after three-thirty when Little parked in front of a small trailer house on the outskirts of Cash, a tiny community thirty-five miles northeast of Dallas, collected money from the others, and went inside. In minutes he was back with an eight-ball of crank—three and a quarter grams. They headed toward nearby Greenville, stopping at a roadside grocery to buy distilled water, cotton balls, and a canned soft drink.

Then they found an isolated spot in a parking lot behind a shopping mall to enjoy their purchase.

Cynthia emptied the soft drink and spread a thin layer of cotton over the can's concave bottom. She then placed a small piece of the crystallized methamphetamine on the cotton and carefully poured the distilled water over it. While waiting for the crank to dissolve she removed a package of disposable syringes from her purse and drew the clouded liquid into each of them.

The rush from the drug was quick and effective. Even before they pulled back onto the highway leading south toward Dallas the mood of the three travelers had lifted dramatically. The quiet tension that had prevailed during the trip to Cash was quickly replaced by frantic laughter. At times all three talked at once, drowning out the knocking of the worn engine of Cynthia's car as they made their way toward home.

Energized by the "bump" she had taken in the parking lot, Cynthia began talking rapidly of her plans for making her apartment more attractive. There were, she said, some things she wanted to pick up at a south Dallas apartment she had shared with a friend before moving to Oxford Square.

She directed Little to a run-down apartment complex and urged him and Castle to come inside and help her get her belongings. First, though, all three took another bump.

By the time they had loaded several knickknacks, a wall clock, some dried flowers, and stereo speakers into the trunk of the Valiant they were all feeling the giddy sense of carefree adventure that is a by-product of the drug they had injected.

The five o'clock traffic, Cynthia said, was building. There was a cheap motel just around the corner. Why not rent a room for an hour or so?

In the motel they took their third bump of the afternoon, and by the time they ventured back onto the interstate for the final leg of their trip home, the flow of cars traveling southward had thinned and was moving steadily.

"Now," Cynthia said coyly, "aren't you glad I suggested we make that little rest stop?"

Sitting in the front seat with Jay, she was feeling better than she had in weeks. For the moment her troubles were far away, shielded by the chemically induced sense of well-being.

As they neared Midlothian, the late afternoon sky dimmed to a dull, overcast gray and the newscaster on the car radio was warning of the possibility of evening showers.

Cynthia laughed. "I ain't gonna let it rain on my party," she said. "Not tonight." If they paced themselves and some sonuvabitch didn't get greedy, the plastic bag in her purse still contained enough little magic rocks to keep all three of them happy until the wee hours of the morning.

Don Castle sat in the back seat, his eyes glazed and a crooked smile frozen on his face.

Before returning to her apartment, Cynthia wanted to stop by the house of a girlfriend she had worked with at the Road Runner. She owed Lindsey Tounds thirty dollars and had agreed to pay her with some of the crank.

Jay and Don waited in the driveway as Cynthia entered the small brick house on South Fifth. Across the street, the men could see a Midlothian school bus parked in front of the football stadium field house, waiting to take the team to Red Oak.

Richard and Jonathan had not seen Greg when school was dismissed. After sitting through homemaking, their last class of the day, the boys had waited as Becky and Gina McLemore put books away in their lockers, then went directly to Jonathan's pickup. Relieved that another school week had ended and two days of freedom loomed ahead, they all squeezed into the cab of the truck and drove to the Goeglein house to watch rock videos on television.

It was a little after five when the telephone rang. Jonathan answered, placing his hand over one ear to block out the blaring music. It took him a few seconds to realize that the whispering voice on the other end of the line was that of Knighten. "Okay," Greg began, "this is the plan. . . ."

For several minutes Jobe listened as Knighten talked in rapid, breathless sentences. Then Jonathan motioned to Richard. "Greg wants to talk to you," he yelled over the music.

Richard glanced over at Gina, rolling his eyes. She moved across the room to stand near him as he took the receiver. "What's going on?" Richard answered.

Again the conversation was one-sided, with Richard listening as Greg outlined his plan. Gina, leaning against the living room wall with her arms folded, did not take her eyes off Richard as he went through a variety of facial expressions.

"Where the fuck did you get the gun?" she heard him ask. "Is it registered?"

By the time Richard hung up, Jobe was sitting with Becky on the living room floor, his attention again focused on the television. Richard walked across the room and stared down at Jonathan. "Greg wants us to meet him at his house at six-thirty," he said.

Gina McLemore, upset by what she had overheard, glared at Richard. "I want to know what's going on," she demanded.

Richard looked at her for several seconds, then nodded in the direction of his bedroom.

Seated on the side of his bed, he sighed heavily. "Greg says he's going to kill this guy who's an undercover cop," he began.

"Who?"

"That dude named George who he's been hanging around with lately."

For a moment Gina considered the possibility that it was another of Richard's bizarre jokes, but the strained look on his face told her it wasn't. "I heard you say something about a gun," she said.

"His dad keeps a thirty-eight revolver in the house," Richard said. "Greg's got it."

Gina was speechless, suddenly cold and scared. She knew Greg Knighten had an explosive temper and was prone to do crazy, impulsive things. He had been that way even when he was her boyfriend back in the seventh grade. But this was too far out, even for Greg.

"Listen, Richard," she finally said, "this scares me. Is he really serious about this?"

Goeglein stood up and broke into a smile. "Naw," he said. "Hey, you know how Greg is. He's just talking."

Richard's lack of concern was reassuring. She did know how Greg was, always lying, talking big, trying to impress people. He had told everyone how his dad was going to get him a new car as soon as he turned sixteen, but his birthday had come and gone, and he was still riding the bus to school. Gina, like everyone else, had learned to dismiss most of what Greg Knighten said.

By the time Richard's mother arrived, they were listening to a new tape by a heavy metal group called Grim Reaper. It was a few minutes after six when Gina said she had to be going. She was supposed to watch her baby sister while her parents went out to dinner.

She heard Richard tell his mother that he was going to spend the night with Jonathan as they walked out the back door.

It wasn't until they dropped her off in front of her house

that Gina again began to feel uneasy about the earlier conversation. "Where are you guys going?"

Richard grinned. "We're going to go pick up Greg," he said. "I'll call you later."

Nelda Knighten strongly believed in the importance of her family sitting down together for dinner. It helped promote unity, she felt, and provided one of the few opportunities for all of them to share their thoughts, talk about any problems they might have, and just let each other know how their day had been. Many of her friends' families kept such hectic schedules, particularly during the school year, that they were rarely together. With parents working and kids in and out, homes sometimes took on the atmosphere of a hotel. Nelda worked hard at making sure the Knighten family spent some time together each day, even if it was just for half an hour around the dining room table for the evening meal.

On that Friday evening, Greg was more talkative than usual. Though it was still a week before Halloween, his girlfriend was planning a party and hayride for Saturday night, and he had volunteered to help her with the decorations. He talked about the old-fashioned party that would begin at the Cadenheads' country home, then proceed along the back roads in a hay-filled trailer to be pulled by Jamie's father's pickup. Greg asked his father if he knew where he might get some pumpkins that could be carved into jack-o'-lanterns.

He also mentioned that his friend, George Moore, was going to stop by later and give him a ride out to the Cadenhead house so he could help Jamie with preparations.

In town, George was feeling far from festive. He had seen Knighten briefly that afternoon, just before he got on the school bus for the ride home. Greg had asked if he would stop by at around seven. He had something "exciting" he wanted to tell George about.

Normally, with several hours to kill and nothing to do, George would have taken an out-of-the-way route back to his apartment and remained there, escaping his role as a high school student for a few hours before traveling to the Knighten house. But for the past couple of weeks he and Martha had been arguing more than usual. The move to the new job in Cedar Hill, being away from her family, and spending so much time alone had begun to wear on her. George had tried to reassure her that he would be working a more routine schedule soon and talked of the vacation they would take together once his undercover assignment was completed. Such promises would calm the situation for a time, but within a matter of days the old complaints would surface. More and more of their time together was spent in tense silence, as each tried to find privacy in the small apartment they shared.

Over the weekend, George had thought, he would make it up to her. They would do whatever Martha wanted. He had already told her that Lieutenant Fowler had instructed him to stay away from Midlothian on Saturday and Sunday. They could see a movie, maybe stop by to visit her parents, then go out to eat. Already, he had invited his sisters and their husbands to drop by on Saturday for a relaxing evening of dinner, talk, and listening to music.

So he had decided to remain in Midlothian until it was time for his trip out to Greg's house, thereby avoiding another confrontation.

George drove around town for a while, waving at other students weaving along the same route to pass the time before going to Red Oak for the game. Soon bored with the aimless cruising, he headed for the Pizza Inn. He had plenty of time to eat and play the video games before picking up Knighten. His favorites were the machines lining the wall in the far corner of the restaurant. One was called All Points Bulletin, the other Dead Angle. Both allowed the player to act out the role of a police officer exchanging gunfire with cartoon criminals.

It was fifteen minutes before seven when he went to the pay phone and checked in with Billy Fowler. As usual, Fowler did most of the talking.

"You got anything going tonight?"

"Naw, I'm just going out to pick Sparky up in a few minutes and mess around with him for a while."

"We're going over to Waxahachie for dinner," Fowler said, "but we'll be in early. Give me a call when you get home." Raffield smiled at the reminder. It was the same one he heard from the lieutenant every time he telephoned him.

"I'm not planning on staying out late," George added.

Tom Knighten was watching television when Jonathan and Richard knocked and asked if Greg was home. Paying the youngsters little mind, he told them his son was in his bedroom.

They entered to find Greg sitting on his bed, already wearing a jacket. "Are your parents home?" he asked Jobe.

"I didn't see the car when we drove by."

"Let's go over to your house," Greg said.

As they walked through the living room, Greg asked his father to tell George to pick him up at Jonathan's house.

Tom Knighten didn't look up from the television. "Be in by midnight," he said as the boys walked out the front door.

A gentle mist had begun falling, and the boys broke into a jog as they hurried toward Jobe's house. Instead of going inside, they went into the garage and pulled the door down behind them.

Greg immediately lit a joint and began passing it around. As he unbuttoned the flannel shirt he wore as a jacket, Jobe and Goeglein saw that he had the black .38 tucked into the front of his jeans. He had, he explained, taken it from its hiding place in a stack of towels in his parents' bathroom. They also noticed that Greg appeared to be wearing several T-shirts.

Knighten drew on the joint with a deep hissing sound, then began pacing back and forth on the concrete floor of the darkening garage as he outlined his plan. "When George gets here," he began, "I'm going to tell him I've set up a crank buy and that we're supposed to meet a guy at this place I know out in the country. When we get him out there I'm going to kill his ass."

Neither Jobe nor Goeglein said anything, standing mesmerized as Greg spoke matter-of-factly about what he intended to do.

"Richard," he continued, "I need you to go with me."

"Fuck you, man."

"You've got to," Greg said. "I'm not sure I can do it by myself." A tone of pleading had crept into his voice. "I need you."

Goeglein shook his head, but Greg ignored his protest and continued outlining the plan. "You wait about thirty minutes," he said to Jobe. "Then drive out and pick us up."

"You're not really serious about this," Jobe responded.

"I goddam sure am. Wait about thirty minutes; then drive out to 875 and pick us up. We'll be watching for you. That's all you've got to do."

"What if George doesn't show up?" Jobe asked.

"Then I'll hunt the motherfucker down," Greg said, a look of grim determination fixed on his face.

"This is bullshit, man," Richard said.

"Dammit," Greg repeated, "you've got to help me. I need you."

Richard lifted the garage door and walked out toward the street. Greg and Jonathan followed and saw George Moore's red pickup turning onto Sir Lancelot Circle. It was seven o'clock. He was right on time.

As Greg and Richard approached George's truck, Jobe turned and walked toward his pickup. "I've got to go to town and get some gas," he said, waving at his friends. Though still far from convinced that Knighten would actually carry out his cold-blooded plan, Jonathan felt a shiver of excitement as he walked away.

Richard followed Greg to the passenger side of George's truck, then stood back for a moment as Knighten opened the door and greeted Moore. "Richard's going with us, okay?" he said.

George smiled. "Sure. Get in."

Richard still hesitated, standing in the street, his hands jammed deep into his pockets, his shoulders hunched against the damp twilight chill.

The driver did not see the quick, menacing glare Knighten shot at Goeglein. "Come on, man, let's go," Greg said.

Richard climbed into the cab of the pickup, settling in next to George, saying nothing as he stared ahead at the slow movement of the windshield wipers. Greg, next to the window, leaned forward to face George. "I've got us a helluva deal set up," he said.

Even before Raffield had put his truck in gear, Knighten was explaining that he had arranged a meeting with a crank dealer. "We're supposed to meet him out in the country," he said.

"Where?" George asked.

"The Ramsey pasture."

George nodded, aware that Knighten was referring to the wooded spot where they had gone one evening a few weeks earlier to smoke marijuana.

Greg had discovered the well-hidden place quite by accident in early September when he went there with some friends for an afternoon of target practice.

He had been walking along Farm-to-Market Road 663, having just stepped from the school bus, when he noticed Jeff Grigsby approaching in his pickup. Flagging him down, Greg saw that two other high school students, Chad Calvert and Brian Askew, were with him.

Knighten asked what they were up to and, when told they were going out to do some target shooting with Chad's father's new rifle, quickly invited himself along.

In the isolated pasture owned by Calvert's father the four boys took turns shooting at tin cans and small trees. To the surprise of those he had joined, Greg was by far the most accurate shot. Seldom did he miss one of the cans they had placed along a ridge and in the forks of trees. When a one-inch limb was designated as a target, Knighten had been the only one to hit it, snapping the branch on his first shot. Pleased that he had impressed the others with his marksmanship, he explained that his father was once an instructor at the Dallas police target range and had taught him to shoot.

As they were walking back toward Grigsby's truck Greg

stopped to admire the isolated terrain. It was a great place, he said. "You know, if you killed somebody out here," he remarked, "nobody would ever find the body."

None of the others acknowledged the strange observation as they continued toward the pickup. They drove in silence back to the entrance to the Camelot Estates where they let Knighten off. It was the last time he was invited to go target shooting.

All that remained of the October sunset was a hazy gray cloud cover as George drove south on the farm road, past damp hay fields and cattle grazing lazily under the drizzling skies. At the intersection of 875, he turned right onto the meandering two-lane blacktop that led to the community of Venus, eight miles away.

The three passengers talked little, instead listening to the music that blared from the radio, as they drove past the entrance to the Salvation Army's summer children's camp, by craggy gravel pits, and out beyond the isolated Hopewell Baptist Church and its cemetery. Once, years earlier, there had been a community there. Now all that remained was the little white frame church and a field of ancient tombstones.

George slowed as he crossed a narrow bridge and made his way up a small hill.

"It's right up here," Knighten said.

Off to the left, almost hidden by a stand of mesquite trees and crape myrtle bushes, was a new house under construction.

"We're going to turn in just past that house," Greg instructed.

George had to slow almost to a stop to find the opening in the barbed-wire fence and the makeshift road that led into the Calvert property. He followed the winding road into the pasture for several hundred yards, then made a sharp left turn down an incline toward an open area that was shielded from the road by trees and thick underbrush.

The nocturnal croaking of the frogs that inhabited the small stock tank on one edge of the clearing fell silent at the sound of the approaching pickup.

Only after George had parked and joined Greg and Richard on the tailgate of his truck did the night sounds of the countryside resume. Crickets began to compete with the music that blared from the open doors of the pickup. Eventually the frogs, sensing no danger from the invasion of their privacy, resumed their chorus.

For the next fifteen minutes, as darkness settled around them, they shared the joint that Knighten had brought with him, made idle talk, and listened to the music.

Soon the waiting began to get to Goeglein. "Maybe the dude's not coming," he offered. "This deal's not coming down. Let's get the fuck out of here."

"Naw, he said he'd be here," Greg insisted. "What's the hurry? Just chill out, man." There was a nonchalance in his voice that disturbed Richard. From the time Greg had begun talking of his plot to kill George, Richard had never been fully convinced that he would carry it through. Now, though, he was beginning to wonder.

Richard shrugged, slipped down from the tailgate, and walked off toward a row of trees to urinate. From his private vantage point he looked back at Greg and George as they sat talking quietly, their feet dangling from the tailgate.

Richard realized he was shivering and pulled his collar tighter around his neck. Instead of returning to the tailgate, he climbed in the passenger side of the pickup and sat sideways so that he could keep an eye on Greg.

He had been there only a couple of minutes when he heard Knighten ask George to change the radio to another station. Out of the corner of his eye Richard saw George moving toward the cab while Greg walked along the opposite side of the truck. He was standing near the rear wheel well when he called out to George.

"Hey, man, look over there," Greg said, pointing in the direction of the stock tank. "Fireflies."

As George turned, Knighten was already pulling the gun from beneath his shirt, gripping it with both hands.

Three rapid shots echoed across the pasture. At the police academy they would have called it "reflex shooting," a technique that calls for quick aim and a series of shots as fast as the trigger can be pulled. It was one of the many lessons Tom Knighten had taught his son.

The first shot exploded into the back of George's head, causing blood to splatter across the side of the truck and sending fragments of fractured skull into his brain. He was already falling toward the open door of the pickup when the second shot grazed his scalp. The third bullet hummed harmlessly into the darkness.

Neither the second shot nor the third was necessary. The first bullet had accomplished what Greg Knighten had set out to do.

From the seat of the pickup, Goeglein watched as Greg fired across the bed of the pickup, aware only of a painful ringing in his ears. Then, in the fuzzy glow of the dome light, he saw George slump toward the door on the driver's side. It had all taken just a few seconds, but Richard had a sense that everything was moving in slow motion. His suddenly dry lips moved in a private whisper. "Oh, shit," he said.

Outside, Knighten was pacing alongside the truck in quick, jerky movements. Then, after a few seconds, he tucked the gun back into his belt and began yelling at Goeglein.

"Get his billfold," Greg ordered.

Richard slid across the seat of the pickup and looked down at George's lifeless body. He lay on his side, his back to the truck, blood still flowing from the fatal wound. Goeglein put his foot against the body, braced himself against the door of the truck, and rolled George onto his stomach.

He then reached into the dead man's back pocket and removed the wallet. As he handed it to Greg, Richard realized why Knighten had worn several layers of T-shirts. After peeling one off, Greg tossed it to him. "Start wiping the truck down," he said. He wanted no fingerprints or traces of blood left on the pickup.

The two teenagers went quickly to their grim task, the silence interrupted only by more instructions from Knighten. It was clear to Richard that Greg had thought out his plan even more carefully than he had indicated. Once they had wiped the truck clean of fingerprints, they lifted the tailgate back into place. Goeglein stepped across George's prone body to retrieve the keys from the ignition and lock the doors, though it never crossed his mind to wonder why they needed to be locked.

He handed the keys to Greg, who threw them into the darkness. "Okay," he said, "let's get the fuck out of here."

Avoiding the road on which they had entered, the boys ran through the tangled underbrush to the place where Jobe was to pick them up. It wasn't until they reached the road and found that Jobe was not there that Knighten gave any indication that the event had shaken him.

Cursing loudly, he began walking along the edge of the road at a pace Goeglein had trouble matching. "Oh, man," Greg moaned, "I said I would never get myself into this kind of shit again."

It was as if he was talking to himself, and for a moment Richard feared that Greg's wild ramblings signaled that he might be going into shock. Looking at the dark silhouette in front of him, Goeglein suddenly was concerned that if he did the slightest thing wrong he, too, might be killed. "What the fuck are you talking about?" he asked.

"Something that happened over in Duncanville a long time ago," Greg said as he kept walking. "I killed this policeman over there. They never even found the fucking body."

Goeglein was relieved when he saw the headlights of Jobe's pickup slowly approaching.

Unsure exactly where he was to pick up Greg and Richard, Jonathan had driven past the spot and gone almost all the way to Venus before turning around. He had been about ready to give up when he finally saw them walking alongside the road.

As they scrambled into the cab, neither said anything until Jobe put his truck in gear and headed toward town.

"Well?" he said, looking over at his obviously shaken companions.

"It's done," Greg answered.

"Is he dead?"

"He's dead," said Goeglein.

"Are you sure?"

"Greg shot him in the head three times, man."

Jobe's face betrayed his shock. "I can't believe it," he said. "Jesus . . ."

Knighten jerked around in the seat and glared at the driver. "Just shut the fuck up, okay?" he said. "Take me over to Cynthia's. I've got to talk to Cynthia."

He said nothing more until they neared town. As they approached a small combination grocery–gas station, Knighten instructed Jobe to pull in.

"What the hell for?"

"I want to get a Coke," Greg replied.

Before leaving the truck he pulled George's wallet from his pocket and opened it. Silently he counted the eighteen dollars it contained, then handed a five and a one to Jobe. He gave six one-dollar bills to Richard, then stuffed the remaining five and one into his own pocket.

The fifty dollars in buy money that George Raffield always kept in his shirt pocket had been overlooked.

13

Word spread quickly that Cynthia Fedrick and her friends had returned from Cash with an eight-ball of crank. Several people dropped by the Oxford Square apartment in the early evening to join the party.

Little and Castle were preparing to give each other another injection when they heard a knock at the door shortly after eight o'clock. Cynthia, confident that the visitor was another friend she had invited over, laughed at the men's caution as they hurried to hide in the bathroom. She opened the front door to find Greg Knighten, Jonathan Jobe, and Richard Goeglein standing in the glow of her porch light.

"I've got to talk to you," Greg said, as he quickly walked past her into the living room. "I think I'm in trouble."

Irritated that her drug-induced high was being interrupted, she said, "Hey, the last thing I want right now is any trouble."

"I just need to talk for a minute, okay?" Greg motioned for Richard and Jonathan to wait in the living room as he followed Cynthia into her bedroom.

As soon as the door was shut he erupted into a frenzied

retelling of what had happened. In her foggy state, Cynthia first had trouble understanding Knighten's rapid, disjointed narrative. He mentioned some kind of strange séance they had had. "That's how we found out for sure he was a narc," he explained. He told her he'd taken his father's gun and replaced the expensive police-issue bullets with cheaper target ammunition—wad cutters, he called them—then lured George out to an isolated field.

At first, Cynthia did not believe him. In the privacy of her bedroom his mood seemed to swing from one extreme to another. He had looked frightened when he entered the apartment, but now he was laughing as he spoke. If he was telling the truth, if he had actually killed a man, why was he laughing? "Shut up," Cynthia finally yelled, interrupting the breathless narration. "Just shut the fuck up. I don't want to know about it."

It was as if Greg had not even heard her. He wanted to tell her everything. Cynthia, suddenly sober, leaned against her dresser and listened as he continued to describe what had happened in the field.

"Dammit," she said, shaking her head. "I don't believe this. You're just bullshitting me."

Knighten's voice took on a new emphasis as he looked at her, drawing his words out slowly. "I . . . really . . . did . . . it," he said, the laughter gone. "We've got the guy's wallet. I've got to get rid of it. What should I do?"

"Where is it?"

Greg opened the bedroom door and told Jobe and Goeglein to go out to the pickup and bring the wallet inside. "She wants to see it," he said.

In the three-fold nylon billfold was a temporary driver's license made out to George William Moore. Cynthia studied it for a minute, noticing that it bore a Temple address. "I thought he was from Midlothian," she said.

Greg took the license from her. "We've got to flush it down the toilet or something," Greg said.

As the three boys stood in the crowded bedroom, Cynthia

studied their faces. Only Richard seemed nervous, frightened. Jobe joined in the effort to convince Cynthia that George lay dead out in a field.

"Did he know he was going to die?" she asked.

Greg shook his head. "Hell, no."

"You didn't talk to him about it before you killed him?"

Again Greg answered. "No."

"That license won't go down the toilet," Cynthia said, taking it from Greg's hand. She picked up a cigarette lighter from her dresser and began to burn the piece of paper. As the flame grew larger, she let it fall to the floor and they watched as it disappeared into a small charred pile of black dust.

Outside the bedroom, Jay and Don emerged from their hiding place and stood, curious about what was taking place. Randy Marcott, having just brought Cynthia's daughter home, was surprised to see Jobe's pickup parked outside.

Seconds after Cynthia's half brother arrived, she and Greg emerged from the bedroom. Knighten looked at Randy. "I took care of business," he said.

Thinking back to their conversation earlier in the week, Marcott felt sure he knew what Greg was talking about. "Oh, yeah?"

"Damn right," Greg replied, then returned to the bedroom. Cynthia signaled for Jay Little to follow. Don Castle joined them, standing in the doorway.

"Tell Jay what you told me," Cynthia said to Knighten.

Again Greg recounted the murder at the Calvert place. As he talked he held Cynthia's lighter to George's billfold, unsuccessfully trying to get it to burn.

Going into the kitchen to get her cigarettes, Cynthia could hear Greg again telling of their sitting on the tailgate of George's pickup, of how he had told George to change the radio station, and how he had fired the shots.

What she didn't hear was Greg telling Jay and Don of his plan to use some kind of a wire brush to alter the inside of the gun barrel before returning it to its hiding place. That way, he explained, it would be impossible to trace the bullets fired at George to his father's revolver.

"Man, I don't think that's going to work," Don observed.

"I know it will," Greg shot back.

Cynthia, walking back toward the bedroom, was surprised when she heard Jobe pick up the story, insisting that he had used his shirt to help wipe down the truck. Just minutes earlier, Greg had told her that it was he and Richard who had done it, that Jobe had only picked them up. Now Jobe seemed eager to involve himself. The whole story was too bizarre. It didn't make sense.

"If what you're saying is true," Little finally said, "you guys really fucked up."

Greg did not respond.

Cynthia took the wallet from him, examined the charred, melted edge, and walked back into the kitchen where she tossed it into a plastic garbage sack. "I want you guys out of here," she said. "Right now."

After the boys had left, Cynthia put her daughter to bed. Then she and Jay sat at the kitchen table, talking about the story they had been told. "I don't believe them," Cynthia said. "They didn't really do it. Sparky's just not capable of doing anything like that."

"You goddam better believe it," Little said. "And we're going to be in big trouble if anybody finds out they came here."

Cynthia knew that Jay disliked Knighten. Only because he served as Greg's occasional drug connection had Little tolerated her friend. They sat silently for several minutes as Cynthia nervously rolled the tip of her cigarette against an ashtray. "You think this is for real?" she asked, frightened for the first time since the boys' arrival.

"All I know," Little replied, "is that if it is, we're in deep shit."

Cynthia Fedrick leaned forward, laying her head on her folded arms. "Damn," she said.

As she and Jay talked, Jonathan, following Greg's instructions, was driving along the winding road that led to Jamie Cadenhead's house.

Now sitting between the driver and Richard, Knighten told Jobe to slow down as they neared an S-shaped turn just outside of town. Reaching into his pocket, he gathered the empty shell casings he had collected after the shooting, leaned across Goeglein, and tossed them into a thick stand of cane that bordered a small gully near the roadside.

At school earlier that day, Greg had told Jamie that he would be at her house around eight o'clock. He was thirty minutes late, and she was beginning to wonder if he was coming. She had thought about calling his home but dismissed the idea, and had gone out into the yard to smoke a cigarette when she saw Jonathan's pickup pulling into the driveway.

The three boys got out, and Greg ran to Jamie and embraced her. Burying his face in her hair, he said nothing for several seconds, then backed away and forced a smile. "It's okay," he said. "Everything's okay."

Jamie turned away, looking toward Jonathan and Richard who had walked into the yard near the pickup and begun taking turns tossing Goeglein's knife into the grass. She waved, and they waved back. Both boys were smiling.

"Hey, dude, we're going on back to town," Jobe yelled at Greg as he and Richard began walking toward the truck.

"Call me in the morning," Knighten acknowledged, then turned to go into the house with his girlfriend.

Jamie had never seen Greg so nervous. He had always been hyper, seldom able to sit still for any amount of time, constantly moving, talking, and laughing; that, she felt, was the main reason he got into so much trouble at school. But this was something different. She had seen him angry and messed up on dope, acting silly and showing off. This, however, was the first time she had sensed that he was scared.

"Where's your purse?" he asked.

Instead of answering that it was in the bedroom, Jamie started walking in that direction with Greg closely following. Picking it up from her dresser, she handed it to him and watched as he pulled the gun from the front of his pants. As he put it into her purse, he said, "I need to keep this in here until I go home."

Jamie stared at him but said nothing. Fearful that she already knew what he had done with the gun, she didn't question him. She didn't want to know.

"Let's go back outside," Greg finally said.

The rain had stopped and the two teenagers walked to the side of the house and leaned against the front fender of Jamie's brother's pickup. Again they embraced, and Greg kissed her. "You've got to promise me that whatever happens you'll stay with me," he said. "You've got to promise. I need you so much." And then he began to cry.

Jamie put her arms around him. Suddenly he was not the person she knew—the young boy battling so hard in his passage to manhood; the confident, almost cocky, Greg who had assured her that he was an adult and could provide for her when they were married. There, in the clouded darkness of that October night, he was a frightened little boy, sobbing so hard that his shoulders were shaking even as she held him.

"Oh, God," Greg began to pray, "forgive me of my sins and what happened tonight. I'm so scared. And I'm sorry. Please keep Jamie and me together. Please . . ."

As she listened to Greg's pleading voice, Jamie Cadenhead, more frightened than she had ever been in her life, also began to cry.

For the rest of the evening, until her parents returned shortly before midnight, she sat silently, holding her boyfriend's hand and gently stroking his hair as he wept and prayed.

Greg accepted Jim Cadenhead's offer to drive him home and was making his way toward the front door when Jamie whispered a reminder that the gun was still in her purse. While her father walked out onto the porch, Jamie stood in the doorway, making sure no one saw Greg enter her bedroom and slip the weapon back into his pants.

On the fifteen-minute drive to the Camelot Estates, Jim Cadenhead thought it strange that Greg, generally talkative and eager to discuss fixing cars when they were together, said little.

After dropping Knighten off, he remarked to his daughter

that Greg had seemed troubled. "You two have a fight or something?" he asked Jamie.

"No," she said. "Everything's okay. I think he was just tired." She then quickly changed the subject. "He's going to come out tomorrow and help me get things ready for the party."

That was good news to Jim Cadenhead. He had promised to do the driving for Jamie's hayride, but had made it clear that the preparations were her responsibility.

Upon returning to town, Jobe and Goeglein had stopped by Gina McLemore's house shortly after nine. Mr. McLemore, lying on the couch watching television when their knock came at the door, answered and explained to the two boys that Gina was busy putting her younger sister to bed and could not talk.

Richard, aware that his girlfriend's father was not altogether pleased that she had begun dating him, thanked him politely, and they left.

"Let's go home and get out of these wet clothes," Jobe suggested. "You can call her later."

When the telephone rang at the McLemore home thirty minutes later, Gina's grandmother answered. After checking the clock and deciding that nine-thirty wasn't too late to be calling on a Friday night, she informed Gina that she was wanted on the phone. Gina, listening in on the extension, already knew.

As soon as he heard the click of her grandmother replacing the receiver, Richard began telling his girlfriend what had taken place.

"It happened," he said.

Gina, sitting on the edge of her bed, looked up to make sure the door to her room was closed. "Are you serious?"

"It happened," he repeated.

"You didn't do it, did you?"

"No, but Sparky did. I tried to talk him out of it, but he did it anyway."

"Are you okay?"

"Except for being scared shitless," Richard said.

"Richard, are you sure? Did you see him do it?"

"When I saw that it was really going to happen," he said, "I walked off. I didn't see it, but I heard the shots; three of them. He shot him in the back of the head and in the neck. I saw the dude lying face down by his truck. We took his wallet out of his pocket and split up the money."

Gina gasped, thinking that Richard's story sounded like something from a movie or a TV show.

"Where are you now?" she asked.

"I'm at Jonathan's. He picked us up. Listen, I've got to go. My clothes are soaking wet. I'll call you tomorrow."

"Richard," Gina said, her fragile voice barely audible, "where's George?"

"He's still out in the field."

While Goeglein was talking to Gina, Randy Marcott, home from his visit to Cynthia's, spoke on the phone to Anna Roscoe. He told her of hearing Greg and Richard brag to his sister and friends about killing George. "Sparky had blood on one of his hands," he said, "and they were both real muddy when I saw them. They said it happened out in some field."

"I don't believe it," Anna said.

"I do."

"Where did they get a gun?"

"I don't know. Sparky's dad is a policeman," Randy said. "Maybe they took one of his."

As soon as their conversation ended, Anna dialed the number of Dale Janson. She had to tell someone the incredible story she had just heard.

Much the same discussion was taking place at Cynthia Fedrick's apartment where Dennis and Joyce Brown, the people with whom Jay Little lived, had stopped by shortly after the other boys had left. They listened in stunned silence as the story was related to them.

George Raffield had been dead less than two hours and already Midlothian's grapevine rang with the horrifying news.

But at the police station the telephone remained exceptionally quiet. With so many people out of town for the football game, there were only a few routine calls, alerting the dispatcher to a couple of minor accidents on the city's rain-slicked streets.

At home, Lieutenant Fowler watched the ten o'clock news, then made sure his answering machine was switched on before preparing for bed.

It really wasn't necessary. A light sleeper, he was certain Raffield's check-in call would wake him.

Part
THREE

I find myself still looking for you and listening to hear your voice. I love you so dearly and miss you terribly.

—*from a letter written by Sheryl Zanolini to her dead brother*

14

Roy Vaughn stood at the window of his small office, looking out into the graying twilight at the crowd that had gathered after the discovery of Raffield's body. He counted a half-dozen television minicams bearing the logos of stations from Dallas and Fort Worth. Reporters and photographers, elbowing for space among a number of curious local citizens, encircled Mayor Maurice Osborne and Chuck Pinto as they answered questions about the investigation.

Vaughn crushed out the Camel he had just lit and tried to wash its bitter taste away with coffee. His body ached with fatigue as he stood looking out on the press conference. Normally it would have fallen to him to answer the questions being asked of the mayor and city manager, but he was not ready to face reporters. Their deadlines, their right to know, were of little concern to the chief. He was too preoccupied with the fact that he had a dead officer in the medical examiner's office and two teenagers in custody, telling a story that sounded like a dark nightmare.

There was, too, a more private reason for Vaughn's decision to avoid the media. The chief, his strength depleted, feared he would be unable to keep his fragile emotions in check.

While Vaughn was with the Dallas Police Department, he had forced himself to look upon man's cruelty to man in a dispassionate, detached way. He had adopted the homicide investigator's golden rule: Don't get personally involved. It was, he had learned, the only way to deal with the seemingly endless horror of violent death.

Now, though, there was no way to put his feelings aside; this time he would not be able to lock them safely away in some far corner of his mind. Even the Valium his wife had persuaded him to take earlier in the afternoon had done little to calm him.

The phone call he had just made to George Raffield's parents had left him even more drained, and now he was contemplating some way to summon new strength for what was to come.

George's relatives were on their way to Midlothian. They would want to know what had happened, how this unbelievable tragedy had played itself out, and it was his responsibility to explain to them something he did not yet understand himself.

Outside Vaughn's office, the foyer of the police station was jammed with officers, who, having returned from the crime scene, now wandered aimlessly, wondering what else they could do. Though most of them had been on duty since early morning, no one wanted to leave. Some helped themselves to the ham and tuna salad sandwiches Margie Vaughn had prepared and delivered to the station, others sipped coffee from Styrofoam cups. A few stretched out on the bunks in the empty jail cells while awaiting new orders.

Ellis County District Attorney Mary Lou Shipley had been tending her cattle when word of the crime reached her. She had driven to her home in Waxahachie to change her jeans and flannel shirt and was now sitting in Vaughn's office.

In a room just a few feet away, Lieutenant Fowler was taking a statement from Jonathan Jobe. Sheriff's Deputy Jeff Bryant took it upon himself to stand sentry at the closed door, warding off interruptions. Down the hall, George

Turner told Richard Goeglein's parents it would be some time before he completed his interview with their son. In that case, Richard, Sr., said, he would like to take his wife home. Turner said good-bye and returned to his interview with Richard Goeglein.

Entering the room carrying a soft drink and a sandwich, he placed them on the desk in front of the drawn-looking teenager. "You better eat something," the Ranger said.

Richard nodded as he peeled the plastic wrapping from the sandwich. "I threw Terry away," he said.

Turner, his mind occupied with the lengthy list of questions he planned to ask, didn't know what Richard meant. "What are you talking about? Who's Terry?"

"Terry's heart," Goeglein said. "You saw it when you were in here earlier. I threw it away."

The Ranger sat on the edge of the desk as Richard explained that he had used the plastic amulet to contact the spirit of a girl he had known when he lived in Arizona. "She tells me things," he said.

"Like what?"

"She told us that George was a narc," Richard said, as he reached for his soft drink.

The weary Ranger sighed deeply and moved to a chair on the other side of the desk. Great, he thought, on top of everything else the kid's a certifiable nut case. "Maybe you'd better explain," he said.

Richard began to describe the meeting in Greg's room, how the murder plot had taken form, and the questions he had posed to the Ouija board. With only occasional prompting from Turner, Richard told of the trip out to the field and of the three rapid shots that he swore he had never believed Knighten would fire. They had taken George's wallet, wiped the truck down, and walked back up to the road to meet Jobe.

The fear he had shown earlier in the day had disappeared. Now he told the story in an unemotional voice that chilled the Ranger. If there was remorse, Richard Goeglein was hiding it well. "Where's the wallet?" Turner asked.

"Over at Cynthia's. Greg gave it to her."

As soon as Richard told of the visit to the Oxford Square Apartments, Turner hurried from the room in search of someone to go to Cynthia Fedrick's apartment. Seeing Sonny Pfeifer near the dispatcher's desk, the Ranger approached him and began to relate the information Richard had just given him.

"I was just on my way out the door," Pfeifer said. "The Jobe boy told Fowler the same thing."

"We need that damn wallet," Turner said, "and this Cynthia, whoever she is."

As the sergeant made his way toward the door, Turner called out to him. "One more thing. We need a warrant for Greg Knighten's arrest."

As he spoke, Turner noticed a woman in her late thirties entering the station. She had gained a few pounds since he had last seen her and wore her hair differently, but George had no difficulty recognizing her. Sharrell Jobe had just returned from an afternoon of shopping when her sister telephoned with news that Jonathan had been taken to the police station.

Walking directly to Turner, she asked where her son was being held. "I want to see him," she demanded.

"He's giving a statement," George said.

"Has he signed anything?"

"No," the Ranger said, "but he's about to. They're typing it up right now."

"I don't want him signing anything," Sharrell said, "until he's talked to a lawyer. Do you understand?"

"Sharrell, he's already told us—"

"I said I don't want him signing anything," she repeated, then turned and hurried out the front door. Making her way through the still-growing crowd that had formed in front of the station, she walked across the parking lot toward Dee Tee's Restaurant. By the time she reached the front door she had already dug a quarter from her purse for the pay phone.

In Vaughn's office, Fowler handed Turner the two-page statement Jonathan had dictated to him. Rubbing his eyes, the Ranger sat down and began to read:

About three or four days ago I was riding through town with Richard Goeglein in my truck. We saw George and Greg Knighten riding in George's truck in the opposite direction. Greg motioned us over to Del's Drive-in, and we got out of my truck. They got out of their truck. We all were standing there and Greg said hello and George introduced himself to me. I had seen him at school but never knew his name. I told them I had to leave and left at that time. Richard left with me. The next day Greg told me he thought George was a narc, and he was sure of it. He said he needed to do something about it. Yesterday, on October 23, 1987, when we got to school he told me and Richard Goeglein that he had come up with a plan. He didn't tell us what he was talking about until after school. After school me and Richard Goeglein went to my house. Walked over to Greg's. Greg said that the plan was in action, that he had already called George to come over and pick him up or that he had already told George to pick him up. I don't remember which. He said George was supposed to pick him up between 6:30 and 7:00 P.M. He said when George got there he was going to take him out on a road out at the end of FM 663 and hang a right and that he would take care of George. He asked Richard Goeglein if he would go with him when George got there because he didn't know if he could do it by himself. We were in Greg's room in his house and he had a black pistol stuck down in the front of his pants. Richard told Greg he didn't know if he would go with him or not. Richard, Greg, and I were out in the street when George drove up. Richard and Greg got into George's truck and George drove off. Greg had told me while we were in his room to pick them up out on that road that crosses the end of FM 663 about thirty minutes after they left. After they left I went and got some gas and then drove out on the road Greg had told me to come to. I went way down the road past a bridge and turned around and came back up the road. I drove back and forth on the road. The second time I was coming back toward the city I saw Greg and Richard walking down the road. I stopped and picked them up. Greg said everything was taken care of and he couldn't really believe this had happened. I couldn't either. Greg told us to just shut up and never talk about it again. Greg told me to take him to Jamie Cadenhead's house because he had to talk to her. Before we got there I asked Greg if he was sure he had killed George. He said he was sure, he had shot him three times and he was sure he was dead. Richard said yeah, he was shot three times very fast. Richard said he was sure he was dead, too. I let Greg out at Jamie Cadenhead's house. Jamie Cadenhead came outside when I let Greg out. He told her he had did it. He then told me and Richard we had better protect ourselves.

Turner silently handed the first page to Mary Lou Shipley, then began reading the second page. It had been dictated almost as an afterthought:

I forgot, but before I took Greg out to Jamie's house he said he wanted to go by Cynthia's apartment over behind the Dairy Queen. Greg had a wallet and said it was George's wallet. He said he wanted Cynthia to get rid of the wallet for him. When we got to Cynthia's we went in. She was there and her small daughter. There was some guy there I didn't know. Greg and Cynthia went into one of the back rooms to talk. He came back out and had the wallet in his hand. He said there had been $18 in the wallet and that we would all get $6 apiece. He handed me $6 and I used it today, October 24, to put gas in my truck. I saw Cynthia burn something from George's wallet. I think it was his temporary driver's license before he got his real license. Cynthia laid George's wallet on her dresser in the bedroom. We all left and that's when I took Greg to Jamie's. Since last night, today, October 24, Richard told me again Greg had shot George three times and that he felt kinda sick about it. He spent the night with me last night. Today before we went to Waxahachie to a flea market, we went to Del's Drive-in. Richard used the pay telephone and I think he called someone in Arizona.

At the bottom of the page, the signature line remained blank.

Turner sat for several minutes, silently pondering what he had read, allowing the district attorney time to finish. She had placed the second page of the voluntary statement form in her lap when he finally spoke.

"Based on what I've read here and what the Goeglein kid is saying," Turner said, "it doesn't look like Jobe was all that involved. At this point, it looks like Greg Knighten is our triggerman and Richard is his accomplice. Right now I'm not sure how Cynthia Fedrick fits into it.

"Jobe's mother has gone to get her lawyer," Turner continued. "I want to get his signature on this statement. I may be making a mistake, but I'd like to offer Jobe a deal as an unindicted witness if he'll sign the statement and testify against the others."

The district attorney, already thinking ahead to the mountainous preparations that would be required to prosecute the case, nodded her head. "Okay," she said.

Outside, Sharrell Jobe had returned. Standing with her was her husband, Johnny, who had just arrived. Turner shook hands with his old high school teammate. Before he could speak, Sharrell informed Turner that she had talked with Connie McGuire, their attorney, and had been advised not to allow her son to sign any statement.

Though Turner tried to explain that her son's signature on the statement would ensure that he would not be arrested or prosecuted, Sharrell steadfastly refused. "Do you mind if I talk to your attorney?" George asked.

Dialing the number Sharrell had given him, George counted several rings before hearing yet another voice from the past. Connie McGuire had also been a classmate during his student days at Midlothian High School.

"Connie," he said, "this is George Turner."

There was no hint of warmth in her response. "Has he signed anything?"

"No," George answered, "but let me tell you what I'm prepared to do." With that he again outlined the proposal he had made to the Jobes. He assured the attorney that if she agreed to allow him to sign the statement and volunteer to serve as a witness against the defendants in the case, Jonathan would face no charges, no indictment.

"I'm not about to let him sign that statement," McGuire replied, her voice even cooler than before.

"Connie, I'll have my offer put in writing. The boy walks out of here as free as a bird. I've already talked to the district attorney and she's agreed to—"

"George," the attorney interrupted, "I trust you, but I don't trust Mary Lou Shipley. My client will not sign anything."

Turner resisted the urge to slam the phone down after hearing the click when Connie McGuire hung up abruptly. He had accomplished nothing except once again to remind himself that he had precious little use for most lawyers. A look of resignation on his face, he turned to Jonathan's parents, Sharrell and Johnny Jobe, and told them that they could take their son home.

In need of some fresh air before returning to his questioning of Goeglein, Turner walked outside and watched as Johnny Jobe stopped to talk with Steve McLemore and Ricky Pennington while his wife and his son, now free, hurried past the crowd toward the car.

George stood there, letting the night chill sweep over his tense body, and found himself reflecting on the ironies of the situation into which he had been thrown. The investigation seemed to be turning into a damn class reunion. He had forgotten how many of his old acquaintances had stayed behind, how closely entwined with the town their lives had remained. First Sharrell and Johnny Jobe, then Connie McGuire. And now Turner was nodding acknowledgment as Ricky Pennington looked in his direction. They had been good friends back in high school, before their lives had taken different paths. While George had gone in search of something Midlothian didn't have to offer, Ricky had stayed.

The last time George had heard anything about him, Ricky had very nearly drowned in a boating accident on Lake Whitney. The local chapter of Woodsmen of the World had honored Johnny Jobe at a dinner and given him a citation for saving Pennington's life.

After Jobe had left to join his wife and son, Pennington made his way over to Turner.

"What in the world are you doing, hanging around here?" George asked, extending his hand and forcing a tired smile.

Gina McLemore, Pennington replied, was his niece.

Mention of the girl who had been brought to the station with Richard and Jonathan brought Turner's thoughts back to the task at hand. Throughout all the confusion, Gina had sat patiently in a corner of the waiting room. Though Turner had no idea how she might figure into the case, he had wanted badly to talk with her. Now, though, too many other things were demanding his attention. Gina McLemore would have to wait.

Turner walked into the crowd and told her father to take her on home. "Just tell her I'll be in touch with her when I get time."

As he headed back toward the front door, Turner felt a sudden sadness sweep over him. He knew that his hometown, robbed of its innocence by an act he could not begin to explain, would never be the same. Nor would those who called it home. He wearily shook his head and buried his hands deep in his pockets, wishing he was home talking with his son about a soccer game that now seemed to have been played a lifetime ago.

By the time he entered the room where Richard waited, Turner was fighting to keep his anger in check. "Richard," he said, "I believe you're telling me the truth. Now the question is, are you ready to write it all down in a statement for me and sign it?"

Goeglein nodded. "Yes, sir, I am." With that, he began

dictating a confession to Turner, aware the statement he would later sign could be used as evidence against him.

In her apartment, Cynthia Fedrick looked across the kitchen table at Sonny Pfeifer and Detective David Bennett. No, she told the officers, there had been no visit from Greg Knighten or any of his friends the previous evening. "I don't know what you're talking about," she said in a controlled, even voice.

"Our information is that they brought a wallet here," Sergeant Pfeifer said, "and left it with you."

Cynthia rested her elbows on the table and shook her head. "I don't know anything about that."

Only after Pfeifer pulled a card from his pocket and read the Miranda warning to her did Cynthia show signs of uneasiness. Looking across the apartment toward her daughter who was watching television in the living room, she told her to go to her room.

"Okay," Cynthia said, "the boys did come by. But it was earlier this morning, not last night. Sparky said something about a wallet he needed to get rid of. I think he threw it in the garbage before they left."

Pfeifer asked what the boys had talked about during their visit.

"They seemed real excited about something, but I told them I didn't want to hear it. Greg just kept saying he needed to get rid of the wallet. I told him I was busy and asked them to leave."

David Bennett, who had watched Cynthia closely as his partner questioned her, sensed that she was getting more nervous. Her hands were trembling slightly as she lit a cigarette and waited for Pfeifer's next question.

"Ma'am," he said, "did you burn a driver's license that was in the wallet?" Bennett suppressed a smile when he saw Cynthia's surprise at how much information they had.

"I don't know anything about any driver's license," she insisted. Then, after several seconds of silence, she spoke again. "I did see the wallet, though. Sparky gave it to me and I tossed it in the trash."

"Where is it?" Pfeifer asked.

"I took the trash out after I cleaned house this morning," she said. "I'll show you."

She led the officers to a fenced area in the apartment complex where residents left trash. Bennett and Pfeifer looked at the large mound of plastic bags and glanced at each other. Though they said nothing, their thoughts were the same. Neither looked forward to sorting through the plastic bags of stale garbage for the evidence.

"It's in one of those," Cynthia volunteered, pointing to the only two white bags in the pile.

Bennett retrieved the bags and placed them on the sidewalk. He was relieved when he found the charred wallet in the first one he opened.

"We'd like you to come to the station with us," Pfeifer said, "so we can take a statement."

"Am I under arrest?"

"No, ma'am, we'd just like to get your statement so we can clear this matter up as quickly as possible."

Cynthia nodded. "That's what I'd like to do," she said. "Can I drive my baby over to my parents' house first?"

The officers waited as she dressed her daughter, then followed as she drove to a house just south of town.

"What do you think?" Pfeifer asked.

Bennett looked down at the plastic evidence bag in which he had placed George Raffield's wallet. "I think she's telling us just enough to make us happy . . . and not involve herself."

Still, the fact that she had admitted throwing the wallet away was just cause to press charges of hindering an investigation. When they got to the station, Sergeant Pfeifer again read Cynthia her rights, then placed her under arrest.

At the police station, Richard Goeglein had completed his statement and was placed into one of the small cells. He had been locked up less than an hour when he saw Cynthia being escorted into an adjoining cell.

Though the cinder-block wall that separated them prevented him from seeing her, Richard knew she was angry. As soon as the officer left the jail area she began ranting.

"What the fuck is going on?" she demanded. "What have you told them?"

Richard's answer came in a scared, pleading voice. "I didn't tell them anything," he swore. "It's Jonathan. They've got him somewhere and he's telling them everything."

"Shit."

As Cynthia paced in her cell, hoping her parents would soon arrive with bail money, Richard remained silent, saying nothing for several minutes.

Then she heard his voice again. "Cynthia," he said, "something's really wrong. This doesn't make any sense."

"What do you mean?"

"Greg's not here. Why the fuck isn't Greg here?"

Following his visit to the police station, Greg Knighten had gone to Jamie Cadenhead's house to help decorate for the party and hayride. Both of the youngsters had avoided talking about the night before as they busied themselves stringing black and orange crepe paper in the living room and along the eaves of the front porch.

Greg, though unusually quiet, appeared composed to the early-arriving guests. That changed, however, after Jamie's mother told them about a phone call from a friend who had just heard something on her police scanner about a young boy having been found dead in a deserted house.

Unaware that the report had come from the Dallas Police Department and was in reference to one of its investigations, Greg slumped on the couch, his face pale. Jamie sat next to him, placing her arm around his shoulders as he began to shake.

"Greg, honey, what's wrong?"

After making sure Jamie's mother had left the room, Greg lowered his head and stared at the floor. "She's talking about Jonathan," he said. "He must have gone to that old house and killed himself."

A few hours later George Turner stood in the dim light above the entrance to the Midlothian police station, scanning the grim faces of officers from a half-dozen law enforcement agencies who would compose the search party for the last remaining suspect.

"Greg Knighten's daddy says he's supposed to be on a hayride," the Ranger said. "I want everyone to spread out and start looking. When you find him, treat him gently. I want everything by the book on this. The first thing I want you to do when you locate him is to contact me. I don't want anybody 'cowboying' this deal. I know everybody here would like to snatch him up and beat the shit out of him, but I'm telling you right now . . . no rough stuff. Just find him."

Areas were assigned, and the officers walked silently to their cars. Billy Fowler, who would accompany Turner on a search along the back roads in the area near the Cadenhead home, stood beside the worried Ranger, watching as the crowd dispersed. "A lot of those guys have blood in their eyes," he heard George say.

Across town, Midlothian High School counselor Perry Elkins and his wife were finishing dinner and discussing the news of George Raffield's death. Though no names had been released, the television report had indicated that a local juvenile was a suspect.

"How in the world could a kid do something like killing a police officer?" his wife asked.

"Someone like Greg Knighten could," Elkins replied.

No one had anticipated that there might be more than one hayride on that particular Saturday night. What they soon found, however, was that at least a dozen pre-Halloween parties were taking place. Several times a message was radioed into the station that a hayride had been located, only to be followed shortly by word that it was not from the Cadenhead house.

A sheriff's deputy drove to Cedar Hill and, unaware that Jamie Cadenhead worked there, stopped at the Dairy Queen to ask the night manager if he had seen a hayride. Steve Womack, who had been working since early afternoon and had not heard news reports of Raffield's death, asked whom they were looking for.

"A suspect in a murder," the deputy replied. "A kid from Midlothian shot a police officer."

Womack, standing behind the counter, felt his knees weaken. "Oh, my God," he said.

Unable to locate the hayride in the vicinity of the Cadenhead house, Fowler suggested they drive to the Camelot Estates. "I'd like to tell Tom Knighten what's going on," the lieutenant said. "I called him earlier and asked him to gather whatever guns he's got at home."

As Turner knocked at the front, Tom Knighten was walking out through the back door. Nelda, looking weary and drawn, answered and directed the Ranger to the garage. "He was just on his way to the police station," she said.

Seeing Turner and Fowler approach, Knighten got out of the car, carrying a briefcase. "They're in here," he said. "I was just bringing them down." Inside were two .38 caliber Smith & Wesson revolvers, a .22 caliber Smith & Wesson revolver, and a .44 caliber Smith & Wesson pistol.

"Tom, we've got a search party out looking for your son," Turner said as he took the briefcase. "A warrant for capital murder has been issued."

Opening the briefcase, the Ranger glanced hurriedly at the handguns. His attention immediately focused on the black .38, a model that included a shroud covering the hammer. In describing Greg Knighten's gun, Richard had recalled that it did not appear to have a "cocker." Making no mention of the fact, Turner closed the briefcase, certain that he now had the murder weapon in his custody.

As he stood at the entrance to the garage, Fowler extended his hand to Knighten. "We just wanted you to know," the lieutenant said. "I think we'll have the boy in custody shortly, if you want to come down to the station."

Tom Knighten's eyes were lifeless, his broad shoulders slumped. "I can't believe this," he said, his voice breaking and barely audible. "It's just not possible."

A few miles away, in the office of the city manager, the

victim's mother, Shirley Moore, nervously twisted a hand-kerchief through her fingers, expressing the same doubt.

Chuck Pinto looked into the agonized faces of George Raffield's family and fiancée, knowing that nothing he could say would be of comfort. The horrifying details of the day's activities, he knew, would only add to their grief. Still, it was important that they hear the facts firsthand.

A distraught-looking Chief Vaughn stood at his side, joined by the mayor. Red Oak Chief John Gage, who had become a friend of the family while George worked for him as a dispatcher, was there to express his sympathy. Jesus Chao, assigned by Vaughn to assist the family in any way he could, stood near Don Moore.

The family and Raffield's fiancée, Martha, had come directly from the Moore house as soon as Vaughn called, dreading what they would hear, yet desperately anxious for answers after the long day's wait. Sherrie Prine, George's half sister, had brought her young sons, one of whom played quietly at her feet while the other sat in her husband's lap.

For several minutes everyone in the room was silent as the city manager told of the search, of finding George's body, and of the suspects the police already had in custody.

It was George's fiancée who asked the first question: "Did the boy who slapped George shoot him?"

Vaughn answered. "No, ma'am. Right now, we have good reason to believe it was a boy named Greg Knighten."

Shirley Moore had begun quietly weeping even before the chief had completed his answer. "I told him to get out," she cried. "I told him his cover was blown and he was going to get hurt. I told him . . ." Don Moore cradled his wife in his arms and the remainder of her sentence was blurred in muffled sobs.

Finally composing herself, she sat erect in her chair and looked at Vaughn. "I want to see him," she said. "I want to see what they've done to my baby."

"Mrs. Moore," Vaughn said gently, "they haven't per-formed the autopsy yet."

"I want to see him," she repeated.

The chief nodded. "I understand," he said, suggesting that she go home and try to get some rest. "I'll be over to pick you up first thing in the morning."

The meeting had lasted less than thirty minutes, yet to those gathered in Pinto's office it had seemed like an eternity. For several minutes after Chao had pulled away, escorting the family back to Red Oak, Vaughn, Pinto, and the mayor stood in the darkness, watching as the taillights faded in the distance, then finally disappeared.

As they stood, each struggling with emotions frayed by the unpleasant duty just fulfilled, a gentle rain began to fall.

In one of the cars silently making its way back to Red Oak, five-year-old Adam Prine climbed over the back seat to be near his father. "Daddy," the little boy said, "Greg did it. He killed Uncle Tiger."

"I know."

"Are you going to kill Greg?"

Mark Prine did not immediately answer the question. Then, gripping the steering wheel tightly and fighting back tears for his brutally murdered brother-in-law, he said, "No, son, the police will have to take care of him."

It was a few minutes before 10:00 P.M. when off-duty Ellis County sheriff's deputies Darrell Carrington and Jim Welch, returning home from a weekend of deer hunting in south Texas, heard of the search for Knighten on their scanner.

Without even bothering to check in, they began driving back roads, looking for the hayride. Only ten minutes had passed before they saw a flatbed trailer parked in front of the entrance to an elementary school on Farm-to-Market Road 664.

As the deputies pulled up alongside the pickup, Jim Cadenhead leaned out the driver's window and began explaining that he had just pulled under the roof of the driveway to get out of the rain.

"Is a boy named Greg Knighten with you?"

"Yes, he's back there with my . . ."

Not even waiting for Cadenhead to finish his sentence, the deputies, guns drawn, hurried to the trailer and called Knighten's name. "He's back there," a teenage voice volunteered.

The beam of Welch's flashlight swept the bed of the trailer until it came to rest on the angry face of a young boy huddled beneath a blanket with his girlfriend.

For a split second both deputies wondered if it was possible that the boy at whom they were pointing their guns could be a murder suspect. Kids didn't kill people; at least not kids in their part of the world.

"Are you Greg Knighten?" Carrington asked.

"Yes."

"You'll have to come with us," the deputy said. "You're under arrest." Even before Greg climbed down from the hay-covered trailer, his rights were being read to him.

Tom Knighton had walked into the Midlothian police station just minutes before his son was escorted inside, a jacket covering his head to shield him from the television cameras that had been poised to record his arrival.

Wet and shivering, Greg was immediately taken into one of the interview rooms where Justice of the Peace Ayers read him the same juvenile rights he had read to Jonathan Jobe earlier in the day.

Feeling a sudden burst of new energy, George Turner was pacing outside the door, anxious to begin his questioning, when Ayers opened the door and signaled him over. "The boy wants to talk with his father," the J.P. said.

Turner's first impulse was to say no—hell, no—but he pondered the request for several seconds and glanced at Tom Knighten. Then, going against his better judgment, Turner called him over. "Greg wants to talk to you," he said, "but you'll have to make it short."

Knighten was in the room only a few minutes before he reappeared and walked over to the waiting Ranger. "I've told him not to say anything," he said.

Turner responded with a steel-hard glare but said nothing. He had made the mistake of thinking of Tom Knighten as a fellow law officer instead of a father of a sixteen-year-old kid charged with cold-blooded murder.

Knighten turned to leave, then stopped near the door and looked back at Turner. "George, he says he didn't do it."

Turner felt his anger melting away. There was no way, he realized, that he could begin to imagine the agony that Tom Knighten must be feeling, no way to know how he might react under the same horrifying circumstances. At that moment he felt a rush of pity for the police officer who walked out into the rain, leaving his son to be taken to jail.

It was after midnight when Cedar Hill Police Captain Phil Hambrick walked into the Midlothian station. Though littered with the remnants of the day's frantic activity— empty Styrofoam cups and stale sandwiches—the small building was quiet, as if resting. Most of the officers from other agencies who had come to lend a hand were on their way home, and the district attorney and justice of the peace had left. Richard Goeglein and Cynthia Fedrick had long since been transported to the Ellis County jail, leaving the Midlothian cells again empty. Turner, after realizing he had not spoken with his wife all day, called home to tell her he would be there after he delivered Greg Knighten to the Cleburne jail. About the only luck he had had all day, he told her, was that the nearest juvenile detention facility in the area was the one just a few miles from their house.

Hambrick had been working an off-duty security job at a Dallas department store when he heard the news that an undercover officer had been killed in Midlothian. Rushing to the appliance department, he had watched aerial shots of the crime scene on one of the demonstration television sets.

Then, for the next two hours, he had frantically tried to get in touch with Jack Wallace. When he had been pulled from his Midlothian undercover assignment at the end of the summer, Wallace had repeatedly expressed disappointment that he was unable to complete several cases on which he had been working. More than once he had suggested that he "just might go back and take care of unfinished business."

Though he had told Wallace not to do so, Hambrick, unaware that Vaughn had put another undercover operation in motion, had feared the worst until Jack finally answered his phone, assuring him he was okay.

Relieved that his own officer was safe, Hambrick had driven to Midlothian after work to see how Vaughn and Fowler were doing and to offer his help.

For almost an hour he sat listening as Vaughn told the tragic story. Hambrick, sensing the sadness in the tired chief's voice, praised the swiftness with which the suspects had been apprehended. "It sounds to me like you people have done a remarkable job today."

Vaughn ignored the compliment. "I can't for the life of me understand how in God's name they thought they would be able to get away with it," he said as he stared down at his desk.

As he drove slowly back toward Cedar Hill, Captain Hambrick thought with sympathy of the burden weighing down on his friends. And he wondered how a police officer would begin to deal with the fact that his own son had killed a fellow officer.

It wasn't until he was almost home that the name Tom Knighten began to ring a faint bell. Though he didn't know him personally, Hambrick remembered that he had spoken with him on the phone almost a year earlier.

The chief had taken a juvenile burglary suspect into custody and, convinced the youngster had committed a series of thefts in Cedar Hill, asked his mother for permission to search the boy's room. Among the stolen items Hambrick found was an expensive target pistol.

After running a check of the serial number and registration, he had learned the pistol belonged to Tom Knighten. He had been surprised at the lack of interest Knighten displayed when he telephoned him to tell him that the gun had been recovered. Tom, in fact, said he was not aware that it was missing. The last time he had seen the gun, it was in the garage. He would check and get back in touch.

The following day Knighten telephoned Hambrick to say he had mentioned the gun to his wife, who reminded him that he had sold it at a flea market.

At the time, the story had seemed strange to Hambrick. He would have to remember to tell Roy Vaughn about it.

15

Midlothian awakened Sunday morning to a somber sense of disbelief. In homes where families quietly prepared for church, the still sketchy details of the murder were discussed in hushed tones. Subscribers to the Dallas newspapers read the blaring front-page headlines in silent horror, faced with the disquieting realization that death was no longer reserved only for the old, the feeble, and the sick; that their comforting invisible barrier against outside evils had been ripped away. They pondered the town's newfound vulnerability while ministers prepared to deliver impassioned sermons on the strength and faith necessary to deal with the cataclysmic event that had visited their small corner of the world.

In a town where the adults had always cheered on the youth, lavishing praise on them for touchdowns scored and honors achieved, a bitter, almost paralyzing sadness swept through the streets. How was it possible that some of their children had turned into such monsters?

Convenience store owner Bobby Sims, who for the past twenty years had made a practice of staying away from his store on Sundays, rose early and drove to town. Standing alone in the parking lot, he raised the flag to half-mast. Within hours other businessmen had done the same.

As his hometown grieved, Texas Ranger Turner, after only a few hours of restless sleep, was leaving Cleburne to continue the investigation. His face was flushed, and he was perspiring freely despite the damp chill in the air. Every muscle in his body throbbed with a dull ache. His cold, he feared, was turning into a full-blown case of flu.

That, however, was not his greatest concern as he drove toward the Midlothian police station. His mind was filled with the lengthy list of things that had to be done. For the next several days, he knew, time would be his greatest adversary. A number of people would have to be questioned as quickly as possible, while memories were still fresh. He would have to meet with the district attorney to update her on the case and seek her advice on specific legal matters. He wanted to do a thorough search of the crime scene, and the weapons Tom Knighten had given him would have to be taken to the forensic lab in Dallas. He wanted to visit the Ellis County jail and talk with Richard Goeglein again. Evidence had to be collected and reports written.

There was, he decided, too much for one man to do. His first move, then, would be to request additional help from the Texas Rangers. Though Vaughn and Fowler had volunteered to help in any way possible, Turner knew they would be tied up with normal police business and funeral arrangements for the next couple of days. George was also keenly aware of the heavy loss his two friends were facing. Both had appeared near the breaking point several times during the previous day's hectic activity. Though he knew they would continue to assist with the investigation, it was now officially a Texas Rangers case, and Turner had already decided on the two men he would request to assist him.

It was a few minutes past eight in the morning when Dr. James Weiner stepped from the elevator into the vast sterile basement of the Southwestern Institute of Forensic Sciences in Dallas. His name had come up in the rotation of pathologists assigned to work a Sunday shift, an assignment roundly disliked by the medical examiner, since it routinely promised a long, busy day. Pathologists working Sundays could anticipate dealing with the tragic aftermath of Saturday night murders resulting from barroom quarrels, domestic hostilities, and dope deals run afoul.

Walking through the examining room, weaving his way among the lifeless bodies lying on gurneys, the pathologist sought out JP3212, the case number assigned to George Raffield. He had heard of the officer's death on the ten o'clock news the night before and had mentally assigned it priority. Investigators, he knew, would be impatient for his report. They always were when a police officer was killed.

As was his practice, the doctor stood for several minutes, looking down at the rigid body before he actually began his examination. Two things struck him: Raffield looked far too young to be a police officer, and the watch on his left wrist still kept perfect time.

It was 8:20 A.M. when the coroner went to work, first studying X rays, which revealed one bullet still lodged in the head, then removing the bloodstained jacket from the body.

The procedure was routine, one the doctor had dispassionately gone through hundreds of times before. Then he took photographs, made fingerprints and palm prints, recorded an inventory of clothing, and weighed and measured the body.

Speaking into a tape recorder in a soft monotone, Dr. Weiner made note of the fact that fly eggs had been laid on the right side of the head and along the neck and shoulder. Dried grass had stuck to the clothing, and there were insect bites on the officer's abdomen. Lividity was evident, and the eyes were closed, hiding the clouded corneas that always accompany death. Blood had seeped from the mouth and nose, coagulating on the right side of the face.

There was a gunshot wound three-eighths of an inch in diameter at the base of the skull, causing a one and three-quarter-inch fracture of the mid-occipital bone. The doctor removed the deformed bullet and placed it gently on a steel tray.

He then turned his attention to a graze wound near the top of the head. Though there was no way to determine which wound had been inflicted first, Dr. Weiner's report would note that the one that had pushed the skull into the brain would have been instantly fatal. As he completed his examination, the doctor wondered if it would give the family any comfort to know that George Raffield had died quickly.

In Waxahachie, Raffield's mother and fiancée met with Roy Vaughn and Chuck Pinto to begin making funeral arrangements. When they were escorted into a back room to choose a casket, Shirley Moore's knees buckled and she fainted into the arms of Mark Prine, her son-in-law.

Still, after she had been revived, she again insisted to Vaughn that she wanted to see her son's body before it was prepared for the funeral. "I've got to know what they did to him," she demanded.

Despite gentle attempts by the police chief to dissuade her, it was finally agreed that the funeral director would contact her as soon as Raffield's body was delivered to Waxahachie.

It was midafternoon when the wary mortician appeared at the Moore home in Red Oak to escort Shirley back to the funeral home. Apologetically, he handed her a form, explaining that she would be required to sign it before seeing the body. The document stated that she would not file suit against the funeral home or any of its employees in the event she suffered a heart attack while viewing her son's body.

Shirley Moore, trembling but walking steadily in the company of the funeral director and her son-in-law, was escorted into the embalming room where her murdered son lay. A sheet covered his body, and a white towel was draped over his head.

Pressing a clenched fist to her mouth, Shirley muffled a scream, then began to sob uncontrollably.

She had not been told her son had been shot in the head.

Several miles away, in the field where Raffield's body was discovered, Turner and several other officers joined Billy Fowler and his wife, Jeanie, in a search for the ignition keys, which Goeglein had said Knighten tossed away. It wasn't until darkness made their efforts fruitless that they abandoned the task.

By the time they walked wearily back toward their cars, the lonely night chorus of insects and frogs, which George Raffield had heard on the night of the murder, had begun.

Turner did not notice the sounds. He was lost in thought, already contemplating the blur of furious activity he knew loomed ahead of him in the days to come.

Sitting behind a desk in his cramped office on the fourth floor of the Ellis County courthouse, Assistant District Attorney Kevin Chester listened silently as George Turner, Billy Fowler, and Roy Vaughn outlined the case. With D.A. Mary Lou Shipley in court in the early stages of a jury trial, it had fallen to her chief assistant to coordinate the efforts of her office with those of the police.

Already that Monday morning Chester had appeared before a juvenile judge who had granted a ten-day detention of Greg Knighten. That accomplished, he wanted a detailed account of everything that had been done on the case.

In his wire-rimmed glasses, Chester looked every bit the confident attorney. His three-piece suit was immaculately tailored, his shoes were polished to a reflective sheen, and not a strand of his thinning blond hair was out of place. He asked few questions as Turner recapped the events, only giving an occasional nod or writing a brief note on the legal pad he had pulled from the mound of paperwork and law books that cluttered his desk.

Having unsuccessfully campaigned against Mary Lou Shipley for the office of D.A., Chester had been surprised when, after the election, she had offered him the position of chief felony prosecutor. Although he had been assigned most of the trial cases since coming to work for her, nothing he had prosecuted even remotely approached the magnitude or complexity of the crime being described to him. This one, Chester knew, promised to become the most highly publicized case in Ellis County history. Members of the media had even been on hand for Knighten's fifteen-minute detention hearing. Chester had already received word that a film crew from New York was en route, planning to do a story for the Fox network's nationally syndicated news program, "A Current Affair."

A meticulously ordered man, Chester had confided to his wife, Darla, that he badly wanted to be put in charge of the case. Not only did it offer a challenge unlike any he had ever met, but it promised the first real opportunity to test his talent as a prosecutor.

Privately, Chester had long disapproved of the manner in which many felony cases were handled by various law enforcement agencies in Ellis County. Citizens constantly criticized the number of dismissals and plea bargains by the D.A.'s office, unaware that the improper preparation of the cases by arresting officers had often left no other option. With this case, he wanted to make certain that did not happen.

One thing he had learned during his five-year career as an attorney was that police and lawyers worked together under the most fragile of trusts. While sworn to work toward the same judicial goals, their approaches were often light-years apart. Cops, he knew, were all too often ruled by emotion. A crime is committed, an arrest is made. Then comes the officers' immediate demand for justice in the courts. To them it was that simple. To Chester, it was important to remain emotionally detached, to view the evidence brought to him with a critical eye. His focus had to be firmly fixed upon the law, concentrated only on what would or would not hold up in court.

In the days to come, Chester knew, he would be regarded as the devil's advocate by the men he worked with. No doubt they would be wary of his inexperience, questioning his ability to handle the enormous task that lay ahead. They would quietly check and find that he had tried only two other murder cases—one as a defense lawyer, the other as a prosecutor. He had lost the first, then, after doing much of his own investigative work on the second, won a guilty verdict.

Though he did not know Vaughn well, Chester had been impressed with the way cases from his department were prepared. And he knew the thorough manner in which Fowler approached his work. The fact that Vaughn had had the foresight to call in the Texas Rangers to head the investigation was another plus.

Still, Chester was firm in his instructions. Although it had rarely been done in the past, he wanted every statement, no matter how trivial the information, to be submitted in writing. "We're going to be dealing with a lot of sixteen- and seventeen-year-old kids in this thing," he said. "By the time we get to trial they may have forgotten what they said or decided to tell a completely different story. I want to have something in my hand that will refresh their memories."

His instructions completed, he leaned back in his chair, lit a cigarette, and studied the three men seated across from him. By all rights, Turner should have been home in bed nursing the flu. The faces of Vaughn and Fowler were lined with grief and exhaustion. That the two men remained functional was a testimony to their energy and sheer willpower.

Aware of the magnitude of the task at hand, Chester had requested that Turner phone his commanding officer in Waco and ask for assistance. Rangers Fred Cummings and John Aycock, two of the most highly regarded investigators in Company F, were already on their way to Waxahachie. Additionally, Chester had asked Ellis County Sheriff Barney Boyd to assign Deputy Ronnie Harris, who the assistant D.A. felt was the most capable officer on Boyd's staff, to assist the Rangers.

By Monday afternoon the process of interviewing those who might have any knowledge of the crime was under way. And the first unforeseen twist in the case had developed.

In the Ellis County jail, a female inmate had a story she wanted to tell.

Ranger Aycock, though still not thoroughly briefed on the case, sat in the office of the jailer, listening as the young black woman told of being locked in the same cell with Cynthia Fedrick.

As a tape recorder ran, she described a conversation she and Cynthia had had. "She told me how they killed that policeman over in Midlothian," the woman said in a whining, nervous voice. "It was right before her folks came and bailed her out." According to her, Cynthia said she had accompanied the youngsters to the field outside of town and watched as Greg Knighten fired the first shot, which knocked the officer to the ground. Then, Cynthia had told her, he handed the gun to Goeglein, who shot the officer a second time as he lay unconscious beside his pickup.

As the woman told her story, George Turner was driving in the direction of the crime scene, Richard Goeglein seated next to him. While Knighten was being returned to the juvenile detention facility in Cleburne following his court appearance, he had volunteered to Sheriff's Deputy Jim Welch that the spent rounds from the gun used in the murder had been tossed out near a railroad crossing on the road leading to Jamie Cadenhead's house.

The deputy had relayed the information immediately after turning Knighten over to the jailer. While the admission was valuable, Welch knew that it would be of no use in the event Knighten went to trial. Not expecting any conversation en route to Cleburne, the deputy had not advised Knighten of his rights. By law, the remark about the discarded shells would be inadmissable in court.

Unfamiliar with the area, Richard had difficulty pinpointing the location of the shells until Turner had retraced the route the boys had taken from the field. At first Goeglein had indicated the area was on the farm road that led from the murder scene back into town. Then, after considerable thought, he recalled they had only thrown out Raffield's comb in that area.

Finally, after almost an hour, Richard sat upright as Turner negotiated an S-shaped turn on Farm Road 1387. Pointing across a ditch, he said, "That's the place. Jonathan slowed down to make the turn and Greg leaned across me and threw them somewhere over in that direction."

Turner pulled to the side of the road and, leaning against the steering wheel, looked out at the head-high stand of wild cane growing on the edge of a small stock tank. Important evidence lay somewhere among the impossibly thick tangle, and finding it, he feared, would be like the proverbial search for a needle in a haystack.

Still, Turner mentally added it to his growing list, then headed back to Waxahachie to return Goeglein to jail.

That done, Turner drove to the nearest hospital and spent the better part of the next hour arguing with a doctor who warned him that his flu appeared well on the way to developing into pneumonia. The frail-looking but insistent doctor recommended that Turner allow himself to be admitted to the hospital immediately.

His patience worn threadbare, Turner stepped down from the examining table and glared at the white-coated man, who was six inches shorter and fifty pounds lighter than he was. "Look, goddammit," he said. "I've got a murder case to work on, and all hell is breaking loose. I don't have time to lie around in a hospital. I don't even have time to be sick. All I want is a shot or a prescription that will knock this shit out so I can get back to work."

Even before his tirade ended, the doctor was writing out a prescription.

For the next several days, the men and women putting the case together rarely saw each other until they gathered for late night meetings. A steady stream of teenagers, generally accompanied by parents with sad, strained faces, appeared at the Midlothian City Hall, where their statements were taken. Those who didn't come voluntarily were sought out in the halls at the high school.

For a while, each story the officers heard seemed to lead to the need to talk to someone else who had another fragment of information, another small piece of the puzzle. In time, Aycock and Cummings came to share the same disbelief expressed to them earlier by Turner. Half the kids in town, it seemed, had heard that a murder plot was taking shape, yet they had said nothing. The other half seemed to have learned about the murder after it happened, but still long before the police knew.

Aycock, who had spent years as a Department of Public Safety narcotics investigator before joining the Rangers, looked down at the pile of statements and shook his head. "Maybe it would be simpler just to go through the Midlothian phone book," he said.

Alerted to Cynthia's claim that a second shot was fired after Raffield had fallen, Chief Vaughn had immediately called the medical examiner's office and was told that it would be impossible to determine whether one of the wounds had been inflicted after Raffield had fallen to the ground.

Though convinced that the story Cynthia had told her cell mate was nothing more than the kind of "jail talk" commonly used by inmates to convince others that they were tough and not to be messed with, Turner, Vaughn, and Aycock returned to the crime scene and collected soil from an area twelve inches deep and approximately two feet in diameter directly below where Raffield's head had lain. Back at the station, George and Lieutenant Fowler spent most of one afternoon straining the rocky dirt through wire mesh, searching for a bullet that might have embedded itself in the ground. Their efforts, as they had expected, yielded nothing.

"She was just trying to convince people she's a bad-ass," Fowler said.

If either harbored doubts that Cynthia was making up stories, they were put aside soon after Captain Hambrick called from the Cedar Hill Police Department. He had a female prisoner in custody, he said, who'd had a conversation with Cynthia in the Ellis County jail. "I don't know if it's anything," Hambrick said, "but I thought you might want to hear what she has to say."

Suppressing the urge to offer a guess about what Cynthia might have said, Fowler told Hambrick he would be there right away. Upon his arrival he was ushered into an interview room where a small, frightened woman sat at a table, alternately sipping from a canned soda and taking deep drags from a cigarette.

"I'm not telling you anything," she said, "unless you promise me that she won't know about it."

Fowler smiled and nodded. "Cynthia's got much bigger problems than you to worry about. Why don't you just tell me what you know?"

"Everybody in the jail was scared to death of her," the woman said, "even the goddam guards. In just a couple of days she was running the place."

Fowler maintained his patience. "Did she talk about the murder?"

"She said she went out to this field somewhere with two boys who were going to kill this narc that had been hassling them. But when they got out there, the boys chickened out. They said they couldn't do it. So she got pissed and just grabbed the gun out of this one dude's hand and shot the narc in the back of the head. She's the one who killed him."

"Anything else?"

The woman took another drag from her cigarette and thought for several seconds. "Yeah," she finally said, "and this is fucking cold-blooded. She said she ground her heel into the hole in the back of the dead man's head so the medical examiner wouldn't be able to tell what kind of bullet he was shot with."

En route back to Midlothian, Fowler vowed to waste no more time chasing Cynthia Fedrick's fairy tales. There was too much else to do.

A city maintenance crew was dispatched to the area where Goeglein said the spent shells were thrown, and the cane was cut away so a search could be made. Even with the aid of metal detectors and officers searching the ground on hands and knees, the effort was fruitless.

Finally, after every inch of the area had been gone over thoroughly, Vaughn, in frustration, suggested an experiment to Fowler. Gathering five .38 caliber shells, they drove to the same area and simulated the speed at which Goeglein indicated Jobe had been driving. As they crossed the railroad tracks and neared the area where the cane had been, Fowler tossed the marked shells out the passenger window. Despite an all-day search, they were only able to retrieve two of the five Fowler had thrown.

On another visit to the Knighten house, Cummings and Deputy Harris returned all but one of the handguns that Tom Knighten had turned over and gathered samples of his ammunition in the hope of matching the wad cutters that had been used in the murder. Additionally, Nelda Knighten turned over articles of clothing she thought Greg had been wearing when he left the house the previous Friday evening.

Neither of the officers commented as she handed them a sleeveless white T-shirt with a skull and crossbones and the word *Headhunter* emblazoned across the front.

On an unseasonably warm Tuesday, George Raffield's funeral was held in Waxahachie. As the ceremony was being conducted, George Turner and his fellow Rangers were examining the bloodstains on the dead officer's pickup and preparing the ballistic evidence to be taken to the forensic lab in Dallas.

They had talked the night before about attending the services, but had finally agreed that it was essential to continue work on the case.

It was, they decided, the best way of showing their respect.

16

The first days of November gave warning that the chilling discomfort of winter would soon arrive in north Texas. The blustery winds that swept across Ellis County took on a hard bite that sent dairy farmers in search of heavy jackets and wives to the closets for additional quilts for the bed. Outside chores were accomplished with a quicker step, the reward for their hurried completion being a return to the warmth indoors.

Men lingered longer over coffee at Dec Tee's and Amie Ann's, and women quick-stepped from their cars into the grocery store or post office, no longer stopping to chat in the parking lot. To the casual observer, it appeared the people of Midlothian had fallen back into a normal routine. Below the surface, however, a pervasive feeling of despondency shrouded the town.

Over evening meals, worried parents questioned children about their friends. At school, teachers tried at first to discourage classroom discussion of the tragedy, then decided it was healthier to allow the students to talk about their feelings. Traffic into Dallas for drug purchases had slowed almost to a stop. The dopers, according to the word on the streets, were scared.

Mixed among the familiar faces was a steady invasion of visiting reporters, some from as far away as New York, Washington, and Los Angeles, all with the same assignment: to learn the effect of a drug-related tragedy on small-town America.

And as journalists went about their interviews, virtually every high school student they spoke with claimed that he or she had suspected all along that George Raffield was an undercover narcotics officer. He looked too old and was generally better dressed than the other kids; teachers never made him do homework; he could be late for school, but was never sent to detention hall.

A classmate of Raffield's named Rob Summers recalled that everyone in his English class had kidded George about being an undercover officer. "Yeah," Summers said, "we called him 'Twenty-one Jump Street,' after the TV show."

Yet, after being questioned by Turner or other investigators, few members of the same English class verified the youngster's recollection. Many students, in fact, began reluctantly admitting they had never even met Raffield. But with television cameras and reporters from *Time* and *Rolling Stone* in town, hungry for interviews, everyone seemed to want in on the act.

Still, after two weeks of around-the-clock preparation, Turner was comfortable that more than enough evidence had been gathered to convince a grand jury to indict Knighten and Goeglein for capital murder.

He had also become convinced that Jonathan Jobe was far more deeply involved in the crime than he had originally thought. In the first week of November, Turner asked Justice of the Peace Ayers to prepare a warrant for Jobe's arrest.

In Waxahachie, meanwhile, the legal wheels began to turn and Turner found himself facing a new cast of adversaries when a judge appointed attorneys for Knighten and Goeglein.

George Turner was sitting in his office one morning when a long-distance call came from Detective Jeffrey Greene, the

Coconino County sheriff's deputy who had investigated the assault Goeglein had been involved in in Williams, Arizona. Turner had spoken to him during the early stages of the investigation, briefing him on the case and asking for details of the beating of Elliott Smith.

"Listen," Greene said, "I got a strange call from a police officer in some place called Carl's Corner, Texas, yesterday. He told me he was working on the Raffield murder and asked if I would send him the files on this case here. Also said he would like to come out and talk with me. I didn't think too much about it and told him it was okay with me. Then, last night, I got to wondering if something fishy might be going on."

"It damn sure is," Turner replied immediately. "Did you mail the file to him?"

"No, it's sitting here on my desk. I thought I'd better give you a call first."

Turner leaned back in his chair, the phone cradled against his ear, wondering why the police in a tiny community sixty miles away would be interested in the Raffield case.

"Who was the guy who called?" he asked.

"I don't have his name here in front of me . . ."

"That's okay, there can't be but one officer there. The place isn't anything but a truck stop on the highway."

Greene laughed. "I felt like there was something squirrelly about the deal."

"I'm going to check him out," Turner replied. "I'd appreciate it if you wouldn't send him anything or talk to him," Turner said.

"That's all I needed to hear," Greene said.

After promising to keep him updated on the case, Turner hung up and sat staring at the phone. After a few minutes he began to nod and smile to himself. What was it Shakespeare had said? Something about society being a helluva lot better off if somebody would kill all the lawyers.

He remembered an article that had appeared in one of the Dallas papers just a few days earlier. Though he had read it hurriedly, he recalled that Jim Jenkins, Greg's attorney, had argued that his client was not the triggerman in Raffield's murder. He said Greg had admitted accompanying Raffield and Goeglein to the field but had no idea that the purpose of the trip was murder. Greg, the attorney had told the reporter, was shocked and horrified by what happened.

All pretty standard defense-lawyer talk, Turner thought.

But then, near the end of the article, Turner recalled, the incident in Williams, Arizona, had been mentioned. And there had been an interesting quote from Jenkins. He said he wanted to learn more about Goeglein's involvement.

Turner reached for the phone. After several rings the Carl's Corner officer answered.

As Turner questioned him about his interest in the case, the officer sounded nervous to Turner. No, he explained, the deputy in Arizona had misunderstood. He hadn't told him he was working on the Raffield case. "See," he tried to explain, "we've been hearing rumors about a lot of devil-worshiping going on around here. I got some information that this Goeglein boy had been hanging around down here, and I thought it would be a good idea to check him out."

Turner fought to keep from laughing at what was, in his opinion, a lame story. "Where did you get this information?" he asked.

There was another long pause before the officer answered. "I'm not real sure offhand. I'd have to check my files."

"Don't bother," Turner said. "I'm telling you that Richard Goeglein doesn't even have the foggiest notion where the hell Carl's Corner is. He's never been there, believe me."

The officer seemed to sputter for a few seconds, then said if that was the case he had no interest in the matter.

"That's good," Turner said, "because I'd hate to think any other law officer would be low-life enough to try to run under me on this investigation."

It was Turner's concern that the man might have been acting in behalf of Knighten's attorney. If so, Turner had learned what course the defense planned to take. It would attempt to switch the blame from Knighten to the devil-worshiping new kid in town.

Knighten's attorney, however, was not Turner's only concern. Immediately after learning of the interest the Carl's Corner officer had expressed in the case, Turner drove directly to the Ellis County sheriff's office and requested that a notice be posted in the jail stating that no other law enforcement officer but him was to be allowed to interview Goeglein.

Two days later Turner arrived to find that the notice had been covered by a letter signed by Lee Johnson, Goeglein's attorney. It stated that no one, including Texas Ranger Turner, was to be allowed to talk with his client.

The games had begun.

On November 10, a grand jury was called to consider whether Goeglein and Knighten should be indicted on charges of capital murder. Jurors listened silently as Kevin Chester carefully went over the evidence, outlining the plot to kill Raffield, then reading statements which made it clear that both Greg and Richard had been at the crime scene. It did not matter, the assistant D.A. pointed out, who actually pulled the trigger. In the eyes of the law, both shared the guilt equally.

When Lieutenant Fowler was called upon to describe Raffield's duties and his relationship with Knighten, he wept as he told of learning that Raffield was dead. Several of the grand jurors cried along with him.

They voted to indict.

Earlier, while several Midlothian youngsters sat nervously in the witness room waiting to be called to testify, Cynthia Fedrick had glared at them from the head of the table. For several days her brother, Randy Marcott, had been passing the word at school that Cynthia had said anyone who made her look bad was going to get his ass kicked. Now, facing several of the youngsters to whom the threat had been passed along, she had the opportunity to express her feelings in person.

Looking at sixteen-year-old JoAnne Dupree, who had been summoned to testify about Jamie Cadenhead's call to her from the Dairy Queen, Cynthia began talking of the brief conversation she and Richard had in the Midlothian jail the Saturday after the murder. "The only reason I'm here," she said, "is because that fucking Jonathan told the cops about them coming over to my house that night. He talks way too much. Somebody needs to kick his fat ass."

Then she turned her attention to Jamie. "The next time you visit Sparky, tell him I need to see him. I want to talk to him." It was a demand, not a request. Then, smiling, she said, "You know why he did it, don't you?"

Jamie did not reply.

"He did it because I scared him."

Two days later Greg Knighten was certified as an adult following a three-hour hearing. He was immediately ordered moved from the juvenile detention facility in Cleburne to the Ellis County jail where he would be held without bond.

On the same day District Judge Knize set Richard Goeglein's bail at $500,000.

As the wearying investigation began to wind down, the role played by Cynthia Fedrick became a subject of growing debate. While Turner doubted that she had actually instructed Sparky Knighten to carry out the murder, Vaughn and Fowler stood firm in their belief that she should be charged with soliciting the crime and had argued their point to the district attorney repeatedly.

Concerned that making anything more than a circumstantial case against her was impossible, Turner persuaded Cynthia to take a polygraph test. He picked her up at her apartment and took her to the DPS regional office in nearby Garland where she answered questions posed her by the polygraph operator. Results of the test indicated that she had been telling the truth when she denied having orchestrated Raffield's murder.

If anything, Turner argued, she was guilty of hindering the investigation by destroying Raffield's driver's license. He had briefly considered such a charge but decided that she would be more valuable as a witness against the three boys. He had wrestled with the same decision in regard to Jamie Cadenhead. By hiding the gun Greg had brought to her, she had left herself open for prosecution. But he knew a good defense attorney would play heavily on the innocence of young love, making it difficult for a jury to return a guilty verdict. They would have to be satisfied with her testimony.

With the facts of the case now gathered, Turner was surprised to find himself thinking like a lawyer.

While Vaughn and Fowler reluctantly agreed with him on Cadenhead, they were unyielding on the matter of Cynthia's involvement. Finally, Mary Lou Shipley and Chester were persuaded to their side after reviewing the statement of Grant Donley, who had heard Cynthia say "they were going to get George."

On Friday morning, November 23, Lieutenant Fowler, accompanied by several other Midlothian officers, drove to the home of Joyce and Dennis Brown, just a few blocks from the police station. Cynthia, they knew, had left her Oxford Square apartment after her parents had bailed her out following the initial charge and had moved in with the Browns.

When Cynthia appeared at the front door, Fowler told her he had a warrant for her arrest.

"What for?" Cynthia asked, assuming it was for unpaid traffic tickets in Duncanville.

"We'll talk about that later," Fowler replied. "Just come with us."

Cynthia hugged her daughter, then asked Joyce Brown to follow them to the station and arrange bail.

"I don't think she'll be able to afford it," Fowler interrupted, taking Cynthia by the arm and escorting her to the car.

The arrest warrant he had brought with him was for solicitation of capital murder. By the end of the day Cynthia Fedrick's bail would be set at $100,000.

On the day before Thanksgiving, Jonathan Jobe was scheduled to appear at the Waxahachie courthouse for a hearing that would determine whether or not he would be certified to stand trial as an adult despite his adolescent age.

To accomplish their goal, Shipley and Chester would have to present evidence to the judge that the sixteen-year-old Jobe was mentally mature and understood the charges against him. To help in their argument, they had solicited the services of local psychiatrist Roberto Schack.

A staff member at the newly opened Willowbrook Psychiatric Hospital in Waxahachie, Dr. Schack had also testified in the Knighten certification hearing, stating that during his half-hour interview with Greg he had been "scared to death" by the youngster. He had immediately detected psychopathic and sociopathic disorders in Knighten but felt he was competent and mature enough to stand trial as an adult.

The report that the doctor turned over to the district attorney's office several days earlier, however, indicated that the doctor had reservations about Jobe. He felt the boy to be immature for his age.

Suddenly facing the concern that the doctor might turn into an adverse witness on the stand, Chester called him to his office. There, with Vaughn and Fowler joining them, the assistant D.A. reviewed the case against Jobe.

Dr. Schack reluctantly admitted that he had not been made aware of much of what they were telling him. His brief interview, he said, had been conducted in the company of Jobe's mother, who had answered most of his questions. He also admitted that he had privately spoken with Jonathan's attorney, Connie McGuire, about the youngster on several occasions prior to the interview.

The picture that had been painted for him was drastically different from the one that Chester was providing.

"I'm not surprised," the prosecutor said. He had dealt many times with Connie McGuire when she had come to his office to plead the cases of her clients. As he saw it, her manner, the touching of a hand or arm, the laughter that seemed all too cheery, and the flips of her frosted blond hair, served as warning signals. It was no secret around the courthouse that it was Kevin Chester's opinion that she was one of the most manipulative lawyers in town.

At the conclusion of the meeting Dr. Schack said he would immediately submit a letter to the judge, stating that he needed to investigate the matter more thoroughly before reaching a decision.

The date for the certification hearing arrived without the letter having been written. The doctor submitted his original findings, and an angry Chester prepared to question him as a hostile witness.

On the stand, Dr. Schack was asked about his conversations with Connie McGuire: "Isn't it true that she spoke with you on several occasions, emphasizing the fact that her client was immature?" And Sharrell Jobe: "Wasn't Jonathan's mother allowed to sit in on the session you conducted, answering many of the questions for her son?"

By the time he told the judge that he had no further questions, Chester privately felt he had done the best cross-examination of his career.

That done, Sharrell Jobe was called to the stand and questioned by Mary Lou Shipley. In a soft, almost inaudible voice, the district attorney established that Jonathan hoped to pursue a military career, following in the footsteps of his two uncles and both of his grandfathers. "The fact that he has already begun making plans for his future," the district attorney said, "would indicate he is a mature-thinking young man, would it not?" Even before Sharrell Jobe could answer, the D.A. stated that she had no further questions.

Stepping from the witness stand, Mrs. Jobe walked past the table where Shipley sat, looking down at her legal pad in preparation for the next witness. She glanced up when Sharrell stopped just feet away from her.

"You bitch," the angered mother spat, glaring down at the prosecutor.

Before the hearing was completed, Jamie Cadenhead added another strike against the defendant. Yes, she admitted to Chester, she had heard Jonathan mention George at school the day before he was murdered.

"Do you recall what he said?" Kevin asked.

Cadenhead's answer was barely more than a whisper. "He said he was dead meat."

Jobe was certified as an adult and ordered to jail for the first time since the murder.

In a separate ruling, Judge Gene Knize denied Connie McGuire's request that the court appoint her as Jonathan's attorney. Having earlier indicated that her services had been retained by the family, she now told the court that the Jobes could not afford legal counsel. Knize ruled that her initial statement that she had been hired by the family represented a circumvention of the judicial system and refused her request.

The following day, Lon Earl Hayes, Jobe's grandfather, posted $50,000 bail and Jonathan was released. It would be Hayes's final gift to his grandson. He died of a heart attack just days later.

Connie McGuire, however, refused to completely remove herself from the case. One afternoon Chester entered the court reporters' office to find her talking with Joe Grubbs, the newly appointed attorney for Greg Knighten, and his investigator, Mike Yarbrough. Eavesdropping, Chester learned that they were planning a trip out to the crime scene.

Though unaware of the purpose of their trip, Kevin Chester telephoned Billy Fowler in Midlothian and suggested that he follow them and attempt to see what they did.

Fowler had a better idea. Following his conversation with Chester, he quickly called Weston Ramsey, owner of the property on which the crime had been committed. "I just thought you might like to know," he said, "that some people are on their way out to your place."

"Lawyers for those damn kids?"

"That's what I heard."

Ramsey needed no further explanation. "They won't be there long," he said.

McGuire, Grubbs, and Yarbrough had just stepped from their car when Ramsey drove up behind them and ordered them off his property.

* * *

When the Thanksgiving holidays ended, Jonathan was back in school, walking the halls with girlfriend Becky Goeglein. If he harbored any concern over the dramatic turn in his life, he hid it well. Instead, he seemed to enjoy his newfound status as a campus celebrity.

With no legal means to prevent Jobe's return to school, Principal Roesler and many of the teachers were incensed that an accused murderer would be allowed such freedom.

There was no way, they knew, that the remainder of the school year could be conducted normally. Despite efforts to divert the attention of students back to the academic routine, the death of George Raffield hung over Midlothian High School like a cloud. In the halls and lunchroom the murder was a primary topic of discussion. Eventually the student body divided into two camps: one, headed by Jamie Cadenhead, stood firm in the belief that Richard Goeglein had fired the fatal shots; the other, led by Becky, pointed accusing fingers at Greg Knighton. One afternoon the argument became so heated that a fight broke out between Jamie and Becky in the parking lot, prompting Roesler to send both girls home for the remainder of the day.

In an attempt to defuse the angry climate that was polarizing the community, an anti-drug rally was planned, complete with a downtown parade and a ceremony at which a scholarship named in George Raffield's honor would be announced. A traveling evangelist, promoting himself as a born-again Christian who had once served as a satanic high priest, spoke to a turn-away crowd at the high school gymnasium. While students participated in the Just Say No program, adults formed an organization called REACH in an effort to join forces in the battle against drugs. Store owners placed "We Care" signs in their windows, and a citizens' group raised over $6,000 to purchase bulletproof vests for the police department. An impassioned editorial appeared in the *Midlothian Reporter*, urging the townspeople to put the tragedy behind them and again focus on the positive aspects of the community.

For all the effort, however, the devastating wound would not heal.

Turner, however, was dealing with another kind of problem. Each evening at almost the same time, the number 666—a satanic sign of the beast—would appear on the digital beeper he wore clipped to his belt. At first he suspected a practical joker, perhaps his neighbor, who worked as a narcotics investigator for the DPS. The trooper, however, denied any game-playing, and Turner thought little more about it until one evening when he and his family returned home from a restaurant. His son had asked to be allowed to check the answering machine for messages as they entered the house. Turner had returned to the kitchen after taking his sleeping daughter to her bedroom to find Josh standing by the phone with a horrified look on his face. On the answering machine was a growling chant.

The following day Turner made a trip to Midlothian High School and spoke to several students he knew to be friends of Richard Goeglein. If they were trying to hassle him, he said, it was okay with him. Frightening his family, on the other hand, was a different matter and there would be hell to pay when he found out who was doing it.

Thereafter, the daily messages stopped coming in on his beeper and his answering machine recorded only routine calls.

In the Ellis County jail, tension was mounting. Though efforts had been made to keep Knighten and Goeglein separated, they exchanged angry words on several occasions when Richard passed Greg's cell en route to the exercise yard. Once, in a fit of anger, Goeglein threatened to kill Knighten. Knighten, in turn, solicited the help of several other inmates, offering money to anyone who would "knock Richard's fucking teeth out."

Frightened, Goeglein began to palm the medication given him daily by one of the guards, going through the mock gesture of taking the pill prescribed to reduce his anxieties. After several weeks of collecting the tranquilizers and hiding them beneath the mattress of his bunk, he swallowed them all and furiously began doing push-ups in an attempt to speed his heart rate and blood flow. Guards found him lying unconscious on his cell floor following his apparent suicide attempt and he was rushed to a nearby hospital where his stomach was pumped. Later Richard insisted that he had no intention of killing himself. He just wanted to get high and escape, even for a short time, from the misery of jail life.

In Midlothian, Roy Vaughn was wrestling with talk of another kind of agony. Late one evening, as he was preparing to leave for the day, the chief went into Billy Fowler's office and suggested they take a ride out to the Knighten house.

Vaughn had received a call from a friend who worked at the southwest substation in Dallas. The man had told him that Tom Knighten was thinking about resigning from the Dallas police force.

At the Knighten home, the two Midlothian policemen drank coffee and urged Tom not to toss away his career. What had happened, Vaughn and Fowler gently tried to assure the distraught parents, was not their fault.

Moved by the gesture, Knighten asked their advice on mortgaging his home in order to pay for a lawyer to represent his son. "Tom," Fowler said, "a trial like this could cost thousands and thousands of dollars. You and I have both seen families ruined financially by this sort of thing. The courts are obligated to appoint an attorney for your boy, and I have to believe the judge will be careful to pick a good one."

Knighten glanced at his wife and nodded silently. "Billy," he finally said, "I've got to ask you one other thing. Do you think Greg was the one who did it?"

The question sent a shiver of empathy through the lieutenant. He sat looking across at his friend's agonized face for several seconds before answering. Then he nodded. "Tom," he said, "I'm afraid so."

On the way back to the station, Vaughn and Fowler said little, lost in their own private thoughts. Both remembered when Tom Knighten was an instructor at the pistol range in Dallas, always smiling, eager to help. Shortly after Vaughn was sworn in as Midlothian police chief, Tom had come by the station to say that he had an extra spot at the summer boys' camp sponsored by the Salvation Army and wondered if Roy might recommend some youngster in the community to whom it could be given. A good cop and a strong Christian, Knighten did not deserve the burden that had been placed on his shoulders.

There was a widespread sense of relief when it was finally announced that trial dates had been set. District Attorney Shipley, stating that she would personally prosecute all four cases, had decided that Richard Goeglein would be tried first. Jury selection would begin early in the spring.

17

Turner slowed his car as he reached the section of Highway 287 that abruptly becomes a tree-shaded residential area of Midlothian. It was early in December, and he was on his way to Waxahachie for yet another strategy meeting with Mary Lou Shipley and Kevin Chester.

Since the indictments of the defendants, he had made countless trips from Cleburne to the district attorney's office. The routine seemed always the same. He would receive a call alerting him to the fact the D.A. had a break in her schedule and wanted to discuss the case. Turner was expected to drop whatever he was doing and come running.

On this day a meeting had been scheduled for 10:00 A.M., and as usual, he was pressing it to make it to Waxahachie on time.

As he drove, Turner found himself pondering his involvement in the case. For two months it had consumed him, becoming the driving force in his life. He and Dana had spent precious little time together since that Saturday morning call had first summoned him to Midlothian. Her schedule as an emergency room nurse in Fort Worth and his role in the investigation had turned their relationship into one of hurried meals together, brief telephone conversations, and notes left on the kitchen counter. All too regularly his children were tucked into bed and sleeping when he finally arrived home.

Turner had begun to worry that his obsession with the case was taking too great a toll. His priorities had undergone a change that he found discomforting.

But while a part of him longed for the case to be over, he had invested too much time and energy to slow down before the job was completed. He would have to see it through, regardless of the personal sacrifice. Only when it was all over could he feel comfortable taking some time off to spend with his family. Maybe they would get away from town for a long weekend on the Texas Gulf Coast.

Mentally reviewing the events since that October weekend, he felt a brief surge of comfort in the fact that despite trouble spots along the way, he had done a good job. He had been particularly relieved when ballistics experts at the Bureau of Alcohol, Tobacco and Firearms, using a newly designed high-powered microscope, had successfully matched the bullet taken from George Raffield with Tom Knighten's handgun, despite attempts to alter the interior of the barrel. The evidence he had collected and turned over to the district attorney's office, he felt, provided the foundation for strong cases against Greg Knighten and Richard Goeglein. Though less comfortable with the chance of gaining convictions of Jonathan Jobe and Cynthia Fedrick, he was convinced that all that could be done had been. The case was now out of his control, in the hands of the lawyers. Still, he couldn't let go.

The truth of the matter was, he admitted to himself, that he would be making regular trips to Waxahachie even if his presence was not requested.

As he neared the Midlothian business district, Turner saw his father sitting on his front porch. As was routine with Texas weather, winter had taken a brief hiatus, and the elder Turner, who had been in and out of the hospital with heart problems in recent months, was enjoying the early morning sun.

George slowed and considered pulling over to talk for a few minutes, then looked down at his watch. Instead, he honked and waved, then sped on toward his meeting.

Only later, after arriving to learn that scheduling problems had developed and the meeting had been postponed for a couple of hours, did the decision begin to grate on Turner. Was the conviction of a collection of no-good kids so important that he could not take time to spend a few minutes with his sick father who might, in fact, be dying? The question angered him. Then, later in the day, after learning that his dad had been rushed back to the hospital just hours after he had driven past, it sent him into a fit of depression.

The case was taking over his life, pulling his loyalties in the wrong direction. Suddenly he felt the oath he had taken and the badge he proudly wore demanded too much. What if he had to live the rest of his life with the knowledge that the last time he saw his father he did not even take the time to say hello, if the last chapter of their loving relationship was nothing more than a honk and a quick wave?

The next day things just had to wait for George Turner. Before making a scheduled trip to the crime scene for an experiment arranged by Ranger John Aycock, Turner paid a visit to his father in the hospital.

Although Aycock had returned to his regular duties, he had made several visits to Midlothian to check on the progress of the case. His role in the investigation had officially ended after the two weeks of statement-taking and evidence-gathering immediately following the crime, but his interest had continued.

Aware that the defense would in all likelihood attempt to discredit Richard Goeglein's story, he had telephoned Turner with a suggestion. Aycock had recently attended a seminar on a relatively new form of forensic investigation that he felt might prove useful. He suggested to George that they conduct a blood-splatter experiment.

A scientific re-creation of the crime, wherein the same

kind of gun was fired into a mannequin from the position described by Goeglein, could help determine the truth of his statement. Aycock briefly described the technique, then said that Sergeant Dusty Askew of the Austin Police Department, an expert in the field, had agreed to conduct the experiment.

The suggestion had excited Turner and sparked the curiosity of Kevin Chester when it was relayed to him. Chief Vaughn quickly agreed to help gather the materials Askew would need. Only Mary Lou Shipley expressed reservations about the idea; she declined to accompany the others to the crime scene.

On the day the experiment was to be conducted, the weather turned cold and bitter again. The sun was hidden by heavy gray clouds by the time Turner, Chester, Aycock, and Ellis County Deputy Sheriff Ronnie Harris arrived at Weston Ramsey's pasture.

Vaughn had arranged for a pickup that was the same make and model as Raffield's to be driven to the crime scene and parked in the same location. At Askew's request, George's truck had been towed from storage and was parked nearby so that comparisons could be made as the experiment was conducted.

Methodically, Askew went about his task of setting things in place for the strange exercise. A tripod was erected on the spot where Raffield had been standing when he was shot; a Styrofoam head, much like those used for storage of wigs, was placed at its top. Askew measured the bizarre-looking apparatus to make sure it was exactly five feet eight inches tall, Raffield's height.

That done, he stretched cloth across the crown of the mannequin head, explaining that the fabric had the same consistency as muscle and tissue. Human blood donated by a local hospital was poured onto the cloth, then quickly covered with a piece of dried pig's skin. Finally Askew took a wig with hair length similar to that of the victim and attached it to the Styrofoam head.

Using a .38 revolver and wad-cutter ammunition that Vaughn had provided, Aycock—the member of the group nearest the height of Knighten—stood across the bed of the pickup from the dummy, aimed, and fired.

Chester jumped at the sound of the shot. Though the target hardly resembled a human form, he felt a chill as the head nodded forward and blood spurted from the spot where the bullet had entered. For the first time since he had entered the investigation, it occurred to the assistant D.A. how quickly Raffield's death had come. Although the temperature had dipped into the twenties, he was perspiring and a growing knot swelled in the pit of his stomach.

For almost two hours the tests continued. After each shot, each splatter of blood on the truck was logged and measured, then wiped away. The head was reassembled, and then Aycock moved to a slightly different location and fired again.

Only one blood-splatter pattern matched that of the crime scene photographs. The shots that had struck Raffield in the back of the head had come from the spot where Goeglein had said Greg Knighten was standing.

Silently examining the specks of blood yielded by the shot fired from just in front of the wheel well on the passenger side, Askew found tiny traces atop the cab of the borrowed truck. Concerned, he checked the reports and photographs and found no mention of similar findings. When he and Turner walked to Raffield's truck and looked on top of its cab, however, they could clearly see specks of dried blood identical to those that had appeared on the test vehicle.

Embarrassed that the specks had gone unnoticed in earlier examinations, Turner smiled nonetheless. Aycock's suggestion had paid off. Askew's experiment had provided further evidence that the murder had taken place just as Richard Goeglein had claimed.

Additionally, the newly discovered bloodstains would destroy any argument that the fatal shot had been fired after Raffield was on the ground.

Sergeant Askew, shaken by the obvious violence of the crime he had re-created, volunteered to testify as an expert witness for the state, saying that he would waive his usual $200-per-day fee. "What happened out here was nothing but a cold-blooded assassination," he said as he put away his equipment. "The people who did this need to pay dearly. You can tell your D.A. that I'll even buy my own lunch."

With the Christmas holidays approaching, Turner made a concentrated effort to stay away from Waxahachie and Shipley's office and to catch up on long neglected work in Cleburne. With months remaining before even the pretrial hearings, he badly needed to distance himself from the case for a time and made up his mind to stay home and enjoy the season with his family.

There was a matter that he wanted to discuss with the D.A., an idea he had been privately considering for weeks, but it could wait for the beginning of the new year.

Still, getting completely away from the case was an impossibility. It was always there, even on those rare occasions when Turner did manage to push it into some remote corner of his mind. There was, it seemed, always something to remind him.

George and Dana wakened early on Christmas Day, watched as their children opened their gifts, then traveled to Midlothian for a family dinner at his parents' home.

That afternoon, after Turner had put away ample portions of turkey and dressing and pecan pie, his nephew called him aside. "I've got something I want to show you," the youngster said.

He reached into his hip pocket and produced a letter. "I got this in the mail from Greg Knighten the other day," Lance Turner said, handing it to George. "I don't know what to make of it. I hardly even know the guy. We were in the same Sunday school class a few years ago. All I remember is that he usually slept through it."

Turner opened the letter and read. There was a chatty opening in which Greg reminded Lance that they had attended church services together. "I suppose you know that I've been involved in some trouble over the death of an undercover police officer," he wrote, "but I'm hoping it will all work out since I had nothing to do with it. What I would like to ask is that you and the others at church pray for me."

He closed by wishing Lance a merry Christmas and saying that he looked forward to a reply to his letter.

Lance waited until his uncle had finished reading, then asked, "Do you think I ought to answer him?"

George looked at his nephew and smiled. A deeply religious youngster who had already begun talking of entering the ministry, the teenager was obviously troubled. His concern for a fellow human being was at odds with the knowledge that his uncle was working diligently to prove Greg a murderer.

Turner put his arm around Lance's shoulder. "Don't you think it a little strange that someone you hardly know would suddenly write you a letter like this?"

Lance shrugged.

"See, I think you've done exactly what Greg wanted you to do," Turner continued. "You showed me the letter. Hell, he knows we're kin to each other. So, just as he planned, I've read how innocent he is, how badly he needs his friends' prayers, and all that crap. If you want to write him, that's your business. But if you do, be sure to tell him I'm not buying any of his bullshit."

Lance Turner decided not to reply to Greg's letter.

On the drive back to Cleburne that evening, Turner pondered the innocence of his seventeen-year-old nephew. He, rather than the Greg Knightens and Jonathan Jobes and Richard Goegleins, represented the youth of Midlothian. That he and others like him had to be touched by the evil of the world at such a young age saddened the Ranger. Turner sighed and glanced into the rearview mirror at his sleeping children, wondering what kind of world they would be forced to deal with in their teenage years.

Dana moved closer, resting her head on her husband's shoulder. In the two months since Raffield's murder she had seen his warm sense of humor disappear. He only nibbled at the meals she prepared, and often, when the talk was of everyday life, his attention strayed and his sparkling eyes became cold and clouded, as if he were looking at something far away that she could not see.

Though his investigation was finished, she knew that he

did not feel his job was done. The wait for the trials to begin already seemed endless.

A warm spring sun sparkled on the red granite and sandstone Ellis County courthouse, giving Waxahachie's historic centerpiece a look of renewed splendor. Ancient oak trees, bare through the winter months, were again clothed in emerald green, and the grounds beneath them were carefully manicured.

Built in 1894 at a cost of $175,000, the Romanesque building, topped by an ornate clock tower, had long been the city's predominant landmark, drawing photographers and artists to the town square with its unique design and colorful history.

Amid the many gargoyles that silently glare down on visitors from its four entrances, there is the face of a young woman, a long-ago Waxahachie telephone operator with whom, as legend has it, an artisan named Harry Hurley fell in love. While construction was under way, Hurley resided in a room rented from young Mabel Frame's mother. In an effort to win the favor of his landlady's pretty young daughter, the smitten artisan carved her likeness and placed it above the east entrance of the courthouse as a lasting monument to his affection. Not impressed by his gesture, Mabel continued to spurn the young Italian, making it clear her sights were set higher than a common laborer who could not even speak English.

In time, Hurley's love turned to frustration, then boiled into blinding hatred. By the time the courthouse was completed he had carved a half-dozen more likenesses of the young telephone operator, each less flattering. In his final effort, her face was a mask of horror, with jagged teeth, unkempt hair, and a look of madness as terrifying as any of the accompanying gargoyles. In the final hurried days of construction, when it was discovered that a spot high on one of the turrets was devoid of any carving, Hurley volunteered to sculpt a final image to fill the vacant spot.

If one looks high up on the building, just above the monument later erected to honor the county's Confederate war dead, one will see what appears to be the likeness of a vagina, meticulously carved from red sandstone. If legend is to be believed, it was Harry Hurley's final word on the matter of Mabel Frame.

It was not, however, Hurley's handiwork that lured the crowd to the courthouse on the final day of May 1988. After lengthy pretrial hearings and two weeks of tedious jury selection, the trial of Greg Knighten was at last getting under way.

What most of those who filed into the courthouse did not know was that it would be the first and last trial in the murder of George Raffield.

For weeks the enormity of the task of conducting four capital murder trials had been the subject of speculation in the courthouse halls and in Waxahachie restaurants favored by attorneys and law enforcement personnel. It had been announced that Richard Goeglein would be the first to stand trial, with proceedings to get under way on April 11. In rapid order, Knighten would be tried in May, Jobe in June, and Fedrick in July.

Even as a lengthy hearing at which Judge Knize denied attorneys' motions for changes of venue was being held, there were those who doubted that Ellis County, which had not seen a single capital murder case prosecuted since the mid-1960s, would be able to endure a marathon summer of trials. Economics alone would make it impossible.

A county populated by farmers and blue-collar workers whose average income was $20,000 a year could hardly afford four months of attorneys' and investigators' fees and the cost of an endless parade of expert witnesses. Then there was the demand on the sparsely manned court system, forcing the judge to set aside other more routine matters for an entire summer. Several lawyers speculated that preparation and prosecution of the four trials would literally close down the daily operation of the district attorney's office where Mary Lou Shipley and her staff of one felony prosecutor and three misdemeanor prosecutors were hard-pressed to handle the daily flow of business in the best of times.

Though the politically minded district attorney was dealing with the most infamous case of her career, fully aware that the public outcry for justice had not quieted, she would be looking for some way to reduce the work load. In the minds of many, that meant more plea bargains.

Lou Antonelli, editor of the *Midlothian Reporter,* viewed the Ellis County judicial system with a more jaundiced eye than most. "The only reason the kids were even arrested," he assured one fellow journalist, "is because they aren't townies. If they had been, the whole thing would have been swept under the carpet. That's how they've always done things in Ellis County."

In truth, it was George Turner who first suggested the deal-making.

After the Christmas holidays he had traveled to Waxahachie and presented his idea to Shipley. "The way I see it," he explained, "Ellis County can afford one trial. Even if you decide to go to court with the others, it's going to be damn tough for the judge not to rule favorably on a change of venue after all the publicity the first trial is going to get."

The district attorney listened attentively as the Ranger outlined his plan: "Goeglein has the most to lose in this thing. His own statement puts him in on the planning of the murder and places him at the scene of the crime. He's got a past history that isn't going to go down well with a jury. And he's an adult, the only one facing the possibility of a death sentence. Most important, his testimony can help us with Knighten.

"So why not make a deal? Offer him anything less than sixty years, the equivalent of a life sentence, in exchange for testifying against Greg. He'll be crazy not to take it."

"Can we depend on him if he takes the stand?" Shipley questioned.

"He's just a brain-fried kid," Turner said, "but I think so."

Shipley nodded. "I'll request a delay of his trial and get in touch with his attorney."

A week before Knighten's trial was to begin, Richard's

attorney, Lee Johnson, said he and his client were ready to talk seriously about taking the offer. Though admittedly relieved by the prospect of not having to endure a jury trial—there was always the chance that Goeglein, as an adult, would get the death sentence if convicted—Johnson was a hard negotiator. After several weeks of holding out, he managed to persuade Shipley and Chester to agree that his client's fifty-year sentence would be automatically reduced if Knighten was given less time. If Greg received a life sentence, the fifty years would stand, but if a jury gave Knighten a lesser sentence, Richard's would automatically be reduced to match it.

Shipley then called Roy Vaughn and Billy Fowler to her office and told them of the plea-bargain arrangement. While they were there, she asked how they would feel about pleading Jonathan Jobe and Cynthia Fedrick.

With the evidence they had, she explained, it would be difficult to gain a conviction in either case. The judge had ruled that Jobe's unsigned statement could be introduced as evidence, but because he had played only a secondary role in the murder, a jury wasn't likely to find him guilty of capital murder. Probation from the jury was a very real possibility. The case against Cynthia Fedrick, Shipley continued, was even less promising. There were strong hints that she might have set the murder plot in motion, but where was the proof?

"I think we can be assured that they will all serve some time if we plea-bargain," Shipley explained. "If we try them, I don't know."

Vaughn sighed and shook his head, disheartened. An old-school law officer who stubbornly believed in eye-for-an-eye justice, he would be happy with nothing less than jury trials for all defendants, regardless of the risk and the cost to taxpayers. Privately he had even hoped that Shipley might appoint a special prosecutor to the case. Now his worst fears were being realized. Only one of those responsible for the murder of George Raffield would go to trial, and the prosecution would be headed by Shipley, who had never tried a capital case in her life.

Driving back to Midlothian Vaughn grumbled and cursed as Fowler sat silent, a sounding board for his friend's angry tirade. Though he did not like the plan, Fowler reluctantly judged it the best course of action. Unlike Vaughn, he had worked both sides of the fence, as a police officer and in district attorneys' offices, and had come to accept the workings of the system. While he hadn't said so, he felt some form of plea bargain was inevitable. In the time spent working for Shipley, he had come to know how she thought.

Fowler was relieved that a decision had finally been made. Now at least there was an end in sight to the nightmare that had begun with that early morning phone call so long ago. Maybe once it was over, the case would begin to retreat from his mind, freeing him from the agonizing months of restless sleep and second-guessing; removing him, if only for a while, from a world that suddenly seemed populated by rotten kids and misguided parents.

It was, in fact, the parents who had begun to wear on him.

For all his sympathy for Tom Knighten, he could not understand how a knowledgeable, well-trained police officer could ignore the evidence and continue to insist his son was innocent. How could the Jobes allow their indicted son to continue to go to school and drive around town in his pickup, tape deck blaring, as if nothing had happened? And what of those parents who had prevented their children from coming forward to tell what they knew about the murder?

None of it made sense.

Just a few weeks earlier he had received a phone call from Jackie Cadenhead, who belligerently demanded to know why another undercover narcotics officer—this time a young woman—had been placed in the high school.

After assuring her there was no officer in the school, Fowler asked what made her think so.

"This new girl who enrolled has been hanging around Jamie, trying to be friends with her," she said. "She looks too old to be a student."

"Ma'am," Fowler repeated, "there is no undercover officer, male or female, in the school. You would do me a big favor if you would ask Jamie to spread the word." He hung up, convinced that Jackie Cadenhead did not believe him.

Two days later, after completing her mail route, she stopped by the station to deliver a recording of an anonymous call her daughter had received. As she sat in his office, Fowler placed the cassette in a recorder and listened as a muffled male voice spoke: "Do you still love that guy who killed the cop with that Satan worshiper?"

"Who is this?" Jamie had asked.

There was laughter, then the caller saying, "This is my dick talking." The tape ended.

Jackie Cadenhead looked at the lieutenant with a demanding stare. "Well?"

"I'm sorry," he said, "but it sounds like nothing more than some kid making a crank call. There's not much I can do."

The Jobe family, meanwhile, adamantly refused to consider any plea bargain. At one point, Kevin Chester talked with Don Ellyson, Jobe's court-appointed lawyer, about offering Jobe probation in exchange for testimony against Knighten. But while Ellyson was trying without success to persuade Johnny and Sharrell Jobe to consider the offer, Goeglein agreed to the fifty years offered him. With Jobe's testimony no longer so crucial, Chester urged Shipley to forget about offering probation and hold out for at least a ten-year sentence if a deal was made. Twice, Jobe had been afforded the opportunity to avoid going to prison. Chester and Shipley agreed there would be no third chance.

The Jobes had then decided to retain one of Dallas's premier defense attorneys.

Doug Mulder, who was the chief felony prosecutor in the Dallas District Attorney's office when Fowler worked there, telephoned to ask if the lieutenant would arrange a meeting with Shipley.

Among the headline-making cases Mulder had been involved in was the defense of a Dallas ninth-grader named David Keeler who, on a Sunday morning in the summer of 1981, had shot and killed his mother and father as they returned home from church. After hearing of the strictness of the teenage boy's parents and testimony from a battery of mental health experts gathered by Mulder, the judge ordered the youngster sent to Timberlawn, a private psychiatric hospital, instead of jail. Later, the young Keeler was placed in a halfway house where he remained until he reached his eighteenth birthday, then was released and his juvenile records sealed. Not only did the youngster avoid jail but later received a share of his dead parents' $1.2 million estate.

For the flamboyant Mulder, the ruling in the case was a major triumph that gained him national attention.

On a Friday three days before jury selection in the Knighten trial was to begin, Mulder sat in Roy Vaughn's office with Shipley and Chester. He was stunned when the district attorney refused to discuss details of the case.

"Look," he said, "the Jobes have approached me about representing their son. I can't do anything for them if I don't know what the situation is. Can't you just give me something I can take back to tell the family?"

"You can tell them," Shipley said coldly, "that they've been listening to some very bad advice."

Mulder shrugged and lifted his hands in mock frustration. "How much time do I have to make a decision?"

"Until Monday," Mary Lou responded.

"That's pretty short notice."

"Tell young Mr. Jobe he's had two months already." The D.A. got up from her chair and smiled as she shook Mulder's hand. "If you'll excuse me," she said, "I have a trial to prepare for."

Inside Judge Knize's second-floor courtroom, the polished blond wood benches were filling quickly. Elderly couples, most of them retired, hurriedly claimed the spots they planned to occupy for the entire trial. Eager to witness the real-life drama the proceedings promised, to get a firsthand look at the boy charged with a man's crime, their soap operas would go unattended and afternoon naps ignored.

Ceiling fans circled lazily, and morning sun filtered

through tall windows framed by faded portraits of past judges who had dispensed justice from the same elevated bench Knize now occupied. From the open windows on the opposite side of the room, the muted traffic noises of downtown Waxahachie could be heard. The century-old room needed only a balcony—which it had once had, before architects removed it in a frenzy of remodeling—and the presence of Gregory Peck to bring to mind the chambers used in the filming of *To Kill a Mockingbird.*

Long before Greg Knighten appeared, most spectators had picked out the mother of the defendant. Dressed in a pastel print dress, wearing oversized glasses, and carrying a Bible, Nelda Knighten took her place on the front row, directly behind the defendant's table. Her mother and several women from her church were there to lend moral support.

George Raffield's family was more difficult to identify. With the Knighten entourage occupying most of the front row and with no seating reserved for the family of the victim, Shirley Moore and her daughters were forced to sit near the back, where they were lost among the curious townspeople and representatives of the media.

It was a few minutes before nine when Judge Knize walked hurriedly toward the bench, looked out on his rapidly filling courtroom, and nodded to the attorneys. The trial would, in a manner of speaking, be a reunion, since all of the lawyers trying the case were protégés who had assisted Knize during his tenure as district attorney.

Shipley had acted as second chair to him during numerous prosecutions before assuming the responsibility of serving out his term in office when he ran for district judge. Making no secret of her admiration of his courtroom demeanor and legal knowledge, she regularly sought his advice on everything from points of law to how to handle various functions in the D.A.'s office.

Mary Lou Shipley, many longtime courthouse watchers would say, had adopted Knize as role model and mentor. Single, she worked long hours at her job and spent weekends mending fences, hauling hay, and tending the small herd of cattle she kept on leased property outside of town. Her social activities were related to church and politics. One of the precepts she had borrowed from her mentor was an extreme wariness of the media. She had been pleased when, at the outset of pretrial hearings, the judge had placed all involved in the case under a strict gag order.

With Knize's ruling as her excuse, she refused even to acknowledge a woman newspaper reporter who asked nothing more than the time of day. She had ducked her head and shielded her face when a newspaper cameraman tried to photograph her as she walked along the sidewalk near the courthouse.

"She's not trying to be uncooperative," a friend told members of the media. "She's just focused on the job she's got to do."

Although she had her admirers, her critics wondered if she was up to the task and whether she would ever develop the confidence and polished courtroom presence of her predecessor.

Kevin Chester, who had shown promise as an attorney on Knize's staff, then as the chief felony prosecutor for Shipley, had tendered his resignation just a week before the trial began, spawning rumors of discord. Some felt he had agreed to take a position in private practice because Mary Lou decided to serve as the lead prosecutor on the case. Such speculation, he told those who asked, was far from the truth. He had taken the job because it promised three times the $24,000 he earned as a prosecutor. Even then, he had accepted the position only after his new employer agreed to allow him to remain with the D.A.'s office until the Knighten trial was completed. Still, there were many who felt he should be heading the prosecution. Privately, Chester was among them.

Joe Grubbs, seated at the defense table, had answered a notice posted on the Baylor University bulletin board in the fall of 1972, just days after learning that he had passed his bar exams. In short order he was hired by the Ellis County D.A.'s office. For two years he learned at Knize's side, then was elected county judge, a position he held for eight years.

His career continued to flourish when he was appointed to the county court-at-law. Then, in 1984, he entered private practice.

Poised and self-assured, Grubbs quickly gained a reputation as one of the brightest, most sought-after attorneys working in Ellis County. In addition to his knowledge of the law, he was a strong counter-puncher who rarely failed to score points with his aggressive cross-examinations.

After Knighten was certified as an adult, Knize had called Grubbs to his chambers and appointed him to the case as a replacement for Jim Jenkins.

"Jenkins," Knize explained, "has requested that the court allow him to pursue his motion that Knighten's civil rights were violated when he was ordered to stand trial as an adult. Unless you can give me a good reason why you can't take the case, I want you to handle the defense."

Aside from the simple fact that he did not want the job, knowing it would mean considerable time away from his practice, Grubbs had been unable to come up with a legitimate excuse to avoid the appointment.

Once involved, however, he entered into the task with the single-mindedness that Knize expected. After countless meetings with his client and long nights of poring over material gathered by investigators, he had come to two conclusions: he had serious doubts that it was Greg Knighten who fired the shots that killed George Raffield, and he felt he had a good chance of convincing a jury that Knighten wasn't the killer.

In his meetings with Greg Knighten, Grubbs had heard a much different story from the one he had read in newspapers. Yes, Greg admitted, he was at the scene of the crime. But he had no idea Raffield was a police officer or that a murder was to take place.

It was, he told his new attorney, Jonathan and Richard who had talked at length about the possibility of Raffield being an undercover cop. In his own bedroom the night before the murder actually took place, he had heard them discuss killing George, but had not taken them seriously. On that Thursday evening, as they were discussing Raffield in his bedroom, Greg had been called into another part of the house by his father. While he was gone, Richard took the gun that was used in the crime.

In the field, as they waited for a drug dealer whom Richard—not Greg—allegedly had summoned, Greg was standing near the tailgate of the pickup. He had turned away from the wind to light a cigarette when he heard the shots and turned to see Richard holding his father's gun.

Later, Greg said, Richard pointed out that "he had gotten away with it in Arizona and could do it again."

Grubbs's background check on Richard Goeglein, his history of satanic involvement, and his role in the Elliott Smith attack had given the lawyer good reason to believe his client might well be telling the truth.

Long before Knize's gavel signaled the opening of the trial, Grubbs was certain of one thing: if Richard Goeglein had not moved to Midlothian, George Raffield would never have been murdered.

His goal was to convince the ten men and two women on the jury to share his feelings.

18

On the opening day of the trial—after a two-hour delay caused by a juror who forgot the date and reported to work instead of the courthouse—the prosecution outlined the case it planned to make against Knighten. In her opening statement to the jury, Shipley read from a yellow legal pad, outlining the case she and Chester would present, and reminded them that not one but two elements necessary for a capital murder conviction were clearly present: A police officer had been the victim of the crime, she said in her quiet, even voice, and during the course of the murder, a robbery had taken place; eighteen dollars had been taken from Raffield's body. To find the defendant guilty of capital murder, she pointed out, the jury needed only to agree that one of those things actually happened on the evening of October 23, 1987.

"Greg Knighten," she concluded, putting her yellow legal pad aside and focusing her attention on the jury, "eventually became suspicious of his friend George Moore and was convinced that he was a cop, a narc, a pig, working undercover. And once convinced of that, he felt betrayed. He felt he had to do something about it."

It was, however, not until Sherrie Prine took the stand to identify a photograph of her dead brother that the jury got its first real hint of the emotion that would course through the proceedings in the days to come. As Sherrie wept, heads in the jury box were lowered, then, one by one, turned in the direction of the defense table where Knighten was seated. Dressed in a neatly pressed plaid shirt and navy slacks, his hair neatly trimmed, he stared down at the table, hands folded.

For the remainder of the day law enforcement officers paraded to the stand to answer questions asked alternately by Shipley and Chester, each adding to the reconstruction of the grim murder plot and the aftermath of the crime. Physical evidence, including the .38 revolver, was introduced.

Fowler took the stand to describe the work Raffield had been doing, then to relate in detail the statement that Jonathan Jobe had made that Saturday afternoon. Looking toward the jury box, the lieutenant told of the conversation Jobe said had taken place after he picked Knighten and Goeglein up on the farm road: "Jonathan asked Greg if he was sure he was dead. Greg told him, 'Yeah, I shot him three times.'"

At the defense table, Knighten smiled and shook his head. In the back of the room, Shirley Moore reached into her purse for a tissue.

For reporters eager for new revelations, the testimony provided little they had not already known. The big news would come later in the evening, long after the day's proceedings had been recessed.

Fowler was having dinner at home when he received a call from attorney Doug Mulder. "I tried to get in touch with the D.A.," he said, "but haven't been able to reach her. If you would, I'd appreciate your telling her that I'm meeting with Jobe's parents tomorrow to advise them against going to trial. Tell Mary Lou that Jonathan will take the deal."

The news delighted Fowler. In exchange for a ten-year prison sentence, which he knew Shipley would agree to,

Jobe would be added to the prosecution's witness list and would testify against Knighten.

Even as Fowler and Mulder were talking, Chester and Shipley were at the Ellis County jail, finalizing a plea-bargain agreement with Cynthia Fedrick.

For weeks Cynthia had hoped to avoid going to trial. Her court-appointed attorney, Ron Johnson, had indicated to her that his practice was primarily in the area of civil law.

It had, in fact, been Cynthia's mother who first informed Johnson that he had been appointed to the case. Frustrated that her daughter had not seen an attorney since being jailed, she had telephoned the courthouse and learned the case had been assigned to Johnson.

Later, on his first visit to Cynthia, he told her that the D.A.'s office lacked any solid evidence of her complicity. "But," he added, "they feel you were somehow involved, so they have to do something." He then suggested she consider the fifty-year sentence Shipley had offered.

"Fuck that," Cynthia said. "I might as well go to trial if that's the best they can do."

Despite a letter from Cynthia to Judge Knize, requesting another lawyer, Johnson was still the attorney of record when she agreed to plead guilty to charges of conspiracy and solicitation of capital murder in exchange for an eight-year prison term and her testimony.

"I'll take the deal," Cynthia told Chester and Shipley, "because it's the easiest way out. With eight years, I'll just do a turnaround in prison. But there's one thing that is important for you to know."

"What's that?" Chester asked.

"I never told those kids to kill George Raffield."

On June 1, following a lengthy day of testimony from medical examiners and forensic experts, Cynthia Fedrick took the stand. With classes at Midlothian High School dismissed for the summer, many students had made the short drive to Waxahachie to attend the trial, filling the courtroom to capacity.

Occasionally glaring at Greg, Cynthia told of the three

boys coming to her apartment that evening, of Greg telling her that he had shot Raffield. "He came into the apartment and told me that I didn't have to worry anymore, that everything was cool. He said he had gotten his daddy's gun and switched the fancy bullets out. Eventually, he got to where he said he'd shot him," she said. Carefully led through her testimony by Chester, Cynthia told of becoming angry with Knighten for bringing Raffield to her apartment two days before the murder and of hearing rumors that Raffield was an undercover narcotics officer. "The day he brought George over to my apartment I called him into the bedroom and tried to convince him. I said, 'Look at him out there, damn it, he wears his hair like a grown man.'"

In his cross-examination, Grubbs had Cynthia describe her drug habits and her trip to Cash with Jay Little and Don Castle to purchase crank on the day of the murder. Raising his voice for the first time during the trial, he asked about the conflicting statements she had given. "We have one," he said, holding it above his head, "that you gave immediately after the murder took place." Then, walking back to the defense table, he picked up the other. "And, we have this one that you gave in jail after cutting your deal with the district attorney's office. I'd like to know exactly when this second statement that is so much more detailed was written."

"I wrote it last Sunday after church services," Cynthia responded. "It's the real truth."

A look of indignation spread across the attorney's face as he turned to face the jury. "Once you cut the deal," he said, "then you knew what the truth was."

Though he had succeeded in painting Cynthia Fedrick as a hot-tempered drug user, Grubbs did nothing to sway her from her story. She was, Chester felt, an excellent witness.

As Cynthia's testimony ended, the tension grew in anticipation of Jamie Cadenhead's testimony, which was next.

In the law library, just down the hall from the courtroom, Nelda Knighten was joined by a half-dozen women for prayer sessions during breaks in the trial. Raffield's family, meanwhile, sat on a bench just outside the courtroom, checking their watches now and again to make sure they got a good seat when the recess was over.

When Pat Day, a Victims Outreach representative who traveled daily from Dallas to join Shirley Moore in the courtroom, asked the bailiff if it was possible to arrange for places for the victim's family in the front row, she was brusquely informed that it was not the policy of the court to reserve seats during a trial.

Angered, she paced in front of the closed law library that provided the Knightens' privacy. "They have things backwards here," she observed. "The people of the defendant are being treated far better than the family of the victim."

An elderly couple, overhearing her complaint, volunteered to remain in the courtroom during the breaks and lunch hour to make sure that spots were available for Shirley Moore when court reconvened.

David Zanolini, Raffield's brother-in-law, was in the restroom that morning when a deputy escorted Greg in during the break. On his job in Duncanville, Zanolini had heard numerous stories of scrapes that Greg's father had gotten him out of when they lived in the neighborhood. Angered when he heard Greg joking with the deputy, David approached him. "Your daddy isn't going to be able to get you out of this one," he said before walking out into the foyer.

Later, in the courtroom, while waiting for the jury to return for the afternoon proceedings, Mark Prine, Sherrie's husband, found himself seated next to Knighten's grandmother. Several times during the day he had felt her cold stare, and as she sat there, her Bible in her lap, he decided to speak to her.

"Are we really that different?" he asked. "I've been drawn into this in much the same manner as you, and I feel so helpless."

The woman nodded but did not reply.

"I was just wondering how you feel," Mark continued.

Tears formed in the grandmother's eyes. "Young man, I

hate what has happened to your family," she said softly. "I really do. But my grandson's going to go to jail for this."

Mark immediately regretted having started the conversation. Fighting to control his anger, he spat out a reply: "And my brother-in-law is lying in a cemetery." It was the last time he would speak to any member of the Knighten family.

As the afternoon session got under way, a hushed crowd watched as Jamie Cadenhead was sworn in and took her place in the witness chair directly in front of the bench. Lips pursed and looking frightened, she clutched a white Bible.

Her voice barely more than a whisper, Jamie answered Chester's questions reluctantly. "First, Miss Cadenhead, would you please tell the court what your relationship is with the defendant?" the prosecutor asked.

"He's my fiancé," Jamie said.

Chester smiled, privately recalling a conversation a few days earlier with Jamie's friend, JoAnne Dupree. "You know," JoAnne had told him, "Jamie says she's going to stick by Greg through the trial, but as soon as it's over she's going to start dating other boys."

For the next twenty minutes Jamie described trips she had taken with Greg and Raffield into Dallas to purchase drugs, of warnings from her mother the previous summer that there would be a narc in the school, and of Greg's visit to her on the night of the murder. "I was outside smoking a cigarette when they drove up," she said. "As soon as I saw Greg I knew something was wrong." When he asked to hide the gun in her purse, she said, she "kind of figured what he had done, but I didn't ask because I didn't want to know."

As she described what had taken place at her home, Jamie's answers became sketchy and increasingly hostile. Tears ran down her cheeks as the prosecutor asked her to read from the statement she had given to George Turner following Greg's arrest.

"If you would just start here," Chester said, pointing to a place midway down the typed statement.

Jamie glared at the prosecutor, then began to read. "He

started crying and he asked me to say a prayer with him. He said the prayer while we held each other. The prayer said, 'Please, dear Lord, forgive me my sins and for what's happened tonight.'"

"And here," Chester said, pointing to a line farther down the page.

Now crying so that even the jury had difficulty hearing, she continued reading. "Throughout the night we would be sitting there at the house and he would say, 'God forgive me.'"

Grubbs waited until she had regained her composure before beginning the same line of questioning he had pursued with each of the state's witnesses. He asked of her knowledge of Richard Goeglein's involvement in Satanism and if she had ever heard Greg Knighten refer to George Raffield as an undercover police officer.

Grubbs's defense had become obvious. First he would attempt to shift the blame from his client to Goeglein. Then he would try to establish that Greg had never been aware Raffield was a police officer. He pointed out that, in the vocabulary of Midlothian students, the word *narc* did not necessarily mean an undercover narcotics officer. Rather, it meant a snitch—anyone who told on someone else, whether the other student was cheating on an exam or skipping class.

Everyone who took the stand, including the high school principal, provided the same definition. The state, in building its case, had yet to summon a single witness who could testify that Greg Knighten had actually said that he knew George Raffield was a police officer, something the D.A. felt she had to prove in order to get the automatic life sentence that accompanied the conviction of a minor in a capital case. Without that proof, a jury could rule only on first-degree murder, which carried a sentence of five to ninety-nine years.

The exhausting day ended with the question still left hanging, a bothersome loose end that the prosecutors seemed unable to tie up. The following day, even the strongest fabric in the state's case began to unravel.

On Friday morning, Cynthia Fedrick returned to the witness stand for additional cross-examination by Grubbs. Looking far more weary than in her first appearance, she smoothed her dress and stared at her hands as the defense attorney approached, preparing to drop the first bombshell of the trial.

Producing two letters Cynthia had written to Knighten the previous April, Grubbs stood silent for several seconds as if squeezing the final drops of dramatic effect from the moment.

"In a letter written to the defendant and delivered to him by a deputy in the jail," he finally asked, "did you write that Richard had convinced the D.A. that Sparky had done it, but that you didn't believe it?"

"Yes."

"And did you further say that you did not ever hear Greg Knighten say that he shot George Raffield?"

"I was being loyal to a friend," Cynthia shot back.

Grubbs ignored her answer and, turning to face the jury, began reading from one of the letters: "'I don't think you killed him, and I'll never think you killed him. Why did Richard do that to George? That's cold. He's going around messing everybody's life up.'"

Glancing in Cynthia's direction, Grubbs read from a second letter: "'My lawyer said the district attorney wants me to say you did it. I could walk. But, Sparky, I can't do that.'"

At the prosecutors' table, Shipley and Chester sat motionless as Grubbs handed them the letters before continuing his questioning of Cynthia.

"Now that you've cut your deal with the district attorney's office you've changed your mind," he observed. "When your own neck was on the line, you had to put your friends aside, didn't you?"

"I'm telling the truth," Cynthia said.

Again Grubbs ignored her. "When did you tell the truth? When you didn't have anything to gain? Or when your own life was on the line?" They were not questions seeking answers. Rather, they were observations for the jury to consider. "You care about yourself more than you do Greg, don't you?"

Cynthia no longer attempted to disguise her anger. "I care about my daughter," she said. "If it weren't for my daughter I would go to the penitentiary for life for Greg."

She wanted to explain how Knighten had written her repeatedly, begging that she do whatever she could to help him; to tell the attorney how hurt she had felt when every letter she received from Greg was filled with pleas for help but never once did he ask if there was anything he could do to help her. Still, despite the growing resentment, she had tried to help in whatever way she could, and that was why she wrote the letters.

The Greg Knighten she knew simply didn't seem capable of murder, regardless of what he had told her that Friday night in her apartment. She had even sent word to him after making her deal with the D.A., suggesting that he tell his lawyer to try to focus as much of the blame as possible on her. They couldn't hurt her anymore. And maybe it could help him.

She got to explain none of those things as Grubbs dismissed her with an angry wave of his hand and returned to his chair.

He had accomplished what he set out to do. The counter-puncher had made a shambles of one of the state's star witnesses.

As Cynthia Fedrick was accompanied from the court-room by a deputy, Greg turned and smiled at his mother.

Judge Knize, his face showing the strain of the proceedings, was pleased that the first week of the trial was coming to an end, promising two days' relief from the mounting tension. Concerned from the outset that his courtroom might become a circus, he had begun each day with a lecture to those in attendance. He would tolerate no talking, no gum chewing, not so much as a nod of the head during questioning of a witness. If, he said, there were those who felt they might be unable to contain their emotions, he suggested they leave before he called the court to order. "I have to watch the jury, the witnesses, the attorneys, and I have to watch you," he said.

Visitors to the courthouse on Friday were greeted by handwritten signs posted on each doorway, spelling out new rules. No cameras or newspapers would be allowed on the second floor. The third floor, containing the offices of the district attorney and sheriff, was off limits. No one would be allowed in or out while the trial was in session. "If you have an appointment, if you have a phone call to make, if you have to go take a pill, you do not belong in this courtroom. You will not be allowed to leave until we recess."

At the lunch break, reporters gathered in a nearby restaurant to discuss the impact of Cynthia's testimony and the behavior of the judge. A Dallas radio reporter whose hourly live call-in reports were now impossible sipped her iced tea, too angry to eat. One television reporter sat with an artist hired to sketch courtroom scenes, pondering the fact that there would be no way to make the five o'clock news. Another grumbled that he had covered hundreds of trials during his career and had never been locked into a courtroom before. Tom Steyer, on hand to report the events for Channel 4 in Dallas, summed up the feelings of those seated at the table. "The rule stinks," he said as he pushed his half-eaten chicken-fried steak away.

The cameramen, who were forced to wait outside on the courthouse lawn in the hope of getting footage as witnesses entered or left the building, had problems of their own. During the first day of the trial everyone had been escorted in and out of the same door; thus cameras were positioned before each day's noon break and afternoon recess. Later, however, Sheriff Barney Boyd took it upon himself to slowly circle the square in his patrol car, using a walkie-talkie to alert deputies to where the photographers were stationed so that family and witnesses could use another exit.

Quickly realizing what was going on, the cameramen agreed to pool their resources, stationing someone at each exit. Whoever got pictures would share with the others.

With fifteen minutes remaining before the afternoon session was to get under way, *Dallas Times Herald* writer David Bloom lifted his tea glass in a mock salute and suggested they all return to the "Beirut courtroom."

The heavy-handed manner in which Knize ruled over the trial began to grate on many. Victims Outreach president Pat Day grew increasingly upset at the way the judge and D.A.'s office continued to ignore the Moore family and made plans to file a formal complaint. Even the casual trial watchers began making sarcastic comments about the private prayer sessions being held in the law library. "Every time Mrs. Knighten and her entourage come in," said one spectator, "I can't help but compare it to a boxer making his way to the ring for a championship fight, surrounded by bodyguards and hangers-on."

One journalist had begun privately referring to the women accompanying Nelda as "the church ladies," an allusion to a popular character on "Saturday Night Live." "Like it or not," he said, "the judge has a full-fledged circus on his hands."

Another opinion was current among many who had sat through the first week of testimony, keeping private scorecards and monitoring the reaction of the jury: the state's case wasn't looking good.

During the afternoon session that Friday, Judge Knize was called upon to enforce his rules. As Jay Little sat in the witness chair, describing the events at Cynthia Fedrick's house on the night of the murder, a dark-haired young spectator became ill. Clutching his stomach, he stood and began walking from the courtroom.

Despite the judge's orders to return to his seat, the man continued toward the exit. When he had disappeared into the hall, Knize angrily instructed a bailiff not to allow him to return.

The man Knize had barred from the courtroom was David Zanolini, George Raffield's brother-in-law.

* * *

Throughout the weekend Kevin Chester battled the depression that had set in following the revelation of Cynthia's letters to Greg. Though the remainder of Friday's testimony, including ballistic reports matching the Knighten weapon to the bullet taken from Raffield's head, had gone well, the points scored by Grubbs troubled the assistant D.A.

Before the letters were introduced, he had felt sure that the jury believed Cynthia's recollection of the events following the crime. In fact, he had experienced his only feeling of real euphoria after she had initially testified. To have that feeling so suddenly erased by words in her own handwriting had been devastating.

On Sunday afternoon, still unable to relax, Chester went to the jail to have another talk with Richard. He wanted to make sure Goeglein had withheld no surprises. Several times they went over his testimony, and each time Richard assured him that he was telling everything he knew.

Then, on Monday morning, just minutes before he was to take the stand, Richard made an offhand statement that caused a flurry of activity.

He was sitting in the D.A.'s office, listening as Chester briefed him one last time. Roy Vaughn and Billy Fowler, having driven over from Midlothian, sat listening to the last-minute preparations.

"You know," Richard remarked, "Greg said he had sworn he would never do anything like this again." The observation had come from far left field, catching Chester in mid-drink from his cup of coffee.

"What the hell are you talking about?" the assistant D.A. asked.

"That night when we were walking back to the road to meet Jonathan," Richard said. "Greg was telling me he had done that sort of thing before. He found out this policeman over in Duncanville was a narc and talked him into going on some kind of hunting trip. He killed him and hid his body under some brush. He said they never found the guy."

Chester's face turned crimson. "Goddammit, Richard, why are you just now getting around to telling us this?"

Goeglein just shrugged.

Even before Kevin suggested it, Vaughn was on the phone to the Duncanville Police Department. Following a brief conversation with the chief there, he hung up and glared at Richard. "It's bullshit. They have no record of any missing police officer," Vaughn said.

Chester shook his head and felt a new rush of concern. From their first meeting, Richard had been difficult. Every piece of information had been dragged from him. When Chester left a note pad, suggesting that Richard write down everything he could remember he returned the following day to find that Richard had done nothing but draw doodles. Finally, desperate to convince the youngster to cooperate, Chester had burst into a carefully planned tirade as he and Turner visited Richard, screaming obscenities, threatening to call the deal off and vowing that he would make every effort to see that the uncooperative prisoner wound up on death row. Chester's outburst reduced Goeglein to tears. Even Richard's lawyer had become frustrated with his client once the plea-bargain agreement had been reached. During one evening meeting in the jail he, too, had been reduced to screaming at Richard, demanding that he tell the truth. It was only after Chester arranged for Goeglein to have a lengthy personal visit with his mother that Richard finally began to cooperate. Even then, Chester was far from comfortable with Richard.

Now, with the outcome of the case hanging in the balance, the assistant D.A. had to put his faith in the testimony of a witness who might throw him a curve once he took the stand.

It was, then, with extreme care that Kevin Chester led Goeglein through his story.

Occasionally glancing around at the capacity crowd, Richard responded to the prosecutor's questions in a voice devoid of emotion. He told of his relationship with Jonathan and of first meeting Greg on the state fair midway the previous October.

He described in detail the meeting in Knighten's bedroom

and the discussion of ways to kill Raffield. Then he told of consulting Terry's heart about the plan.

Led by Chester's careful questioning he told of waiting in the Jobes' garage that Friday night, then getting into Raffield's pickup for the trip out to the field.

A stillness settled over the room as Goeglein began telling what happened following their arrival.

"The radio was on and we were smoking dope," he said, his pale blue eyes focused squarely on Chester. "We talked about music and cars and some of the girls in school. We sat there for about twenty minutes, and I started getting restless and walked around.

"I finally told Greg that it didn't look like the deal was going down, hoping he would leave, but he said the guy would be there. It still wasn't completely dark by then, but it was cold and misting rain, so I went and sat in the truck on the passenger's side.

"I heard Greg saying something about lightning bugs. George was on the other side of the pickup, and he started to look around. When he had turned his back, Greg pulled the gun and fired three shots . . . very fast.

"I saw the flash from the gun, heard the shots, and saw George fall. Greg just stood there for a minute, then told me to get the wallet."

At the defense table, Knighten smiled and shook his head repeatedly as Goeglein told a story of premeditated cold-blooded murder.

By noon he had detailed the ride back into town in Jobe's pickup, the visit to Cynthia Fedrick's apartment, the drive to Jamie Cadenhead's house, and the events of the following day.

It was when he described the trip to the Waxahachie flea market the following morning that the shock of the spectators could be seen, heads shaking in dismay in the gallery despite the judge's previous admonishments. He and Jobe, accompanied by Gina McLemore, had visited a park before their return to Midlothian. Richard and Gina had played on the swings while Jonathan slid down the slide.

Just hours after participating in a brutal murder, they had played children's games in a park.

After Knize called the noon recess, Shirley Moore walked slowly to a wooden bench in the hall. Lighting a cigarette, she sat staring at the wall as a woman approached and took a seat next to her. "I'm so sorry," the woman said.

Shirley Moore began to weep and shake her head. "I don't know how much more of this I can take," she said. "All of these kids are so cold, so heartless."

The woman waited a few minutes before getting up to leave. She did not want the grieving mother to see that she, too, had begun to cry. Neither did she introduce herself.

It was best, she felt, that Shirley Moore did not know she was Cynthia Fedrick's mother.

Joe Grubbs had been looking forward to the cross-examination of Goeglein since the trial began. If he was to convince the jury of his client's innocence, he felt he would have to do it when he had Richard on the stand.

More animated than at any time during the trial, the defense attorney led the stone-faced Goeglein through the days leading up to the murder, adding new emphasis to Jobe's role.

Goeglein told of Jonathan's suggestion that Raffield be taken to Dallas and stabbed. And he recalled his conversation with Jonathan as they drove home from Greg's after having consulted Terry's heart.

"I said, 'What if the guy ain't a cop?'"

"And what was Jonathan's reply?"

Richard paused for a moment before answering. "He said George was a nerd and deserved to die anyway."

"Do you own a pistol?" Grubbs asked.

"Yes."

"You've done a good deal of hunting with your father, right?"

"Yes."

"And would you consider yourself a good shot?"

"Pretty good."

Grubbs, turning his focus to Richard's background, questioned him about his interest in Satanism and his involvement in the beating of Elliott Smith. The jury sat grim-faced as Goeglein admitted to being a member of a witches' coven in Arizona and described the assault on Smith.

Despite Richard's insistence that he had not been responsible for what happened to Smith, the similarities between the Arizona crime and Raffield's murder, Grubbs was confident, would not be lost on the jury.

"And were you still involved in satanic activities after you moved to Midlothian?" Grubbs asked.

Richard shrugged. "I was kind of interested in it," he said. "I looked at some books about it, stuff like that. But I'm not into it anymore."

"You've now gotten religion?" Grubbs asked sarcastically.

"Yes."

"When did that happen?"

"Since I've been in jail."

"Before or after you made your deal with the state to testify?"

Richard again glared at the attorney. "Before," he said.

Grubbs smiled and turned toward the defense table. Though the young man whom he had been questioning for almost an hour had continued to minimize his role in the murder, the jury, he felt, had at last seen the real Richard Goeglein.

He only wished they could have witnessed the bizarre scene that had been played out in front of the courthouse a couple of hours earlier.

Frances and Richard Goeglein, Sr., had been standing on the sidewalk with their daughter, Becky, waiting for Richard to be escorted from the courthouse and returned to jail for the noon meal. As he appeared, handcuffed and escorted by a lone sheriff's deputy, a television cameraman rushed up and began filming his walk to the car. Richard's father tried without success to block the cameraman's path. The cameraman continued to film as the deputy put Richard in the passenger seat.

Suddenly Becky Goeglein ran toward the cameraman. "Leave him alone, you sorry motherfucker," she shouted. "Leave him alone or I'm going to kick your ass."

Before the cameraman could turn, he was being kicked repeatedly by the cursing teenager. In anger, he kicked back.

As the confrontation continued, Richard suddenly jumped from the car. "You sonuvabitch," he yelled. The stunned deputy hurried from the driver's side of the car and managed to wrap his arms around Richard before he reached the cameraman. At the same time, Becky's father was pulling her away.

Regaining his composure, the cameraman continued shooting, knowing full well that viewers of the six o'clock news would not see the final act of the event he had recorded. From the car, Richard Goeglein was shooting him the finger.

Texas Ranger George Turner arrived at the courthouse early Tuesday morning, anticipating the final day of the prosecution's case. When he left the night before, the plan had been to put Jobe on the stand and then close with testimony from Fort Worth cult specialist Stan Ferguson, who would explain that Goeglein's involvement in Satan worship was far less serious than Grubbs had intimated.

Turner's discomfort with the course the trial had taken had grown daily, and he had been disappointed when Shipley announced her decision not to include the blood-splatter testimony. Turner had briefly argued with her, pointing out that he felt it would lend credibility to Goeglein's story. Shipley, however, said she feared the jury was already weary of complicated forensic testimony.

Seeing that Jonathan Jobe and his mother were already seated in Shipley's office when he arrived lifted Turner's spirits. But only briefly. Stepping into the hallway, Chester pulled the door to the D.A.'s office shut. "We've decided not to put Jonathan on the stand," he said.

Stunned, George sat in a nearby chair. "Why, for God's sake?"

"His story doesn't track with Richard's."

"Jesus. You mean to tell me you've given the kid the sweetest deal in the world and now he's not even going to take the stand?" Turner had been aware for several days that Shipley and Chester had concerns about Jobe's version of the story. Jobe adamantly refused to admit that he was as actively involved in drug use as statements from others indicated. Too, his recollection of who had been at Cynthia's apartment when he arrived with Greg and Richard was hazy. These were, in Turner's mind, minor points. One, at least, could be easily explained. Jobe was never out of the company of his mother when he spoke with attorneys, and he simply did not want to admit to his parents that he had become a doper. Too, his statement of what transpired at Cynthia's included all the important facts. So what if he couldn't remember Randy Marcott coming in or that Jay Little was there?

The prosecutors, he knew, were aware that Jobe and Goeglein had ended their friendship. Becky, weeks earlier, had broken off her relationship with Jonathan and had begun dating another boy. When Jonathan made off-color remarks about Becky, her new boyfriend had sought him out and roughed him up.

"Every time I talk to the kid," Chester said, "all I get is a blank look. If we put him on, there's no telling what he's liable to say. I'm afraid he might get up there and give the defense the ammunition to shove the whole damn case down our throats."

"You don't think Grubbs is going to call his ass up there in a New York minute?" Turner replied.

"I've told Jonathan to plead the fifth to any questions."

Turner slumped in his chair, suddenly feeling exhausted. He silently wondered if the decision had been Chester's or whether he was merely the bearer of the disturbing message.

In truth, Chester and Shipley had jointly decided that putting Jobe on the stand could be disastrous. A prosecutor's nightmare, Chester had called it. Since the state's case now relied so heavily on the testimony of Richard Goeglein, he feared that Grubbs might successfully discredit Richard's version of what happened by hammering at the differences, regardless of how minor they were, in Goeglein's and Jobe's stories. The weary prosecutors feared their increasingly fragile case might be reduced to shambles.

As Stan Ferguson entered the room, Turner looked up at him, then at Chester. "Why don't we put Jonathan and Richard together?" George offered. "Let them talk it out with Stan and see if we can determine what the damn problems are."

"I'm due in court," Chester replied.

Turner stood and pulled on his hat. "I'm going to the jail to get Richard," he told Ferguson.

While Shipley and Chester sat at the prosecution table awaiting the arrival of the jurors, Ferguson sat in the D.A.'s office listening as the two boys once again reviewed their stories. When Jobe insisted that his only involvement with drugs had been an occasional hit from a joint, Richard laughed.

"Jonathan," he said, "that's bullshit. Hell, man, you did crank with me once, remember?"

Jobe grinned. "Oh, yeah, I forgot about that."

Slowly the friendship between the two was rekindled as Ferguson continued his questioning. Now that he was relaxed and smiling occasionally, Jobe's memory seemed to improve as Goeglein told the story as he recalled it.

Ferguson went into the foyer outside the office where Turner had been pacing. "George, they're telling the same story. I don't see any problems."

Downstairs, Judge Knize had already called court to order. Mary Lou Shipley stood, rolling a pencil between her fingers. "Your Honor," she said, "the state rests."

Ferguson, angry that he had made the drive to Waxahachie for nothing, shook Turner's hand. "I'm going back to Fort Worth," he said.

George grinned weakly. "I wish to hell I could go with you."

* * *

Surprised that Jobe had not testified, Grubbs quickly reorganized his plans and had a subpoena issued for Jonathan. He would open his defense with a hostile witness.

The defense attorney wasted no time going to the heart of the matter. He painted a scenario dramatically different from the one posed by the prosecution. It was, in fact, Goeglein who had murdered George Raffield, was it not? Then, after Jobe dropped Knighten off at Jamie Cadenhead's house, didn't he and Richard return to the scene of the crime to make sure that Raffield was dead?

After each of Grubbs's questions, Jobe took the fifth.

"Then," Grubbs continued, his voice rising, "isn't it true that you and Richard went to your house to spend the rest of the night planning a story that would put the blame on Greg?"

"We spent the night at my house," Jonathan answered.

Pressing ahead quickly, Grubbs asked Jobe if he had agreed to testify only after reaching a plea agreement with the district attorney that called for him to serve only ten years in prison. Jonathan said he had.

At that point Judge Knize halted the questioning. "Sir," he said, "you can employ your constitutional rights during this line of questioning or you can answer the questions to the best of your knowledge, but you can't have it both ways. Is your attorney present in the courtroom?"

"No, sir," Jobe said.

Knize turned to Grubbs. "Counselor, this witness must be excused until such time as he is represented by his attorney."

Grubbs nodded. Knowing that any chance of Jobe's responding to his questions was lost, he would not bother recalling the witness.

On Tuesday afternoon, Tom Knighten walked briskly into the courtroom and was sworn in. He looked at his son, who stared down at his hands, refusing to acknowledge his father's presence.

"The day following the shooting," Grubbs said, "you had

an opportunity to visit your son at the Midlothian jail, did you not?"

"Yes, sir."

"And what is your recollection of that meeting?"

"He was crying and shaking. He was very afraid. He told me that Richard did it. Richard shot him."

"How did that make you feel?"

Tom Knighten inhaled deeply before he answered. "It broke my heart."

"And did you have further discussions with your son about the matter?"

"He told me on several occasions that Richard Goeglein pulled the trigger. Richard had been involved in another killing in Arizona. Greg told me that Richard said, 'I got away with it there and I can do it again.'"

His son and George Raffield had become good friends, Knighten continued. He recalled the birthday celebration, noting how pleased he had been that his son was associating with someone so nice and polite.

He emphatically denied having admitted to Midlothian officer Fowler that he had warned Greg his new friend might be an undercover officer. At that point, Chester wrote "Fowler . . . rebuttal" on the legal pad in front of him.

"At any time did you suspect that the young man you knew as George Moore might be an undercover narcotics officer?" Grubbs continued.

"No, sir. It wasn't until the morning after the killing that I learned George's real identity. At roll call we were told that a Midlothian undercover officer was missing and were given a description of his truck."

"Did you know then who that was?"

"Yes," Knighten replied. "It hit me like a ton of bricks."

Shipley's cross-examination was brief and devoid of the compassion Grubbs had shown. She questioned Knighten about his background as an instructor at the pistol range and his son's expertise with handguns. Though he said Greg had no formal training with weapons, he admitted that his son had developed into a good marksman.

"Mr. Knighten," the D.A. questioned, "are you familiar with a technique taught to police officers where they are told to draw their weapon and fire three times as quickly as possible?"

"Yes," he answered, then explained the technique of "reflex shooting." Before he finished, a look of discomfort had spread across his face. The district attorney had forced him to describe the manner in which Raffield had been murdered.

It was, Chester thought to himself, one of the prosecution's finest moments.

The final witness called by Grubbs was a thirty-one-year-old Ellis County inmate named Stephen Britton, who was in jail on forgery charges. Britton related a conversation he'd had with Richard Goeglein in the exercise yard.

"I thought at first he was Greg Knighten," Britton said. "When he told me he wasn't, I asked him if he was the one who had turned state's evidence. He told me that he had to. He said, 'This way everybody goes down, but nobody fries.'"

Grubbs asked if Richard had discussed the murder of Raffield.

Britton nodded. "He said, 'Yeah, I shot the motherfucker, but I'm not going to take the rap for it.'"

"Did Richard say why he had decided to let Greg Knighten take the rap?"

"He said that Greg was a pig."

Questioned by Shipley, Britton admitted that he had shared a cell with Greg Knighten for one day. "And how was it that you came to testify in this case?" the D.A. asked.

"I contacted the boy's dad," Britton said.

With Britton's testimony, the defense rested.

Sitting in the D.A.'s office, Lieutenant Fowler was more upset over Tom Knighten's testimony than that of Stephen Britton. For months he had known the day would come when Tom would have to take the stand in defense of his son. Fowler had agonized over it, trying to imagine how his friend must feel. There had been times, in fact, when Fowler wished Knighten had not made that comment to him in the Red Bird Mall parking lot.

Still, he had been certain that Tom would admit to the conversation. He was, after all, a police officer who had taken an oath before accepting his badge.

When told that Knighten had denied ever saying he warned Greg about Raffield, Fowler was stunned.

"I've got to put you on as a rebuttal witness this afternoon," Chester told the lieutenant.

Fowler nodded, aware that while he was telling the truth, he was going to lose a friend. That afternoon Fowler returned to the stand as a rebuttal witness and repeated the conversation he said had taken place at the Red Bird Mall parking lot.

For several days Chester had been waiting for the right moment to talk privately with Mary Lou Shipley. Never in his life had he wanted so badly to give a closing argument, but he had not found a comfortable way to ask.

Discouraged at the way the trial had gone, fearful that the jury might even vote for acquittal, Turner had asked him several times to persuade Shipley to let him give the final argument. Roy Vaughn and Fowler had also expressed pessimism about the way the trial had gone. Without a strong closing argument, they feared the possibility of a hung jury.

Members of the media, glad that the trial was nearing an end, had entered into a pool. Several had bet their dollar that Greg Knighten would be acquitted. The prosecution, they felt, had been unsuccessful in its attempts even to show that Greg had known Raffield was an undercover police officer. Grubbs, on the other hand, had done an excellent job of clouding the issue by establishing the teenage definition of "narc" and painting Richard Goeglein as an evil Satanist who had a history of violence. Then there was the intangible factor: sitting at the defense table, Knighten simply did not look capable of this murder. Though Grubbs's decision not to allow him to testify had robbed jurors of the opportunity to hear Greg's side of the story, there was little doubt what he would have said: Richard Goeglein fired the shots that killed his friend.

Sitting alone in his office, feeling the exhaustion of the previous two weeks, Chester rose from his chair and walked to Mary Lou's office. "I'm going over to the jail," he said.

Shipley, already preparing notes for the next day's argument, nodded.

"Who's been locked up with Stephen Britton?" Chester asked the jailer.

The jailer put down the newspaper he was reading and checked his files. Britton's cellmate was a man who was locked up on probation revocation for aggravated sexual assault.

"I'd like to talk to him," the assistant D.A. said.

In a matter of minutes a young man, dressed in bright orange jail-issued coveralls, was escorted to a tiny interview room stale with the lingering smell of cigarette smoke.

Chester, in no mood to waste time on casual conversation to make the inmate comfortable, went straight to the point. "Did you ever have any conversations with Stephen Britton about the Knighten case?" he asked.

The prisoner asked for a cigarette and smiled. He waited until he had taken a deep drag, exhaling smoke, then nodded. "Yeah. He said he talked to Knighten one day out in the exercise yard. A couple of days later he told me he was going to testify for the kid."

Obviously scared, he paused for several seconds before continuing. "He said he was going to get on the stand and lie. I asked him why, and he just laughed. He said he was going to do it for the money." Though admitting his concern that he might be labeled a snitch, placing himself in danger within the jail population, he agreed to testify.

Shocked by the ease with which the information had come, Chester quickly returned to the courthouse to relay the conversation to Shipley and suggest that the inmate be put on as a final rebuttal witness the following morning before closing arguments began.

The D.A. listened, then leaned back in her chair. "We

made such an issue of the defense using jailhouse testimony," she said, "that it might hurt us if we suddenly start putting inmates on the stand ourselves. I really don't think Steve Britton did that much damage. Let's leave it alone."

A knot of frustration tightened in Chester's stomach. He argued briefly but without a great deal of conviction, aware that it was a futile gesture. Maybe she was right. Maybe it was time to leave it alone.

But not until he made one last effort.

Seating himself across from Shipley's desk, he said, "Since this is probably the last case I'll ever prosecute, I have a favor to ask."

"What's that?"

"How would you feel about letting me do the closing argument on this one?"

Her response came more quickly than he had expected. "That's fine with me," she said.

Long before Judge Knize entered his courtroom Wednesday morning all available seats had been taken. In the front row, directly behind the prosecutors' table, Don Moore joined his wife and daughters. Tom and Nelda Knighten sat with family members and friends directly behind Greg.

Turner joined Roy Vaughn, Billy Fowler, and Sonny Pfeifer near the back of the room.

Following the tradition of the Texas court systems, the prosecution and defense would each be given an hour and a half to present their closing arguments to the jury. The prosecution would begin with a brief summation of the charges against the defendant; then the defense would have its turn. The final hour of the state's allotted time would follow. It was that last hour that Kevin Chester had been granted.

After Shipley's opening remarks, in which she again outlined the elements of capital murder, Grubbs took his place in front of the jury box. With the strain of the trial showing in his face and in his hoarse voice, he immediately launched an attack on the state's case.

"So much of the evidence," Grubbs said, "has been

bought and paid for. Cynthia Fedrick, for instance, readily admitted that her statements changed after she made her deal with the D.A.'s office. And what about Jonathan Jobe? Why, even after making a deal, did he not testify?"

The primary objective of his attack, however, was Richard Goeglein.

"Terry's heart," Grubbs said, "as absurd as it is, is very important . . . because she was the conscience, she was Richard's motivation. Richard Goeglein, the satanic high priest, is the toughest seventeen-year-old I've ever seen.

"And he is the least credible witness you could ever have in this or any other trial. Satan is described as the great deceiver. And Richard is a disciple of Satan.

"He's a young man who admits that he had no compunction about crawling over a still-warm body to take a dead man's billfold. He had so little remorse after the killing that he bought a Coke and played mumblety-peg with his friend Jonathan."

Finally, Grubbs turned to point at Greg. "We have a sixteen-year-old boy who's been in jail for seven long months. He's been harassed and accused by a seventeen-year-old who orchestrated this as a cover-up for his own deviant motivations."

Tears filled the attorney's eyes as he looked back at the jurors. "All we ask is fairness," he said.

Kevin Chester had slept little the night before. It had been after midnight before he went to bed; then his fitful sleep had twice been interrupted by callers who only breathed heavily into the phone before laughing and hanging up.

He was up by 5:00 A.M., again going over the notes on what he planned to say to the jury. By the time his wife woke, an ashtray filled with cigarette butts sat on the lamp table next to him.

Darla said little to her husband, busying herself with making coffee and laying out the clothes he would wear. Only as he dressed did the tension wane. She walked into the bedroom and began to laugh when she saw him carefully arranging washcloths in the armpits of his coat.

It was his secret way of hiding the fact that he perspired a great deal when nervous.

Now, in the courtroom, his face flushed with anger as he stood to face the jury. "I never thought I would live to see the day that Joe Grubbs would cry over a cop killer," he said quietly.

"The evidence is overwhelming," he continued, "that Greg Knighten not only killed George Raffield; Greg Knighten executed him."

Waving his arms, Chester paced about the musty courtroom, his voice growing louder as he reviewed the case and scoffed at the claim that the murder had resulted from occult practices. Richard Goeglein, he assured the jury, was not smart enough to have invented the story he told from the witness stand. Pointing to the defendant, he reminded the jurors that it was Greg Knighten who had the motive, Greg Knighten who had learned about handguns from his father, Greg Knighten who had access to the special kind of ammunition used. "And," he said, "Greg Knighten knew how to manipulate people."

As Chester spoke, Greg vigorously shook his head, then began to cry.

Moving to the prosecutors' table, Chester slowly pulled two photographs from a folder, then walked back to face the jury. Holding up a picture of George Raffield posing proudly in his police uniform, a hint of a smile on his face, the assistant D.A. said, "George Raffield once had a life."

Then, raising a photograph of Raffield lying dead by his pickup, he said, "But not anymore."

Alternating the photos, he continued.

"He once had dreams, just like the rest of us . . . but not anymore.

"He once had a future . . . but not anymore.

"Why? Because it was all taken away from him with three shots fired by that young man sitting right over there." As he pounded his open hand against the railing of the jury box, the harrowing echo of his palm against the hardwood matched his measured words. "Bang . . . bang . . . bang.

"Greg Knighten," he said, glaring in the direction of the crying teenager, "is a misfit, a druggie. And now he's a cop killer.

"When you start to feel sorry for Greg, think about George Raffield. Think about his family who will never see him again."

Again he picked up the crime-scene photograph the jurors had been forced to look at so often during the trial. "And think about this," he said. "This is the last picture of her son that Shirley Moore ever saw."

The jury deliberated for five and a half hours before announcing to the bailiff that it had reached a verdict. Slowly they filed back into the courtroom and took their seats.

With only the whir of the slow-turning fans punctuating the tense silence that had settled over the room, Judge Knize studied the paper handed him, then announced the verdict.

The jury, he informed the defendant, had found him guilty of murder, a crime punishable by a sentence ranging from five to ninety-nine years.

As the judge spoke, Greg laid his head on the table and sobbed. He did not bother to stand as the jurors filed out. Neither did he hear the judge's instructions that they were to return the following day to begin the sentencing phase of the trial.

By not finding Knighten guilty of capital murder, which would have meant an automatic life sentence, the jury had prolonged its duties. It would now have to determine a sentence.

Darkness had fallen by the time Kevin Chester wearily made his way down the courthouse stairs. Never had he left a courtroom with such mixed feelings. Many, he knew, would consider the jury's refusal to convict Knighten of capital murder as a victory for the defense. On the other hand, several people had approached him with warm congratulations, insisting that his closing argument had prevented outright acquittal.

Despite his exhaustion, Chester was plagued by questions. Did the jurors, despite all the testimony, actually believe that Goeglein, not Knighten, murdered Raffield? Did they really think Greg had not believed that Raffield was a police officer? Even if they did, how could they have overlooked the fact that a robbery had taken place? Even if they doubted that Greg was the gunman, they knew that the theft of the wallet and the sharing of the money called for a capital murder verdict. And how difficult was it, really, for twelve people to overlook the fact that they were sitting in judgment of a sixteen-year-old boy instead of an adult hardened by the same world in which they lived?

Walking into the night, Chester stared up at the gargoyles on the ledge above him. They looked more menacing than he could ever remember.

The glowing accounts of his closing argument on the ten o'clock news did little to lift him from his despair.

The following morning Kevin Chester arrived at the office to find Judge Knize there, drinking coffee while waiting to convene the trial for the last time. The judge reached out his hand as Kevin dropped his briefcase onto his desk. "Congratulations," he said. "You gave a fine closing argument." He then recapped the previous night's television account of the proceedings in which a reporter had referred to "prosecutor Kevin Chester's thundering closing argument."

Then, turning to Mary Lou Shipley, the judge asked, "Who's going to argue punishment today, you or Thunder?"

"I will," the district attorney snapped.

Those crowded into the Fortieth District Court on that Thursday morning were quick to recognize that the passion they had seen in the attorneys the previous day was missing. Grubbs, his voice still raspy, again reviewed the case, urging that his client be given the minimum sentence, ten years' probation. Shipley then argued for the maximum ninety-nine years in prison.

Then the waiting began anew.

As Chester stood in the hallway talking with his wife, a

neatly dressed man approached to ask if he could speak with him. Kevin smiled. "I don't have anything to do but hurry up and wait," he said.

"Well," the stranger said, "it may be that I just don't understand your job. I have no idea whether you are a Christian or not, but if you have read the Bible you know that it instructs us to judge not that ye be judged. I found the things that you said about the Knighten boy yesterday to be appalling."

Chester stared at the man in disbelief. "I assume you are a friend of the Knightens," he finally said.

"I am," the man replied.

"Then what I suggest," Kevin said, "is that you go give your speech to Greg Knighten. He's the one who decided to be the judge of whether George Raffield lived or died." Turning to his wife, he said, "Let's get out of here."

Had he been aware of the discussions taking place inside the jury room, Chester would have been even more disheartened. At least half of the jurors thought a strong possibility existed that Knighten had only served as Goeglein's accomplice.

Foreman Richard Byrd, in fact, quickly made it clear that he did not believe Knighten was cold enough to shoot his supposed best friend in the back. He asked if fellow jurors wanted to consider probation. Gale Davis, the mother of three, stood to say she was shocked that anyone would even think of such a light sentence. "He took the gun, changed the bullets, then led his friend to that field and murdered him," she said.

For over six hours they wrestled with the decision.

It was late in the afternoon when the jurors finally filed into the courtroom for the last time. Few looked toward the packed gallery.

Among those studying their faces as they entered was Texas Ranger George Turner who sat near the jury box, the muscles in his jaws clenched. Shirley Moore gripped her husband's arm. A few feet away, Tom and Nelda Knighten held hands.

Again Judge Knize read the folded paper handed him by the bailiff and looked toward the defendant. "Having been found guilty of murder," he said, "you are hereby sentenced to serve forty-five years in the Texas Department of Corrections."

Turner ran his fingers across the brim of the hat that lay in his lap. After staring at the floor for several seconds, he finally lifted his head and looked across the room to see Roy Vaughn and Billy Fowler, their faces mirroring his own disappointment.

Bending forward, Turner again focused on the floor in front of him. He was faintly aware of someone nearby crying and of the judge dismissing the jury. Then there was the busy shuffle of people leaving. It was over.

The courtroom was almost empty when he stood and let his eyes trail across the railing at the judge's bench and the witness chair, the lawyers' tables and the jury box. The arena of justice was vacant and quiet.

"Shit," he said, then turned and walked slowly toward the door.

Afterword

On September 6, 1988, at the annual gathering of the International Narcotics Enforcement Officers Association, George Raffield was honored posthumously with the organization's Medal of Valor. As Shirley Moore approached the podium in the packed ballroom of a New Orleans hotel, she received a standing ovation from the worldwide gathering of law enforcement agencies. Accepting the award on behalf of her son, she urged those in attendance to "please continue your fight against drugs."

The bitterness that had so overwhelmed her during the months immediately following her son's death had finally begun to subside. Later, sitting on the patio of a French Quarter restaurant, having lunch with her daughters, she reflected on the ceremony. "There are men who spend a lifetime in police work," she said, "and never receive the kind of recognition my boy did today. It makes me feel good to know that he left his mark, that what he tried to do has been remembered."

For the first time, there were signs that pride had overcome her grief. Her daughters were privately pleased that she had managed to get through her brief but poignant acceptance speech without tears. It was Shirley who, following the awards program, suggested they remain in New Orleans for a few hours to enjoy the sunny afternoon and visit the shops along Bourbon Street. To Sheryl and Sherrie it signaled a rebirth of strength, an acceptance, finally, of the tragedy that had shattered their lives.

For Don Moore, the return to a normal life was even more difficult. Following the murder of his stepson, he withdrew, often going for days without speaking more than a few words to anyone. The fishing gear he had once used so regularly on weekends gathered dust in the garage. Moore's performance at work declined to a point where his foreman asked Mark Prine to speak with his father-in-law. It was almost a year after the trial before Don Moore finally began to come to grips with his anguish.

In recent days there has been a happier mood in the Moore household, prompted by the birth of Sheryl and David's first child, a son.

Mark and Sherrie's four-year-old son, Cody, carried a crumpled newspaper picture of his Uncle Tiger with him everywhere he went for months after the murder. It was in his coat as he left for the day care center, in his pants pocket when he went out to play. Discreet attempts by Sherrie to persuade him to put it away resulted in violent outbursts. A child psychologist finally advised the concerned Prines to let him carry his yellowing, crumpled remembrance of George and to talk openly with their son about his uncle's death.

Today Cody no longer carries the clipping, but every time he sees a red pickup he still makes the same observation: "You know," he will say in a quiet, matter-of-fact tone, "Uncle Tiger is dead."

Which is to say the scars of the senseless murder of George Raffield will never completely disappear. They are not healed by funerals or arrests or trials and convictions.

And the list of those victimized by what happened on that rainy Friday night in October 1987 goes far beyond the family of George Raffield.

In Midlothian, the younger brother of Greg Knighten and the sisters of Jonathan Jobe and Richard Goeglein have been welcomed back into the flow of high school society. Greg's brother is emerging as an outstanding pole vaulter on the track team. Jonathan's sister, pretty and popular, dates and maintains a high average. Richard's sister, Becky, is still outspoken, but she no longer gets into fights. Friends of the youngsters admit that there is about each of them a guarded, less happy quality that did not exist before the tragedy. Midlothian High School has established a George Raffield Memorial Scholarship, funded by money-making projects of the students.

Tom and Nelda Knighten continue to hold firmly to the belief that their son did not fire the shots that killed Officer Raffield. Corporal Knighten continues to work for the Dallas Police Department, but Nelda no longer teaches, preferring to spend her time at home, seeing only a close circle of friends and remaining active in the church.

Attorney Joe Grubbs says he plans to appeal Knighten's conviction but still had not done so by the winter of 1989. He was awaiting a long overdue copy of the trial transcript before determining on what grounds he will seek a new hearing.

Richard Goeglein, Sr., worked for a while as a barber in nearby Waxahachie and recently applied to a Dallas-owned firm for a job as a security officer. The Jobes still live across the way from the Knightens, and their son's pickup remains parked at the side of the house.

Unknown to his parents, Greg Knighten, who must serve a minimum of fifteen years of his sentence before being eligible for parole, recently wrote to Jamie Cadenhead from prison, asking that she send him any photographs of him she might still have. In his letter he explained that he wanted to mail the pictures to an unnamed woman with whom he had been corresponding. The woman, he indicated, had expressed interest in adopting him.

Jamie, who no longer refers to herself as Greg's fiancée, recently went to the senior prom with one of Greg's best friends.

Richard Goeglein has developed a letter-writing friendship with a radio announcer in New Mexico who shares his interest in Satanism and the occult. Jonathan Jobe's first request for parole was denied just before Christmas of 1989.

While the Knighten trial was going on, Carolyn Loftis, the former Williams, Arizona, high school principal, was accompanying a group of youngsters to a retreat in Texas. She was feeling fine and enjoying the leisurely trip until suddenly she was overcome with "a terrible feeling" and thought of Richard Goeglein for the first time in months. In minutes she became nauseated and briefly feared she might faint. They traveled only a few more miles before she saw a road sign indicating they were approaching Midlothian, the town she knew Richard and his family had moved to, but which she had no idea would be on her route.

In Williams, curious law enforcement officials tried for some time to determine who Richard's mysterious friend Terry might be. Though the question was never satisfactorily answered, there were those who speculated he might have been referring to a girl named Angelina Estrada, daughter of a Williams High teacher. Angelina had died of a heart attack the year before the Goegleins moved to Texas.

Cynthia Fedrick was paroled on May 15, 1989. She chose not to return to Midlothian and moved with her daughter to another Texas city.

Martha Asbury, the murder victim's fiancée, has married and is no longer in touch with George Raffield's relatives.

Texas Ranger George Turner has not visited Midlothian in an official capacity since the murder but travels there occasionally to see his parents and brother. When time permits, he stops by the Midlothian Police Department for a cup of coffee with Vaughn and Fowler. Rarely do they mention the Raffield case.

In the aftermath of Raffield's murder, Detective Everett Berry, supervisor in charge of undercover training for the Los Angeles Police Department, traveled to Midlothian to review the case. The purpose of his trip was not to pass judgment on the Midlothian Police Department but to determine what he could learn from it to help him in his own program, which places no fewer than ten undercover officers in Los Angeles high schools annually.

After a thorough review of the training Raffield received and the effort extended to provide him with a cover story and a new identity, Detective Berry told Chief Vaughn that he had never seen better preparation for an undercover operation. In fact, he admitted, the precautions taken by Vaughn and Lieutenant Fowler were far more elaborate than any the L.A. Police Department took prior to enrolling officers in any of the forty-five Los Angeles high schools. It was his opinion that nothing more could have been done to protect George Raffield.

"In some aspects," observed Detective Berry, who has been training undercover officers since 1976, "they did a better job than we do. As far as procedure is concerned, they did everything perfectly."

In December of 1989, Roy Vaughn was honored by the Kiwanis Clubs of Texas and Oklahoma as the Law Enforcement Man of the Year. At the presentation, specific mention was made of his ongoing battle against drugs in his community.

Assistant Prosecutor Kevin Chester left the Ellis County District Attorney's office immediately following the Knighten trial and is now in private law practice in nearby Corsicana. Recently, several of Ellis County's influential citizens have approached Chester about returning to prosecution and running against Mary Lou Shipley in the next primary.

Shipley ran unopposed in the last election and is now serving her second term in office. In 1989 she won her first death-penalty verdict in a murder case.

There are signs that the region's woeful financial plight may be ending. A county-wide celebration broke out when an announcement was made in Washington, D.C., that the contract for the nation's first superconducting super collider, a $4.4 billion high-energy physics project, had been awarded to Ellis County. Today plans for the super collider are proceeding apace.

Meanwhile the city of Midlothian continues to struggle with its identity, holding to the past with one hand while reaching out to the future with the other. The cramped old police station was torn down recently, and Chief Vaughn and his officers spent a weekend moving files and furniture into spacious new headquarters. The fire department has been upgraded and a new chief hired. The Chamber of Commerce office has been remodeled, and plans have been made for an energetic promotional campaign designed to alert potential businesses to the benefits of small-town locations. The city manager's office is filled with blueprints for improving city streets, revitalizing the city park, and re-zoning, which Manager Chuck Pinto hopes will ultimately result in the demolition of many of the ramshackle frame houses that ring the downtown area, presenting an eyesore to visitors entering the community.

But many still jealously guard the past.

When it was discovered that the support girders on the old downtown water tower had developed spiderlike fractures and represented a safety hazard, city officials voted to have it torn down. The demolition began, however, only after angry protests from many who felt city funds should be appropriated to restore the tower, making it a historic landmark, a visible link with the town's past. The effort failed, however, and the would-be landmark was razed.

The old deserted house which Goeglein and his friends frequented is gone now, the victim of a still unexplained fire.

At a heated city council meeting recently, city fathers, having decided to enforce a twelve-year-old city ordinance that prohibits the raising of hogs within the city limits, met with angry protests. The pressured council finally agreed to postpone action on the matter after in-town hog raisers agreed to look into ways to make their pens more odor free.

The death of George Raffield no longer dominates the conversations on the streets of Midlothian, but the memory of it is still there, just below the surface, remembered on those Thursdays when the weekly newspapers publish reports of the police department's latest drug bust.

The residents of Midlothian, still conservative and self-protecting, have accepted the fact they now live with the same problems as the world beyond the town limits. A recent drug raid resulted in the arrest of several adults as well as some of the same high school students Raffield associated with during his brief undercover tenure.

Acting on an anonymous tip, Midlothian police later arrested a Houston-based drug dealer as he was delivering $200,000 worth of crack to a local man in the parking lot of the Road Runner truck stop.

Then there was the call last fall from the publisher of the *Midlothian Reporter*, complaining to Billy Fowler that a newly hired editor was stealing money received from the paper's advertisers. Lieutenant Fowler drove to the editor's home to serve the warrant for his arrest on theft charges and woke him from a midafternoon nap. After being invited in, Fowler noticed a bag of marijuana on the coffee table.

The editor was immediately taken into custody. Later Fowler learned that the man, popular with youngsters in the community, had been among those scheduled to speak at a school-sponsored anti-drug rally on the weekend following his arrest.

Recently Fowler had dinner with a friend who had just returned from the Midwest. The man talked of past vacations and meeting people who would ask where he was from. "It was always the same," he said. "I'd explain to them that Midlothian was a little bitty ol' town just outside of Dallas, and that would be it. But this time it was different. My wife and I were having breakfast in a restaurant one morning and struck up a conversation with this couple in the booth next to us.

"They asked where we were from, and when I told them, they both kinda nodded their heads. Then this fella's wife says, 'Say, isn't that the town where the kids killed the undercover police officer a while back?' I thought to myself, Now, isn't that a helluva thing to be famous for? I'll tell you, I liked it a lot better when nobody had ever heard of us."

Billy Fowler agreed.

In July of 1982, on the shores of Lake Waco, Texas, police found the savagely mutilated bodies of three teenagers. After only eight weeks, frustrated authorities marked the case "suspended". The killers were getting away with murder. But their ringleader couldn't resist bragging—and one determined lawman heard his...

CARELESS WHISPERS
THE LAKE WACO MURDERS

The Bestselling Account of the Killings that Shocked Texas

CARLTON STOWERS

"The unraveling of a monstrous criminal offense...COMPELLING."
—*San Antonio Express News.*

POCKET
BOOKS

Available in Paperback from Pocket Books